Postcolonial Literature

Edinburgh Critical Guides to Literature
Series Editors: Martin Halliwell, University of Leicester and
Andy Mousley, De Montfort University

Published Titles:
Gothic Literature, Andrew Smith
Canadian Literature, Faye Hammill
Women's Poetry, Jo Gill
Contemporary American Drama, Annette J. Saddik
Shakespeare, Gabriel Egan
Asian American Literature, Bella Adams
Children's Literature, M. O. Grenby
Contemporary British Fiction, Nick Bentley
Renaissance Literature, Siobhan Keenan
Scottish Literature, Gerard Carruthers
Contemporary American Fiction, David Brauner
Contemporary British Drama, David Lane
Medieval Literature 1300–1500, Pamela King
Contemporary Poetry, Nerys Williams
Victorian Literature, David Amigoni
Modern American Literature, Catherine Morley
Modernist Literature, Rachel Potter
Postcolonial Literature, Dave Gunning

Forthcoming Titles in the Series:
Restoration and Eighteenth-Century Literature, Hamish Mathison
Romantic Literature, Serena Baiesi

Postcolonial Literature

Dave Gunning

EDINBURGH
University Press

© Dave Gunning, 2013

Edinburgh University Press Ltd
22 George Square, Edinburgh EH8 9LF

www.euppublishing.com

Typeset in 11.5/13 Ehrhardt by
Servis Filmsetting Ltd, Stockport, Cheshire,
and printed and bound in Great Britain by
CPI Group (UK) Ltd, Croydon CR0 4YY

A CIP record for this book is available from the British Library

ISBN 978 0 7486 3938 0 (hardback)
ISBN 978 0 7486 3939 7 (paperback)
ISBN 978 0 7486 8980 4 (webready PDF)
ISBN 978 0 7486 8981 1 (epub)

The right of Dave Gunning
to be identified as author of this work
has been asserted in accordance with
the Copyright, Designs and Patents Act 1988.

Contents

Series Preface

The study of English literature in the early twenty-first century is host to an exhilarating range of critical approaches, theories and historical perspectives. 'English' ranges from traditional modes of study such as Shakespeare and Romanticism to popular interest in national and area literatures such as the United States, Ireland and the Caribbean. The subject also spans a diverse array of genres from tragedy to cyberpunk, incorporates such hybrid fields of study as Asian American literature, Black British literature, creative writing and literary adaptations, and remains eclectic in its methodology.

Such diversity is cause for both celebration and consternation. English is varied enough to promise enrichment and enjoyment for all kinds of readers and to challenge preconceptions about what the study of literature might involve. But how are readers to navigate their way through such literary and cultural diversity? And how are students to make sense of the various literary categories and periodisations, such as modernism and the Renaissance, or the proliferating theories of literature, from feminism and Marxism to queer theory and eco-criticism? The Edinburgh Critical Guides to Literature series reflects the challenges and pluralities of English today, but at the same time it offers readers clear and accessible routes through the texts, contexts, genres, historical periods and debates within the subject.

Martin Halliwell and Andy Mousley

Chronology

The historical events listed below are mostly those that have taken place in the former colonies of the British Empire since 1918, but also several global events that have had repercussions throughout the postcolonial world. The literary texts include those covered in this book and other particularly significant works by the writers discussed here; also listed are important works that helped define the direction of postcolonial literary studies, including literary-critical and theoretical works, as well as more directly political texts.

Date	Historical events	Literary events
1918	End of First World War	
1919	Amritsar Massacre, India	
	Versailles conference strips Germany of all its colonies	
	Anglo-Irish War (to 1921)	
1920	Britain granted mandate over Iraq	
	Partition of Ireland	
1921	Gandhi launches non-co-operation movement in India	

Date	Historical events	Literary events
	Anglo-Irish Treaty followed by Irish Civil War (to 1923)	
1922	Gandhi imprisoned for civil disobedience	
1923	Nationalists launch General Strike in Ceylon	
1924	Violence between Hindu and Muslim groups in India	
1925	Cyprus becomes British crown colony	
1930	Négritude movement begins in Paris	
1931	British Commonwealth of Nations founded, granting equal status to dominions	
1935	Italian invasion of Abyssinia	
1937	Declaration of Irish Republic Nationalist riots in Trinidad and Jamaica	
1938		C. L. R. James, *The Black Jacobins* Jomo Kenyatta, *Facing Mount Kenya*
1939	Outbreak of Second World War	
1942	Gandhi launches Quit India movement	
1944	Self-government in Jamaica	Eric Williams, *Capitalism and Slavery*
1945	End of Second World War; bombing of Hiroshima and Nagasaki	

Date	Historical events	Literary events
	Manchester Pan-African Conference	
1946	First assembly of United Nations	Jawaharlal Nehru, *The Discovery of India*
1947	Partition and independence for India	
1948	Independence for Burma and Sri Lanka	
	Assassination of Gandhi	
	Indo-Pakistan War in Kashmir	
	Formation of Israel	
	Establishment of South African apartheid	
	Empire Windrush arrives in Britain	
1949	Mao Zedong declares People's Republic of China	
1950	Korean War begins (to 1953)	
1952	Mau Mau violence in Kenya leads to state of emergency	Frantz Fanon, *Black Skins, White Masks*
1954	Algerian War of Independence (to 1962)	
1955	Bandung Conference of non-aligned states	
1956	Egypt seizes Suez Canal	Sam Selvon, *The Lonely Londoners*
		George Padmore, *Pan-Africanism or Communism*
1957	Independence for Ghana	Patrick White, *Voss*
		Albert Memmi, *The Coloniser and the Colonised*

Date	Historical events	Literary events
1958	Notting Hill riots	Chinua Achebe, *Things Fall Apart*
1959	Fidel Castro takes power in Cuba	
1960	Widespread independence across Africa, including Nigeria, Senegal, Somalia	
1961		Frantz Fanon, *The Wretched of the Earth*
1962	Cuban missile crisis Independence for Algeria, Jamaica, Trinidad and Tobago	
1963	Independence for Kenya	
1964	Nelson Mandela sentenced to life imprisonment	University of Leeds conference on Commonwealth Literature
1965	Rhodesian declaration of independence Mobutu takes power in Zaire	Kwame Nkrumah, *Neo-Colonialism*
1966	Independence for Barbados	
1967	Attempted secession of Biafra; Nigerian Civil War (to 1970) Arab-Israel Six Day War	
1968	Martin Luther King Jr assassinated	
1971	Secession of Bangladesh; Pakistani Civil War followed by Indo-Pakistan war	V. S. Naipaul, *In a Free State*
1972	British direct rule in Northern Ireland	Walter Rodney, *How Europe Underdeveloped Africa*

Date	Historical events	Literary events
	Aboriginal land rights protest outside Australian parliament	
1973	Australian Aborigines given vote	Patrick White wins Nobel Prize for Literature
1974		Nadine Gordimer, *The Conservationist*
1975	Indira Gandhi declares emergency in India (to 1977) US troops withdraw from Vietnam	
1976	Student uprising in South Africa	Les Murray, *The Vernacular Republic*
1978		Edward Said, *Orientalism*
1979	Iranian Revolution	Nadine Gordimer, *Burger's Daughter* V. S. Naipaul, *A Bend in the River*
1980	Robert Mugabe takes power in Zimbabwe	Anita Desai, *Clear Light of Day*
1981		Salman Rushdie, *Midnight's Children* Benedict Anderson, *Imaginary Communities* Édouard Glissant, *Caribbean Discourse*
1982	Falklands War	First publication from Subaltern Studies group
1983	Major escalation of inter-ethnic violence in Sri Lanka	J. M. Coetzee, *The Life and Times of Michael K*
1984	Assassination of Indira Gandhi	Kamau Brathwaite, *The History of the Voice*

Date	Historical events	Literary events
1985		Keri Hulme, *The Bone People*
		Ken Saro-Wiwa, *Sozaboy*
1986		Ngũgĩ wa Thiong'o, *Decolonising the Mind*
		Derek Walcott, *Collected Poems*
		Fredric Jameson, 'Third-World Literature in the Era of Multinational Capitalism'
1987		Sally Morgan, *My Place*
1988		Salman Rushdie, *The Satanic Verses*
		Tsitsi Dangarembga, *Nervous Conditions*
		Peter Carey, *Oscar and Lucinda*
		Gayatri Chakravorty Spivak, 'Can the Subaltern Speak?'
1989	Fatwa issued on Salman Rushdie	Bill Ashcroft et al., *The Empire Writes Back*
	Tiananmen Square massacre	Nissim Ezekiel, *Collected Poems*
	Fall of Berlin Wall	
	Burmese opposition leader An San Suu Kyi under house arrest	
1990	Release of Nelson Mandela	
	Sustained violence in Kashmir	
1991	Repeal of South African apartheid	Nadine Gordimer wins Nobel Prize for Literature
		Derek Walcott, *Omeros*
		Salman Rushdie, *Imaginary Homelands*

Date	Historical events	Literary events
1992	Mabo decision	Derek Walcott wins Nobel Prize for Literature
		Amitav Ghosh, *In an Antique Land*
		Michael Ondaatje, *The English Patient*
1993		Roddy Doyle, *Paddy Clarke Ha Ha Ha*
		Paul Gilroy, *The Black Atlantic*
1994	Genocide in Rwanda	Shyam Selvadurai, *Funny Boy*
		Homi Bhabha, *The Location of Culture*
1995	Ken Saro-Wiwa executed by Nigerian government	Eavan Boland, *Collected Poems*
		Giorgio Agamben, *Homo Sacer*
1997	Hong Kong handed back to China	Arundhati Roy, *The God of Small Things*
		Agha Shahid Ali, *The Country without a Post Office*
1998	Good Friday Agreement signed in Northern Ireland	Derek Walcott, *What the Twilight Says*
1999		J. M. Coetzee, *Disgrace*
		Roddy Doyle, *A Star Called Henry*
		Shani Mootoo, *Cereus Blooms at Night*
		Thomas King, *Truth and Bright Water*
2000		Zadie Smith, *White Teeth*
		Michael Ondaatje, *Anil's Ghost*

Date	Historical events	Literary events
		Caryl Phillips, *The Atlantic Sound*
		Dipesh Chakrabarty, *Provincializing Europe*
2001	September 11 attack on World Trade Center	V. S. Naipaul wins Nobel Prize for Literature
		Michael Hardt and Antonio Negri, *Empire*
2003	US-led invasion of Iraq Zimbabwe withdraws from Commonwealth	
2005	London bombings	Leila Aboulela, *Minaret*
2006	British government 'expresses sorrow' over slave trade	Chris Abani, *Hands Washing Water*
2007		James Berry, *Windrush Songs*
		Mohsin Hamid, *The Reluctant Fundamentalist*
		Tahmima Anam, *A Golden Age*
2008	Australian government apologises to Stolen Generations of aborigines	
2010	An San Suu Kyi released	
2011	'Arab Spring' sees deposing of several leaders in Middle East and North Africa	
2012	Three Kenyans to sue British government for torture at time of emergency	

Introduction

The study of English literature, in British universities at least, is largely a twentieth-century phenomenon, even if, as this book will discuss, it began in other parts of the world before that. As imaginative literature increasingly became seen as an appropriate subject for serious scholarship and formal teaching, these activities focused, initially, on the great works of the English tradition. As Terry Eagleton has noted, this development was at least partially inspired by a wish to reproduce some of the values contained within this tradition of writing; while this might explicitly be framed in terms of their aesthetic power, their moral or spiritual ideals were often those considered particularly worthy of reproduction and dissemination.[1] The body of works to be studied was mainly drawn from a national archive, capturing the best of a British, or usually more specifically English, tradition. However, as the century progressed, literature departments increasingly found it necessary to account for the other traditions of writing in the English language, perhaps most notably the extensive and unavoidable oeuvre produced within the most globally significant former British colony of the United States. Yet there was also a body of writing emerging from other Anglophone locations across the world; a new literature in English produced in such diverse places as Australia, India, the Caribbean and across the continent of Africa. When, in the early 1960s, the University of Leeds formalised the study of this writing, it seemed that this was, and would remain, mostly a minority

interest, an interesting but ultimately fairly insignificant addition
to the central concerns of the English literary canon. Since that
time, though, the study of the literatures that came to be known as
postcolonial has exponentially multiplied, not only among British
universities, but also in their American counterparts, across conti-
nental Europe, and indeed in those former colonies within which
this literature was produced. It is now very rare to find an English
Literature degree that does not include the study of postcolonial
literature, often as an optional element, but increasingly as a com-
pulsory part of the curriculum.

In a very useful 2008 study funded by the Academy of Finland,
Jopi Nyman explored the curriculum of a number of introductory
postcolonial literature courses within a range of universities across
the English-speaking world. He concludes that 'post-colonial literature seems to be taught in various ways and contexts', across
these courses: they are 'both national and transnational, diachronic
and synchronic'.[2] Yet despite signalling this diversity, Nyman also
notes the continuities between many of these syllabuses, with the
same key themes and texts arising in each of the varied locations.
Clearly, something like a canon of key postcolonial writing, and a
set of distinctive themes and approaches, is seen to exist by all of
those university teachers who author these various paths of study
for students of postcolonial writing.

This book is intended to offer a way into the study of postcolonial literature. The expansion of postcolonial literary studies
has been accompanied by an explosion of interest in postcolonial
studies more generally, a transdisciplinary grouping of investigations into the world outside of an enclosed Euro-American set
of concerns, exploring history, culture, languages, anthropology,
political theory, economics and a wealth of other topics. This
constellation of academic endeavours has no doubt expanded the
parameters of academic enquiry and can only be welcomed, yet
the breadth of these enquiries can also serve to alienate the student
of postcolonial literature, suggesting that a seemingly impossible
range of knowledge is required before it is possible to engage meaningfully with the literary texts. The challenge can seem further
intensified by the rise of the body of material known as postcolonial
theory, an amorphous and often difficult set of writing that looks

to transcend and bridge disciplinary boundaries in order to come to a clearer understanding of what intellectual labour might be required to explain adequately the situations within, and relations between, these global sites.

In one sense, then, the aim of this book is to focus deliberately on *literature* and to stage the work of reading postcolonial writing as a comparative literary project, thereby partly deferring some of the important questions raised across and between diverse disciplines. The important work that has been done particularly since the 1980s in theorising the postcolonial is not ignored within this guide, but is rather selectively mobilised in the service of looking at particular literary works; the focus is on the critical analysis of literature and the possibility of successful comparative criticism. It is important to be clear from the start that the work of comparison should never involve minimising differences, or pretending that very different writers in diverse locations may be producing the same kinds of texts. Rather, genuine comparison can only take place through a full acknowledgement of the historical and cultural specificities of particular works of postcolonial writing, and must always remain fully alert to the danger of dismissing important differences between literatures from diverse cultural environments. This book, which examines literature from Africa, Australasia, Canada, the Caribbean, Ireland and South Asia, nonetheless retains a positive focus on the possibility of drawing productive connections between the literatures of postcoloniality. It introduces many of the key themes of the field and addresses the work of several of the most important authors, such as those identified in Nyman's exploration. It is also concerned to introduce some approaches drawn from the cutting edge of research in this area, and to explore the ways in which these concerns might complement or challenge older models. Yet although the introduction of the key concerns of postcolonial criticism in the twenty-first century is a fundamental aim of this book, it is to the texts themselves that foremost attention is paid. The material discussed has been compiled with an eye to what is currently taught on university courses, and the focus is biased towards the contemporary, but this guide will also relate its selection of literature from the most recent period to many of the most significant works from earlier decades available in print.

SOME OMISSIONS

Towards the end of his introduction to his monumental *Cambridge History of Postcolonial Literature* (2012), Ato Quayson reflects on how 'two contradictory principles' can be seen to operate within collections and anthologies that offer surveys of postcolonial writing. The first of these is that of 'coevalness', the idea that every literature from any postcolonial location has an equal significance and value; and the principle of 'hierarchy', which reads some postcolonial literatures as more important than others.[3] Quayson is particularly concerned with the processes that make one location seem 'more' postcolonial than another, the pressures of which will be addressed below. However, it first seems appropriate to highlight some of the other exclusions or omissions that operate within this book, and to justify the reasons behind these decisions. The book is intended as a survey of postcolonial literature from the perspective of 2013, but does not stake a claim to comprehensiveness.

In the nineteenth century, the German philosopher G. W. F. Hegel proposed the idea of 'world literature', a comparative ideal that allows for all global writing to be read together, across linguistic and cultural boundaries, to comprehend its shared project. In recent years, the idea of world literature has seen something of a renaissance and increasingly scholars search for ways to achieve this planetary perspective. In a useful discussion of the relations between postcolonial and world literature, Theo D'haen has treated with scepticism the idea that postcolonial literature might be world literature under another guise. Not only does the category of the postcolonial exclude many global locations, the field itself is marked by the continuing dominance of Anglophone literatures (though increasing attention has been paid to literatures within other major European languages, especially French).[4] This book makes no claims to represent world literature, and recognises its circumscription. In fact, it should be noted that this is by no means a comprehensive introduction to every aspect of postcolonial literature: the focus on Anglophone texts necessarily excludes those numerous and significant works produced in other European languages. More importantly still, there is no discussion of the myriad literatures produced in local languages, those hundreds of tongues used every day within the locations that the subsequent chapters will visit. It is crucial to realise that many vibrant and distinctive literatures exist in these languages, which might not only provide the strongest exposition of local conditions, but in some cases are themselves global and document experiences across the contemporary world (the global reach of Arabic writing is a prime example of this). The sheer diversity of postcolonial languages makes viable comparative work in this field very difficult, as no scholar is likely to have access to more than a handful of these linguistic traditions. But without denying the significance of these literatures, it is possible still to maintain the value of a comparative reading of Anglophone texts alone: the very fact that diverse expressions are channelled through a single language offers concrete ground for comparative work. The acts of comparison are not intended to suggest an essential unity between these texts – they belong to diverse traditions, and can usefully be read in other ways through other comparisons.

It is also worth commenting upon the decision to concentrate on literary texts, and the way in which that category itself has been defined within the boundaries of this book. In terms of postcolonial cultural expression, literature may not always be seen as the most significant creative form. The degree to which postcolonial societies have not only defined themselves locally, but also influenced global culture, through such fields as music, film, or even sport, should be noted. As Simon Featherstone notes, 'the fluid, contested performances of popular culture allow an exploration of points of rupture in dominant cultures': in these forms we can often find a democratic instinct particularly suited to reject cultural impositions in a way that formal writing in a colonial language may not offer.[5] Yet to acknowledge that literature may not always be the most significant form of cultural production in postcolonial societies, and that important insights can be provided by studying other means of cultural expression does not entail literature having nothing to say.

Even within the usual remit of literary studies, however, the book omits a body of texts that might often be seen as essential: there is no discussion here of drama. The reason for this is that while drama can be, and often is, consumed as written texts, so much of its power is frequently to be found within the act of performance. C. L. Innes has rightly pointed out the consistent dearth of attention paid to dramatic forms in postcolonial literary studies, but the dangers of including this writing alongside forms more necessarily scribal in nature entails that this omission is reproduced here.[6] Helen Gilbert's important anthology of postcolonial plays from diverse locations itself recognises the difficulties involved in approaching such work in written form only, arguing that not only are 'some of the most vibrant and popular postcolonial performances [. . .] not easily textualised without extensive pictorial documentation', but that real understanding of them can only begin once the diverse traditions of performance from which they arise are fully accounted for.[7] Regretfully then, such texts are excluded from the present discussion for reasons of space.

COLONIAL SPACES AND COLONIAL IDEOLOGIES

It is increasingly common for the practitioners working within a great range of academic fields to question the limits of disciplinarity, and to challenge whether the boundaries traditionally ascribed to their subject are the right ones, or the strategies for producing new knowledge the most appropriate. As Graham Huggan has argued, postcolonial studies has wholeheartedly engaged in such self-questioning since its inception and the dominant feature of its history is precisely that it has been created in an environment 'in which the value of the term "postcolonial" itself has been continually interrogated, its methodological biases unearthed, the potential applicability of its theories put to the test'.[8] At its worst, Huggan cautions, this self-referentiality risks 'collapsing into elaborate self-parody', but the constant challenging of orthodoxies no doubt has a considerable value in ensuring the continuing vitality of the field.[9]

The questioning of the term 'postcolonial' is frequently related to the historical complexity of the colonial project. It is not always easy to pinpoint when a colonial history begins, and often even harder to decide when it ends. The term postcolonial is rarely used to imply that this era is cleanly over; the continuing relations of economic dominance and dependency in the contemporary world not only frequently echo the colonial global divisions of power, but can often be traced back to historical roots in exactly this formation. European colonialism is usually seen to have its genesis in the exploration and exploitation that followed the 'discovery' of the American and Caribbean New World. Throughout the sixteenth and seventeenth centuries the colonies established in these lands operated variously through asserting European power to bolster European wealth. Notoriously, the labour force used to generate profit was increasingly made up of slaves taken from Africa. As well as looking westwards, however, Britain's imperial ambitions also headed east, and with the 1858 transfer of power in India from the merchant British India Company to the Crown, we can see the establishment of Britain's largest and most impressive colony. The 'Scramble for Africa' of the late nineteenth century saw further acquisition of territory in the east, west and south of that continent. When one adds to this the settler territory of lands like Australia and New Zealand, one can begin to picture the extent of British imperial control by 1914, when a quarter of the globe was under its power.

It is important to realise that the ways each of these colonial outposts operated, and indeed their very nature as colonies, often dramatically varied. Quayson maps four basic 'configurations of colonial space', though notes that 'these were not mutually exclusive but rather mixed and overlapped in specific local contexts'. He adumbrates the following: 'the context of formal colonialism', where a full bureaucratic colonial apparatus was established; 'the context of plantation economies', where the colonial effort was directed towards ensuring the production of (usually agricultural) goods for export, like sugar, coffee or tobacco; 'the context of settler colonialism', where whole populations would relocate to the colony; and 'the contexts of migration and diaspora', the movement of peoples either between colonies (such as the indentureship of Indian workers in the Caribbean) or between the colonies and the colonising power.[10] Very different arrangements of power exist in each of these situations and the effects of these on cultural production within each, during and after the high colonial era, correspondingly vary enormously.

If a single work can be seen especially to have led to the huge growth in postcolonial studies over the last three decades, and to help determine much of the course of these enquiries, then this must be Edward Said's *Orientalism* (1978). A discussion of the ways in which the vast stretch of land running from the eastern edge of the Mediterranean to the western edge of the Pacific, known as the Orient, is figured in mostly British and French writing of the last couple of centuries, *Orientalism* is quite specific in terms of the empirical archive it surveys, but many of the processes Said describes have been seen to have analogies in the history of multiple colonial territories. The key meaning Said attributes to the term 'Orientalism' is as a way of describing 'the corporate institution for dealing with the Orient – dealing with it by making statements about it, authorizing views of it, describing it, by teaching it, settling it, ruling over it'.[11] He sees this body of information gathered across time as not necessarily determining what can be said about the Orient, but certainly conditioning it, significantly setting the parameters of what can be known about this huge and diverse place. Said is concerned to point out that there is a 'real' Orient distinct from the ways in which it is constructed from without, but he also notes that the central Orientalist idea of 'European identity as a superior one in comparison with all the non-European people and cultures' became dominant not only within Europe but also pervasively in those very regions described.[12] Said ends his extremely influential introduction to *Orientalism* by hoping that understanding the processes explored in the book might lead towards some 'unlearning' of this inherited body of knowledge that, while offering convincing and frequently productive descriptions of the world, continues to reproduce a discourse of superiority and inferiority.

One way of thinking about the postcolonial condition is as an ongoing process that looks not only to end the political domination and economic exploitation that characterised the colonial era, but also to challenge the social, cultural and intellectual inequalities that were formed within colonial discourses and continue to shape the world today. The great theorists and activists who directed anti-colonial struggles across the world were often well aware of the inseparability of this cultural project from their political aims, as has been well documented by Robert Young.[13] The degree to which these forebears articulated both theory and practice in overcoming colonial power should not be ignored, and contemporary struggles against political and economic injustice frequently draw on their models and examples. Creative cultural work can also often be seen to reiterate such concerns. However, the cultural sphere retains some degree of autonomy from the economic and political base that may ultimately determine it, and it is important to note that the fight for self-determination in the cultural sense is not always strictly synonymous with that which may simultaneously be waged in the political firmament. Importantly, this takes the form of more than the 'writing back' model, where postcolonial societies 'asserted themselves by foregrounding the tension with the imperial power, and by emphasizing their differences from the assumptions of the imperial centre'.[14] Often the concerns of postcolonial writing can be narrowly local, without reference to their difference from a colonial vision, although this concern to craft a positive sense of identity cannot in turn be wholly divorced from the history that previously has enfeebled it. Elleke Boehmer observes that 'identity was not by any means the single problem which occupied the minds of those who sought to dismantle empire. But it is one that still draws collective attention'.[15] One reason for this prominence surely must be that the dismantling of empire was only ever part of the cultural agenda of postcolonialism. Establishing that which comes after, and sounding whether emergent structures are fit for their purpose, frequently motivates the explorations of identity found in postcolonial writing.

GENERAL CATEGORIES AND SPECIFIC CASES

It is now useful to return to Quayson's suggestion that surveys of the postcolonial frequently establish a hierarchy where, for example, 'Kenyan literature is considered intrinsically more postcolonial than say Canadian literature'.[16] Quayson understands and partially sympathises with the thinking behind this idea, but suggests that it reveals something about the common understanding of postcolonial societies that this conclusion is often jumped to so uncritically. Certain types of colonial history can be sidelined in the attempt to make one particular kind of postcolonial experience paradigmatic. For other important postcolonial literary critics, expressing such intellectual preference seems wholly unproblematic, with Neil Lazarus prefacing a timeline of important events with the frank admission that 'it seems to me that little would be gained by treating twentieth-century developments in Canada, New Zealand, Australia [. . .] in analogy with developments in such societies as Cuba, East Timor, Mali, Malaysia, and Mexico'.[17] It is clear that the very different material situations of these two groups of nations make it hard to suggest any straightforward reason to analyse them together, but to make a decision in favour of one or the other, even if for the purest political motives, risks impoverishing our comprehension of the many different forms that postcolonial experience may take.

Settler societies like Australia and Canada are frequently omitted from discussions of postcolonial culture (even though they may offer especially interesting instances of postcolonial life, with a majority population freed from former colonial rule, yet with indigenous minorities still living in conditions that for many are experienced as a continuing colonial domination). However, the location that perhaps has most frequently slid in and out of discussions of the postcolonial is Ireland. This sometimes seems to be because of the comparative wealth of Ireland, and at other times because British dominance in Ireland stretches far back before the colonial era. The close correspondence between many aspects of British and Irish cultures also seems partially behind the refusal of many to consider it 'properly' postcolonial. Irish texts are included within the purview of this guide, and it is useful briefly to indicate why.

The Norman invasion of Ireland in 1170 actually took the form of the earl of Pembroke responding to a call for military support from the king of Leinster. Only after Pembroke had secured the title of the province for himself did he seek the approval of the English king, Henry II. Henry in turn sought and received the papal authority to declare himself lord of Ireland but this official assertion of sovereignty had little significant social impact on the island until almost 250 years later, when Henry VIII decided to impose authority more directly, stripping power from the Irish lords and restoring it only if full fealty was pledged to him as king. Henry's daughter Mary went further in introducing a system of settlement of English aristocrats in Ireland, intended not only to ensure loyalty to the Crown, but also to 'civilise' the indigenous people. One of these settlers, the poet and author of *The Faerie Queene* (1590), Edmund Spenser, provides an example of how this process of civilisation was imagined in his late 1580s work *A View of the Present State of Ireland*, 'arguably the most sustained and sophisticated treatment of Renaissance concepts of race and identity by a major canonical author'.[18] This text takes the form of a conversation between a curious Englishman and a wise settler and sees the latter advise, without irony, that the best way forward for Ireland is through the complete genocide of its people, brought about by war followed by deliberate famine.

The next few centuries of Irish history were consistently punctuated by failed rebellions, which articulated around often very different demands, frequently political or religious, but only by the nineteenth century explicitly nationalist. The late nineteenth century saw the Gaelic Revival and the earnest promotion of Irish national identity along with parliamentary appeals for Home Rule, but also the formation of nationalist and revolutionary socialist militias; and collaboration between two of these latter groups saw the last great failed rebellion, the Easter Rising of 1916. Despite having little popular support at the time, the brutal response of the British authorities allowed the men of 1916 quickly to become martyrs, and by the time the War of Independence broke out in 1919, the nationalist cause enjoyed overwhelming support in most of the country. The treaty that ended the war in 1922 contained among other conditions the controversial partition of Ireland, and divisions among nationalists over whether to accept this compromise led to a bloody civil war. The Irish Free State that emerged from this conflict began life with a fierce crackdown against the rebels and then settled into extreme political and religious conservatism, whichever of the two main political parties was in power.

In the partitioned north, continuing protests against the legitimacy of British rule were played out against a culture of religious segregation, with a Catholic (and mostly nationalist) minority actively discriminated against by a Protestant (and mostly unionist) majority. This tense situation eventually deteriorated into armed conflict waged by paramilitaries on both sides, frequently against civilian targets. The recent peace process and devolution of power to the region has seen a dramatic reduction, but not a cessation, of this violence. Meanwhile, in the south, a republic since 1949, a boom economy fuelled by overseas investment encouraged by very low levels of corporate taxation has been succeeded by economic crisis and the imposition of a strict austerity regime.

This (extremely) potted history is intended to highlight how the Irish situation shares features with many other colonial locations, from the experience of settlement to the fact of racialisation and segregation, from direct political domination to remote neo-liberal control, from radical anti-colonial movements to repressive postcolonial regimes and so on. This is neither to offer Ireland as a paradigmatic example of colonial and postcolonial experience, nor to suggest that these features of its history are identical to similar moments in diverse other locations. It is interesting also to note that debates within Irish Studies about the validity of postcolonial approaches have themselves frequently tended to be discussed in terms that approach sectarianism, with 'a postcolonial reading [. . .] identified as a stalking-horse for ultra-nationalism',[19] even as such writers as Joe Cleary argue that the work of global comparison is actually vital to overcoming the provincialism, sense of exceptionalism and 'narrow insular Anglo-Irish framework that has conventionally shaped Irish studies'.[20]

Cleary goes on to note that the act of labelling Ireland post-colonial involves 'two *analytically* discreet levels that require different methods of investigation', one concerned with 'matters of consciousness, systems of representation and discursive regimes' and the other with 'structural and socio-cultural correspondences' with other postcolonial locations.[21] To label a text postcolonial is not then an end but rather the beginning of an interrogation of the specific. Boehmer reminds us that 'to do justice to a text's grounding in the now, or in the past, it may be necessary to draw on specialist knowledge: to find out about local politics, for example'.[22] Generalisations about the politics of colonialism or postcolonialism are unlikely to offer a comparable insight. As Ania Loomba neatly summarises:

The word 'postcolonial' is useful in indicating a general process with some shared features across the globe. But if it is uprooted from specific locations, 'postcoloniality' cannot be meaningfully investigated, and instead, the term begins to obscure the very relations of domination that it seeks to uncover.[23]

POSSIBLE UNITIES AND THE USE OF THEORY

The concentration on specificity urged above should not be seen as an encouragement to relativism or incommensurability, the belief that every situation is unique in its particularity and thereby fundamentally resistant to any act of comparison. It is necessarily true that any cultural situation or artefact is unique, but equally the case that it exists within a network of connections and correspondences. To insist on absolute difference is not only to deny the possibility of communication but also risks reproducing the rhetoric of otherness used to justify the worst kinds of racist discrimination. Communication across cultures is undoubtedly difficult, and constant vigilance is required to ensure that the values of one cultural formation are not working to distort the message contained in the expressions of another, but to concede this struggle as impossible seems an unhelpful dead end. In his ambitious attempt to find behind postcolonial literature an unconscious cultural logic, Neil Lazarus suggests that 'postcolonial literary writing' points us in a quite different direction from incommensurability, 'toward the idea not of "fundamental alienness" but of a deep-seated affinity and community, across and athwart the "international division of labour"'.[24] The unity that Lazarus finds might be made more easily imaginable by his selective account of what constitutes postcolonial literature, as noted above, but the impulse to recognise connections, which need in no way entail the neglect of differences, inspires this book also.

John McLeod locates the unity of postcolonial culture in quite a different way, not necessarily within the manifest and latent content of its texts but rather in the methodological approaches of those who 'recognise and explore the inseparable relationship between history and culture in the primary context of colonialism and its consequences'. He finds the 'cohesion' of the field 'in the *configuration* of that relationship between the material world and how we conceptualise it'.[25] The immediate context for his remarks locates this configuration in the work of those who would study postcolonial cultures, but it appears that he equally wants to think about its operation within the work of creative artists. He goes on to describe the postcolonial as a 'hinged' concept, a place where the grounded conditions of history meet with the imaginative construction of ideas that might critique or replace these; the two are connected in a relationship that not only permits but perhaps also predicates movement yet never allows for separation, 'a twisting away from a fixed location which can never be fully unhinged'.[26]

At the risk of mixing other people's metaphors into an incomprehensible muddle, this book would like to preserve something of both Lazarus's unconscious and McLeod's hinge: this is to say that the examples provided throughout this guide suggest that some degree of *substantive* unity can be traced between the literary works produced within various postcolonial cultures, even if this is fleeting and qualified always by the specificity of each cultural context, but also a degree of *processual* unity in that writers of creative prose and poetry find similar techniques to articulate the specificities of their worlds, even if the texts that finally result might seem very different from each other. What is not sought here is *theoretical* unity. The profusion of studies that look to explore the postcolonial situation in terms of the generation of knowledge and its critique have only a limited space afforded to them in the discussions that will follow. Attention will instead be focused foremost on the literary texts, and on the ways in which such texts offer their own 'theorisation' of social conditions and individual and communal dilemmas. This decision is by no means intended as an endorsement of the radically anti-theory stance of such a work as Robert Fraser's *Lifting the Sentence* (2000), which reads the explosion of theory as a cynical exercise and argues that 'most theory made possible little but itself, and empowered nobody but its gurus'.[27] This volume will demonstrate that the insights of theory are often just as important as attention to the more specifically literary features that Fraser reads with flair elsewhere in his book. Rejected here, however, is the suggestion that postcolonial theory can *explain* the postcolonial literary text, a naive form of interpretation that enacts a Procrustean abridgement of the potential of the literary work in favour of whatever explanatory power inheres within the unity of the theory itself. In the chapters that follow, important ideas drawn from the history of postcolonial theory and related fields will be introduced and discussed, but never to reveal the meaning of a literary work. Instead, the reader is encouraged to see these theories as another form of creative intervention, as texts that can profitably be read alongside postcolonial literature (much as the literary texts themselves can usefully be read in the light of comparison with each other), but with no necessarily greater degree of explanatory power. Indeed, it is hoped that considering this range of writings in proximity, but not in terms of hierarchy, will better reveal the specific contribution that the actual literary works can make to the conceptualisation of postcolonial cultures, and how they can offer the imaginative seeds of solutions to persistent and recalcitrant social dilemmas.

ABOUT THIS BOOK

Each of the chapters of this guide is structured around a particular theme. These have been chosen not only because they represent important sets of concerns that resonate across postcolonial societies, but equally because they allow for exploration of the ways in which general situations that can be traced across the postcolonial world as a whole may manifest diversely in particular locations, at particular times, in line with the concerns of particular writers. The ways in which Australian writers have dealt with their particular experience of postcoloniality will necessarily differ significantly from those found in the work of Nigerians, whose history and culture engender very different takes on shared concerns. Stephen Clingman has suggested that there may be something wrong with a system of categorisation that requires us 'to think of both Chinua Achebe and Zadie Smith as "postcolonial"', but this book wants precisely to examine what gains may be made in putting such diverse writers together.[28] The reader is asked to note connections between the very different works that make up the fluid category of postcolonial literature, but also to see how meanings are ultimately always generated at the local level, and need to be understood in relation to specific conditions.

Each chapter contains discussions of a handful of important literary works drawn from a range of places and exhibiting very different stylistic approaches. These texts have been chosen to include a good number of those writings considered to have become part of the always-contested postcolonial 'canon', but also to introduce some slightly less known works, which nonetheless offer interesting examples of how diverse postcolonial literatures have explored issues prevalent in the societies that have produced them. In every chapter the reader will also find introductions to some key ideas that have been put forward to understand post-colonial societies, but these theoretical or conceptual discussions are not used to define narrowly the remit laid out by the thematic ideas. Rather, they are intended to provide suggestions as to how one might explore further the kinds of enquiries staged in the texts themselves.

At times the texts selected within each chapter will relate closely to each other – for example, in mapping the ways in which two Nigerian novelists develop very different responses to the ques-tion of writing in English, or looking at the separate ways in which a pair of Caribbean writers fifty years apart might explore the process of settlement in Britain. At other times, though, this guide will very deliberately jump between times and places, in juxtapos-ing, for example, the experience of community recorded by a white South African and a Native Canadian. This is never done to imply equivalence, and the discussion of each text is always intended to function as a complete unit in itself, rather than as part of a cumu-lative argument that will resolve into clear conclusions, but the reader is asked to think about how particular approaches are some-times mirrored and sometimes find their opposite when placed in a comparative framework. Although some especially prolific poets are represented here by works that may have been written at very different points in their careers, showing some of the continuity of their concerns, more often the focus is on a single work, usually a novel or particular collection of poems. In this way, it is hoped that particular literary responses to social situations can be isolated and explored in some depth, rather than merely surveying the oeuvres of writers in general terms. The reader is of course encouraged to read more widely of any writer whose work particularly captures their interest, but although such single-author study undoubtedly can lead to many exciting critical opportunities, this approach has largely been excluded here in favour of the benefits to be gained in exploring in some detail the writing of a large variety of authors.

The themes chosen to structure each chapter are certainly not intended to be comprehensive and many other ways of grouping these works can easily be imagined. Indeed, several of the works discussed here could easily have been considered within different chapters – Ken Saro-Wiwa's *Sozaboy* (1985) could for example very easily have featured in the chapter on war, while Zadie Smith's *White Teeth* (2000) would slot neatly into the discussion of history. The themes do still provide a degree of structure that allow for the work of comparison to begin. The theme of the first chapter was perhaps inevitable, given the decision to concentrate upon literature in English only. We start therefore by looking at some of the debates that have been staged around the question of what sacrifices might have to be made by the postcolonial writer who chooses to write in English, and why some may nonetheless have made this decision. After first exploring how English literature was explicitly used as part of the colonising mission (notably in India, where its utility as a means of disseminating British values was debated within Britain's parliament), the ways in which two poets – the St Lucian Derek Walcott and the Irish Eavan Boland – have addressed the burden and opportunities afforded by engaging with the English literary canon are discussed. The chapter progresses by looking at how the English language can be manipulated to explore local concerns, drawing on the 'Indian English' poems of Nissim Ezekiel, before turning to an important debate between two African novelists, Ngũgĩ wa Thiong'o and Chinua Achebe, the former of whom argued that English could not be used satisfactorily to write about Africa while the latter believed it could. How Achebe might do this in his classic *Things Fall Apart* (1958) is then explored, and followed by an insight into the more radical techniques deployed by his countryman Ken Saro-Wiwa. The chapter concludes by looking at a celebrated novel from Aotearoa New Zealand that includes much Maori language but also examines the importance of non-linguistic communication.

The second chapter explores the sense of place within post-colonial writing, beginning with a discussion of the contentious issue of how Aboriginal and settler Australians have each laid claim to their land. The literary examples here are Patrick White's historical novel *Voss* (1957) and the poetry of Les Murray. A very different sense of settlement is then explored in looking to how Sam Selvon and James Berry have each written of the ways West Indians found to belong in Britain, forcing a reassessment of that nation's understanding of itself. The final section returns to a settler community, but here explores the processes set in motion by the withdrawal of the legitimacy of white rule in a majority black country through reading J. M. Coetzee's *Disgrace* (1999).

The third chapter moves to exploring a particular literary approach: the decision to focus a work of fiction around the coming to maturity of a child or young person. After beginning by noting how this process might work in part by providing an allegorical structure to understand the struggles of a young nation, Roddy Doyle's *A Star Called Henry* (1999) is read to show how writers rarely accept such a neat correspondence. In Shyam Selvadurai's *Funny Boy* (1994) the development of the protagonist takes place within a context of dual oppression, both as a member of an ethnic minority and because of his homosexuality; in Shani Mootoo's *Cereus Blooms at Night* (1996) a number of discrepant sexualities are explored. The chapter then reads the painful coming of age charted in Tsitsi Dangarembga's *Nervous Conditions* (1988) before concluding with a look at how Zadie Smith explores how young people may be defined by histories that began long before their births.

The next chapter develops some of these ideas by looking at the tension that can exist between individuals and their communities, beginning with Nadine Gordimer and Thomas King's exploration of the very different contexts of white opposition to South African apartheid and life on a Native reservation close to the US/Canada border respectively. The idea of diasporic community and the negotiations this may involve are discussed in relation to Salman Rushdie's *The Satanic Verses* (1988). The global outrage caused by this novel is then used as a way into examining ideas of the global community forged by Islam, endorsed in Leila Aboulela's *Minaret* (2005), but sidestepped by the radicalised narrator of Mohsin Hamid's *The Reluctant Fundamentalist* (2007).

The fifth chapter looks to the challenges of representing war and everyday violence within postcolonial societies. First addressing the Martinican psychiatrist Frantz Fanon's influential view of decolonisation, the discussion moves on to explore V. S. Naipaul's pessimistic account of how violence may be inevitable and constant in societies that can only ever incompletely free themselves from colonial domination. In Tahmina Anam's *A Golden Age* (2007), however, the idea that something positive may emerge from violence is reasserted. In the work of two very different poets, Agha Shahid Ali and Chris Abani, other perspectives on war are introduced, with the former questioning his right as an emigrant to represent his struggling homeland, and the latter tracing how participation in violence might lessen a person's sense of their own humanity. In Michael Ondaatje's *Anil's Ghost* (2000), with which the chapter ends, a variety of strategies for responding to war, and their respective utility, are laid out.

The final chapter turns to the idea of history and examines how the past might be represented in various postcolonial situations. Anita Desai's *Clear Light of Day* (1980) and Arundhati Roy's *The God of Small Things* (1997) each deal with families trying to come to terms with their history, but while the family in the former novel seems successfully to ignore part of their past in order to rebuild their present situation, the characters in the latter book are largely destroyed by their history. The chapter then explores how Peter Carey's celebrated mimicking of the iconic Australian Ned Kelly allows for new ways into that country's past, before examining how Sally Morgan's *My Place* (1987) expands the possibilities of autobiographical wiring to explore a much bleaker Australian legacy. This chapter concludes by examining two further non-fictional works, which each defy straightforward generic classification: in Caryl Phillips's *The Atlantic Sound* (2000) various ways of coming to terms with the painful history of black people in the

West are found wanting; while Amitav Ghosh uses *In an Antique Land* (1992) to present a forgotten history which might provide resources of hope to inspire the present.

Many of these discussions of literary works are accompanied by brief explanations of the historical or social contexts to which the texts refer. On occasion, statements by the writers themselves are also used to allow for greater insight. Rarely present, however, is any account of the extensive critical commentary that already exists around many of these works. This omission is certainly not intended to suggest that this material is not of value in approaching these texts; on the contrary, many of the readings given here have been inspired by some of the approaches developed by others. While extensive discussion of this important critical archive has been left out of the main chapters to allow for as much clarity as possible in discussing the literary works themselves, the reader who is interested in pursuing further study of postcolonial literature is strongly encouraged to engage with this body of writing. The first part of the student resources section that concludes this volume is intended to offer some guidance to the student beginning on a further programme of reading. The extensive lists of further reading given here are by no means comprehensive and are likely only to prove a starting point for further investigation, though they do provide an indication of some of the very best work in postcolonial literary studies to date. It is likely that the reader of this book may well be working towards producing their own writing on postcolonial literature. With this in mind, the student resources section also contains a short discussion of some of the possible pitfalls in writing about this exciting field, and offers suggestions as to how to ensure that your own criticism is alive to the complexities and subtleties of this rich literary archive.

NOTES

1. Terry Eagleton, *Literary Theory: An Introduction* (Oxford: Blackwell, 1983), pp. 22–43.
2. Jopi Nyman, 'A Post-colonial Canon? An Explorative Study of Post-colonial Writing in University-level Courses', in Mark

Shackleton (ed.), *Diasporic Literature and Theory – Where Now* (Newcastle: Cambridge Scholars, 2008), p. 51.

3. Ato Quayson, 'Introduction: Postcolonial Literature in a Changing Historical Frame', in Ato Quayson (ed.), *The Cambridge History of Postcolonial Literature* (Cambridge: Cambridge University Press, 2012), vol. I, pp. 24–5.

4. Theo D'haen, *The Routledge Concise History of World Literature* (London: Routledge, 2012), pp. 133–51.

5. Simon Featherstone, *Postcolonial Cultures* (Edinburgh: Edinburgh University Press, 2005), pp. 29–30.

6. C. L. Innes, *The Cambridge Introduction to Postcolonial Literatures in English* (Cambridge: Cambridge University Press, 2007), p. 19.

7. Helen Gilbert, 'General Introduction', in Helen Gilbert (ed.), *Postcolonial Plays: an Anthology* (London: Routledge, 2001), p. 4.

8. Graham Huggan, *The Postcolonial Exotic: Marketing the Margins* (London: Routledge, 2001), p. 230.

9. Ibid., p. 258.

10. Quayson, 'Introduction', pp. 17–20.

11. Edward W. Said, *Orientalism* (London: Penguin, 2003), p. 3.

12. Ibid., p. 7.

13. Robert J. C. Young, *Postcolonialism: an Historical Introduction* (Oxford: Blackwell, 2001).

14. Bill Ashcroft, Gareth Griffiths and Helen Tiffin, *The Empire Writes Back: Theory and Practice in Post-colonial Literatures*, 2nd edn (London: Routledge, 2002), p. 2.

15. Elleke Boehmer, *Colonial and Postcolonial Literature: Migrant Metaphors*, 2nd edn (Oxford: Oxford University Press, 2005), p. 8.

16. Quayson, 'Introduction', p. 25.

17. Neil Lazarus, 'Indicative Chronology', in Neil Lazarus (ed.), *The Cambridge Companion to Postcolonial Literary Studies* (Cambridge: Cambridge University Press, 2004), p. xv.

18. Andrew Hadfield and Willy Maley, 'Introduction', in Edmund Spenser, *A View of the Present State of Ireland* (Oxford: Blackwell, 1997), p. xvi.

19. Glenn Hooper, 'Introduction', in Glenn Hooper and Colin

Graham (eds), *Irish and Postcolonial Writing* (Basingstoke: Palgrave Macmillan, 2002), p. 17.

20. Joe Cleary, 'Misplaced Ideas? Colonialism, Location and Dislocation in Irish Studies', in Claire Connolly (ed.), *Theorising Ireland* (Basingstoke: Palgrave Macmillan, 2003), p. 93.

21. Ibid., p. 95.

22. Boehmer, *Colonial and Postcolonial Literature*, pp. 239–40.

23. Ania Loomba, *Colonialism/Postcolonialism* (London: Routledge, 1998), p. 19.

24. Neil Lazarus, *The Postcolonial Unconscious* (Cambridge: Cambridge University Press, 2011), p. 19.

25. John McLeod, 'Introduction', in John McLeod (ed.), *The Routledge Companion to Postcolonial Studies* (London: Routledge, 2007), p. 8.

26. Ibid., p. 10.

27. Robert Fraser, *Lifting the Sentence: the Poetics of Postcolonial Fiction* (Manchester: Manchester University Press, 2000), p. 223.

28. Stephen Clingman, *The Grammar of Identity: Transnational Fiction and the Nature of the Boundary* (Oxford: Oxford University Press, 2009), p. 31.

CHAPTER I

Finding a Voice

In a significant scene in James Joyce's *A Portrait of the Artist as a Young Man*, the young Irish hero, Stephen Dedalus, converses with his university's dean of studies on the nature of moral and material beauty. Stephen's intellectual development has been charted through the novel and by this point he has an impressive degree of erudition and articulacy. He seems well able to match the older man's cerebral musings, but an unexpected moment unsettles the conversation between them. The dean has been using the image of a lamp as a metaphor and suggests that one should be careful never to overfill the funnel when adding oil. Stephen, wishing to show off his knowledge, questions the use of the noun 'funnel', suggesting that instead that it should be called a 'tundish'. The dean is unfamiliar with the word, but his ignorance does not have the effect that Stephen wished for; instead, as the dean speaks the word again and again, commenting on how 'interesting' it is, the situation becomes uncomfortable, and a power relationship which has nothing to do with their status as teacher and student swims into view. Stephen suddenly becomes painfully aware that the dean is a 'countryman of Ben Jonson'; in other words, English. He realises the significance of this difference between them, and the mistake he had made in trying to confound the older man with language:

The language in which we are speaking is his before it is mine. How different are the words *home*, *Christ*, *ale*, *master*, on his lips and on mine! I cannot speak or write these words without unrest of spirit. His language, so familiar and so foreign, will always be for me an acquired speech. I have not made or accepted its words. My voice holds them at bay. My soul frets in the shadow of his language.[1]

The dean's nationality allows him to possess the English language in a way that seems entirely denied to Stephen. While English is the only language in which Stephen is fully articulate, and therefore that in which his artistic efforts will be framed, there remains an important sense that it cannot fully belong to him or, by implication, to any Irish person. Even as English is exported across the world, and becomes the tongue of first expression for so many global subjects, colonial and postcolonial English speakers may still be struck by the extent to which the language seems to remain foremost the property of the English. Given this, it can be questioned whether it is appropriate, or even possible, to produce a postcolonial literature in the language of the oppressor.

MACAULAY'S MINUTE

The role of the English language within the process of colonisation, and its subsequent persistence in determining the attitudes of postcolonial subjects to language, has often been a central focus of postcolonial studies. If we understand colonialism to be as much about cultural domination as political oppression, then language is a key tool in implementing this authority. If the English language is imposed upon British colonial possessions, then, this thinking goes, so too are British modes of thought. If not only the language, but also the literature of Britain is transmitted, then this process of intellectual subjugation is all the stronger.

One of the most famous historical incidents where we can see this process in action is within the document that has been known as 'Macaulay's Minute'. Thomas Babington Macaulay was a British politician who took up a position on the Supreme Council of India in 1834 and on arrival in the colony became president of the Committee of Public Instruction. This committee had the responsibility of directing education policy in India. At the time Macaulay joined, one particular issue was central to their deliberations: that of the language in which instruction should be offered. Half of the committee held that the extant system of teaching in Sanskrit and Persian should be preserved; half felt that a modern education system could only function if it instead employed a European language, in this case English. Macaulay initially seemed slow to commit to either side, but in February 1835 he published his 'Minute on Indian Education', which came out strongly in favour of teaching in English. The Minute was issued with the governor-general's 'entire concurrence to the sentiments expressed' and soon determined subsequent policy.

It is worth examining the nature of Macaulay's defence of English as the only appropriate language of instruction in colonial India, for in his arguments we can trace a persistent strand of thought that can still haunt postcolonial writers. Macaulay's essay offers several reasons why English is to be preferred, including his key assertion that it is the language 'best worth knowing':

> I have no knowledge of either Sanscrit or Arabic [sic]. – But I have done what I can to form a correct estimate of their value. I have read translations of the most celebrated Arabic and Sanscrit works. I have conversed both here and at home with men distinguished by their proficiency in the Eastern tongues. I am quite ready to take the Oriental learning at the valuation of the Orientalists themselves. I have never found one among them who could deny that a single shelf of a good European library was worth the whole native literature of India and Arabia.[2]

Throughout, Macaulay's arguments are cast in the language of logic. His decisions are presented as inevitable if only one looks dispassionately at the facts. The argument presented in this section of the essay is therefore rendered in such a way as to suggest objectivity. He openly admits his ignorance of the 'native' languages but suggests that reading translations of key works allows him access to them. Further, rather than simply using his own judgement, he sought the advice of experts who confirmed his suspicions that these were inferior languages, with inferior literatures, to those of Europe. Of course, the 'Orientalists' who Macaulay consults are also Europeans; it does not occur to him to suspect that they might be harbouring biased opinions themselves, nor to seek the opinion of any indigenous language user. In fact, we can see his opinions as deeply conditioned by the very category of 'useful knowledge' which he looks to education to provide: he writes at one point that non-European scientific models 'by universal confession, whenever they differ from those of Europe, differ for the worse';[3] in this statement it becomes quite clear that European and 'universal' often function as synonyms for Macaulay. The utility or otherwise of knowledge is judged by European standards alone. English is the best language for tuition as it is best able to reproduce the standards that have already been assumed superior. This is not to suggest that the science of nineteenth-century Europe may not have possessed great potential value for Indians, nor even that European languages might not possess the best adapted vocabularies for its transmissions; rather, one need only note how Macaulay's arguments rarely achieve the objectivity they wish to purport, and instead too easily slip back into a reliance on a simple understanding of Europe as necessarily superior.

The sense that the teaching of English might not just be about its suitability for passing on knowledge, but actually be concerned with the reproduction of values, is revealed far more explicitly later in the 'Minute'. Macaulay famously writes that, as it is impossible sufficiently to teach all of the millions of Indian subjects,

> We must at present do our best to form a class who may be interpreters between us and the millions who we govern; a class of persons, Indian in blood and colour, but English in taste, in morals, and in intellect.[4]

Here a key motivation of colonial language instruction seems most clearly highlighted. The education given to Indians is intended not simply to improve their situation, but to make them think, and act, more like the English. Yet, it should be noted that this acquisition of knowledge does not serve to make the Indians equal to the English, but rather positions them as somewhere between superior

Englishness and inferior Indianness: '*almost the same but not quite*', as Homi Bhabha puts it, '*almost the same but not white*'.[5] It is the tension created between the idea that values can be transmitted and the persistence of discourses of superiority and inferiority that leaves Joyce's Stephen unable to assert himself against the Englishness of the dean of studies; in using English, the colonial subject seems (usually involuntarily) to affirm its superiority to other languages, but also to accept the pre-eminence of the English people as the owners, and masters, of the tongue.

TRADING WITH TRADITION: DEREK WALCOTT

As Gauri Viswanathan points out, the initial dissemination of English was mostly concerned with language instruction, but before long there came a definite shift toward the sustained teaching of the English literary tradition. In the canon of English literature, it was suggested, lay all the values of Englishness from which the colonial subject could benefit. Engagement with the refined sentiments of these books allowed for the development of the sophisticated principles of the English people. However, the turn to the rarefied space of literature also served a further purpose:

> In effect, the strategy of locating authority in English texts all but effaced the often sordid history of colonialist expropriation, material exploitation, and class and race oppression behind European world dominance. Making the Englishman known to the natives through the products of his mental labor removed him from the plane of ongoing colonialist activity – of commercial operations, military expansion, administration of territories – and de-actualized and diffused his material presence in the process.[6]

The noble and cultivating influence of literature is not only made separate from the often brutal realities of colonial rule, but serves to obscure it. True Englishness is cast as the fine intellectual and moral traditions captured forever in the great books; it is this to which the colonial subject should truly defer, not to the messy manifestations of power in the here-and-now, which are instead pushed into the background.

In his famous early poem, 'Ruins of a Great House' (1962), the St Lucian Derek Walcott engages with the distinction made between the literary and political inheritances of the colonial era. His responses show the continuing difficulty of finding a literary voice that is able to speak outside of the imposition of values supposedly made possible by the use of the English language, and the values embodied in English literary tradition. In the poem, the speaker surveys the ruins of a plantation house, a very specifically Caribbean marker of the colonial past. This house, rotting since its abandonment following the abolition of slavery in 1838, stands in for some of the various imperial legacies with which this young man must deal in coming to articulate for himself. The distinction Viswanathan sees the English literary canon enacting between the profound depth of intellectual and moral inheritance and the exigencies of colonial rule is explicitly refused in the poem:

> I thought next
> Of Men like Hawkins, Walter Raleigh, Drake,
> Ancestral murderers and poets, more perplexed
> In memory now by every ulcerous crime.
> The world's green age then was a rotting lime
> Whose stench became the charnel galleon's text.[7]

The Elizabethan period so often seen as a peak of British achievement is recast as a time of some of its greatest crimes, reminding the reader that the trade in African slaves became established at this time. The manor's decay suggests the dark heart within the great adventures of British expansion. The reference to these men as both murderers and poets also indicts the traditions of English literature. The realm of the literary cannot be split off from the facts of history: as the speaker looks at the great house he imagines 'some slave is rotting in this manorial lake'; so, too, are we encouraged to see the violent legacies that the seemingly-transcendent corpus of English literature may conceal. Up to this point, then, the poem can seem a direct and deliberate reversal of the process of colonial literary instruction where the glories of English were placed separately from imperial politics; Walcott draws them firmly back together.

But Walcott does not end here. No matter what brutality has enabled the creation and dissemination of English language and literature, the poet is unsure that this can entail a rejection. While he recognises and records the violence of the past, he does not allow it wholly to determine the present. In his 1974 essay, 'The Muse of History', Walcott writes that the New World has too often looked to its history and then produced 'a literature of recrimination and despair, a literature of revenge written by the descendents of slaves or a literature of remorse written by the descendents of masters'. Instead, he argues, a different relation to history is required: one in which the past can be explored without recourse to a bitterness which disables one in the present: 'The truly tough aesthetic of the New World neither explains nor forgives history. It refuses to recognise it as a creative or culpable force.'[8] This 'tough aesthetic' guides Walcott in his relation to the literature with which he feels he has to engage in order to be able to write appropriately of his own realities. Walcott does not deny the events of history, but neither are they to be paramount in his explanation of the world to himself and to others. He is not disavowing European culture or dismantling it. Rather, he is claiming it; he makes it his own, or, more correctly, reaffirms that it has always belonged to him. 'Ruins of a Great House' ends by turning to John Donne's famous meditation that 'no man is an island': rather than rejecting the legacy of an inheritance of English, Walcott's speaker finds a way to make a productive link and overcome the possible stultification of anger. In remembering that 'Albion too was once / A colony like ours', he finds a way to reconcile himself to history and profit from a literary inheritance (p. 7).

Walcott's willingness to engage with the language of the former coloniser by no means encourages a historical amnesia. The suggestion instead seems to be that it is only through engaging with the past that one can move forward; history is not to be ignored, just not allowed to stultify the present. In a poem like 'Mass Man' (1969), we can clearly trace a danger perceived by Walcott in an aesthetic that allows only the present. The poem begins by describing the costumed participants in a carnival procession: the masquerade men who are indicated by the title. The speaker, however, retains a profound discomfort about the carnival spirit: while the costumed men insist that he should be dancing, he instead suggests that

> some skull must rub its memory with ashes,
> some mind must squat down howling in your dust,
> some hand must crawl and recollect your rubbish,
> someone must write your poems. (p. 39)

A postcolonial culture that forgets its history is, for Walcott, losing sight of that from which it is formed, and therefore of what it might become. The bleak aspects of history should not stop any positive future, but neither should they be ignored. The newness of post-colonial writing must be based on an engagement with the past; not a dependence on what has gone before, but a willingness to remake it. In his 1970 essay 'What the Twilight Says', Walcott sums up the voice to which he feels the postcolonial writer should aspire, recognising the mixed inheritance of his or her past:

> What is needed is not new names for old things, or old names for old things, but the faith of using the old names anew, so that mongrel as I am, something prickles in me when I see the word 'Ashanti' as with the word 'Warwickshire', both separately intimating my grandfathers' roots, both baptising this neither proud not ashamed bastard, this hybrid, this West Indian.[9]

WHERE LANGUAGE IS CONCEALED: EAVAN BOLAND

Walcott's poetry often contains a palpable anger, but he remains confident in his right and ability to use the language of the former colonial oppressor to articulate the postcolonial world. Other postcolonial poets, however, remain more circumspect about the potential of the English language. In Eavan Boland's 'An Irish Childhood in England: 1951' (1986), the speaker remembers 'the teacher in the London convent who / when I produced "I amn't" in the classroom / turned and said – "you're not in Ireland now".'[10] Recounting the same incident in her memoir, Boland describes her usage of the Irish form as an instance 'of that thing for which the

English reserve a visceral dislike: their language, loaded and aimed by the old enemy'.[11]

Boland, whose father was the first Irish ambassador to the United Kingdom following full independence in 1949, learnt much of what it meant to be Irish while in England. In doing so she became keenly aware of the nature of exclusions. In 'Beautiful Speech' (1994), she writes of preparing 'an essay on / the Art of Rhetoric'. In researching the modes of speech, she comes across the word '*insinuate*' and 'saw that language could writhe and creep / and the lore of snakes / [. . .] came nearer'. The serpentine nature of language is here exposed and Boland draws out the ways in which the meanings that are coded within it are impossible to escape. The degree to which a young Irish woman cannot be admitted into the exclusive space of this language leads Boland to address her younger self, suggesting an alternative conception of how language might be employed:

> we will live, we have lived
> where language is concealed. Is perilous.
> we will be – we have been – citizens
> of its hiding place. (p. 181)

Recognising her marginality both as an Irish person writing in English, and as a woman working in an extremely male-dominated tradition, Boland repeatedly looks to capture the space outside of the snake-like bonds that delineate what might be said within poetry. In 'Mise Eire' (1986), she references an Irish-language poem of the same name, written by the nationalist leader Pádraig Pearse. In Pearse's short poem, the title of which translates as 'I am Ireland', Ireland is imagined as an archetypal female figure, suffering under the wrongs of history.[12] Boland rejects this use of myth to imagine a national story, and the women who people her poem are instead noticeable for their materiality, including a prostitute who serves a garrison and a poor emigrant. Here, as ever, Boland does not wish to ignore the many terrible aspects of Irish history, but insists 'I won't go back' (p. 102). The use of the Irish language seems to her dangerous, in that it too easily makes history part of a romantic nationalism that shies away from political questions:

> the songs
> that bandage up the history,
> the words
> that make a rhythm of the crime
>
> where time is time past. (p. 102)

Instead of this, to use English is to engage precisely with what has happened to Ireland, to refuse the soft-soaping of language such as is seen in 'Beautiful Speech' and instead to trace history precisely as it shows itself in the imported tongue: Boland's 'Mise Eire' ends by noting that 'a new language / is a kind of scar' (p. 103). While this scar may eventually heal 'into a passable imitation / of what went before', it continues to bear the markings of wounds suffered in the past.

Boland often perceives her role as poet as a quest to rescue traces of humanity from the language which consigns the memory of people past to stillness and sterility. In 'Time and Violence' (1994), her speaker stands on a suburban street and sees in a vision the shepherdesses and mermaids who were captured in thousands of earlier poems, written by men. These figures lament to her: 'We cannot sweat here. Our skin is icy. / We cannot breed here. Our wombs are empty.' In becoming trapped in language alone, they can no longer exist as complete women and instead beg: 'write us out of the poem' (p. 208). The task of the poet is to refuse the fossilisation that literary representation can impose and to reignite a sense of a living past and present. This is not always a straightforward task. In 'That the Science of Cartography is Limited', the idea that the world in its reality can adequately be represented at all is questioned. The poem speaks of a famine road in Connaught, built during the Great Famine:

> 1847, when the crop had failed twice,
> Relief Committees gave
> The starving Irish such roads to build.
>
> Where they died, there the road ended. (p. 174)

The narrator goes on to state that she regularly examines the map of Ireland to note that the lines that should mark these roads are missing. Maps are unable to represent these roads that go nowhere, whose physical presence is waning as the 'rough-cast stone' is gradually concealed by 'ivy and the scutch grass' (p. 174). We can envisage literature as akin to these maps: while it is able to offer an illusion of a complete whole, in fact there will inevitably be human stories that have vanished inside its polished version of the world. Boland wants to capture this messiness, and accepting that the dominance of the English language is part of Ireland's history is one part of this.

THE EMPIRE WRITES BACK

In 1989, a trio of Australian academics, Bill Ashcroft, Gareth Griffiths and Helen Tiffin, published a study called *The Empire Writes Back*, which was to prove one of the most influential works within the study of postcolonial literature. One of their major focuses in this study is language; writing on such colonial educational structures as that advocated by Macaulay they suggest that the imposition of English is a central way in which cultural domination may be guaranteed. In the hierarchy that is established between the metropolitan and colonial variants of language they argue that: 'Language becomes the medium through which a hierarchical structure of power is perpetuated, and the medium through which conceptions of "truth", order, and "reality" become established.'[13] To challenge the standard, metropolitan, use of language is, in this view, also to challenge the imposition of values. But this is not to suggest that the language is therefore irredeemably compromised. Rather, as Ashcroft clarifies in a later work, 'language is not simply a repository of cultural contents, but a tool, and often a weapon, which can be employed for various purposes, a tool which is itself part of the cultural experience in which it is used'.[14]

For Ashcroft, Griffiths and Tiffin, Anglophone postcolonial literature is a challenge to the authority of standard English even as the language itself is employed. To make this clear, they draw a distinction between 'what is proposed as a standard code, English (the language of the erstwhile imperial centre), and the linguistic code, english, which has been transformed and subverted into several distinctive varieties throughout the world'.[15] Hence, while English (with the authoritative initial capital letter) might inevitably entail a subscription to the imperial values imposed upon the rest of the world, english offers a set of linguistic codes which can be adapted to local circumstances and can capture the realities of diverse particular social relations within the varied communities of english language users across the colonial and postcolonial world.

Developing this position, *The Empire Writes Back* offers a model of two processes that describe postcolonial literature's engagement with standard English forms. The first is 'abrogation': 'a refusal of the categories of the imperial culture, its aesthetic, its illusory standard of normative or "correct" usage, and its assumption of a traditional and fixed meaning "inscribed" in its words'.[16] Abrogation, then, is about defiance, it is a rejection of the standard language and its implications, a stand against the imposition of set values. The second process at work is 'appropriation': 'the process by which language is taken and made to "bear the burden" of one's cultural experiences'.[17] Here the task is to create the language anew, and to make it work in diverse settings. If abrogation is about the rejection of English, then appropriation describes the creation of englishes, new usages that respond to unique situations. In one sense, what defines postcolonial literatures is precisely that they are 'always written out of the tension between the abrogation of the received English which speaks from the centre, and the act of appropriation which brings it under the influence of a vernacular tongue'.[18]

VERY INDIAN ENGLISH: NISSIM EZEKIEL

In the two poets discussed above (at least in those particular poems), we perhaps see few signs of how the English language itself is abrogated. For both Walcott and Boland the rejection of English outright would impoverish themselves and their writing. In their struggles to engage with representing their particular cultural moment, and the histories that have created it, they insist upon recognising that English plays a vital constitutive role. Yet in insisting that the language can talk of their experiences, that it can be worked to articulate cultural specificities far divorced from the imperial centre, we can nonetheless identify acts of appropriation. While their english may differ little in terms of its appearance, or its lexis or syntax, from the codes of English, the cultural role it is able to play shows a clear disjunction at work.

In the work of other writers, however, the process of abrogation is far more obvious, offering a literature which openly speaks outside of a received code. One set of poems that offers a very definite sense of a language shaped within a local setting is the 'Very Indian Poems in Indian English' written by the Mumbai poet Nissim Ezekiel. In these poems, which appeared in several of Ezekiel's late collections, he uses the rhythms, vocabulary and grammar of Mumbai English, creating dramatic monologues whose speakers are definitely located with specifically Indian contexts. The ways in which the speaker is specifically situated through the use of the vernacular are often highlighted by the content of the poem. A good example of this is 'The Patriot' (1982):

> I am standing for peace and non-violence.
> Why world is fighting fighting,
> Why all people of world
> Are not following Mahatma Gandhi,
> I am simply not understanding.
> Ancient Indian wisdom is 100% correct.
> I should say even 200% correct.
> But Modern generation is neglecting –
> Too much going for fashion and foreign thing.[19]

The 'english' here is obviously not that of the standard code. The constructions are clearly 'wrong' according to the rules of English. This seems particularly ironic when the speaker goes on to tell us that 'Every day I'm reading Times of India / To improve my English language' (p. 237).

This sense that the language used is incorrect leads to an interesting paradox in trying to read Ezekiel's 'Very Indian' poems in terms of the abrogation and appropriation of language that the authors of *The Empire Writes Back* see as defining postcolonial literatures. In their model, such appropriation is to be read as a positive reclaiming of the validity of local experience in opposition to a metropolitan norm that would denigrate it. However, it may seem that Ezekiel's poem actually functions to reiterate the distinction between correct and incorrect forms and the implications of superiority and inferiority these may imply. His 'patriot' can come across as foolish or ridiculous – the reference to ancient Indian wisdom being '200% correct' seems to display significant ignorance – and his use of vernacular may reinforce this. Rather than rejecting hierarchies, the satire of a poem like this might actually confirm them.

Yet if 'The Patriot' is a satirical poem, it is worth asking exactly what is being satirised, and how. In 1965, Ezekiel wrote an important critique of a travel book called *An Area of Darkness*, by the Trinidadian writer V. S. Naipaul. In *An Area of Darkness*, Naipaul found Indian society wanting in many ways, not least because of the relationship it had with the legacies of British colonialism, which it simultaneously venerated and decried. Ezekiel's criticism of Naipaul's book offers a useful insight into his own view of India and into how we might read the 'Very Indian' poems. Ezekiel makes it clear several times that he shares many of Naipaul's frustrations with India, but he rejects the way in which *An Area of Darkness* finds *only* problems in the nation. 'I see India in my own way,' he writes, and insists that alternative perspectives must be used to challenge Naipaul's simplifications.[20] Again and again he finds instances of Naipaul condemning the whole country on the basis of limited examples, and asserts that the true story is always more complex. Ezekiel also wants to decry what he sees as the failings of Indian society, but will not accept that these can be seen as its totality. In contrast to what he sees as Naipaul's withdrawal from the intricate realities of India, he insists on his own proximity:

> I am incurably critical and sceptical. This is what I am in relation to India also [. . .] In this sense only, I love India. I expect nothing in return because critical, sceptical love does not beget love. It performs another, more objective function.[21]

Ezekiel makes a determined claim to be allowed both to love and to critique India.

Given this insight we can perhaps read 'The Patriot' more generously, understanding that its satire is mixed with, and given force by, a concomitant affection. The speaker may be foolish, but he is nonetheless allowed to articulate in his own terms, demonstrating that his bluster does not necessarily negate an invaluable generosity of spirit. We can see Ezekiel's affection for his subjects in another 'Very Indian' poem, 'The Railway Clerk'. In this, the slightly pompous speaker decries his position:

> I am never neglecting my responsibility,
> I am discharging it properly,
> I am doing my duty,
> but who is appreciating?
> Nobody, I am telling you. (p. 184)

Here the mockery seems light and the facts of the clerk's unfortunate situation are viewed with a sympathy that recognises the difficulties of his life. As Ezekiel puts it in 'Naipaul's India and Mine': 'I know those clerks, their background, their problems, their conditions of work, their income [. . .] their sense of dignity of worth, their humanity in short'.[22] This sense of humanity is key to the 'Very Indian' poems and the distinctive voices draw especial attention to it. In other poems, Ezekiel rejects any opinion that too easily simplifies Indian scenarios: in 'Poverty Poem' (1982) he pities the simplistic understanding of a tourist who is impressed by what a 'friendly people' Indians are, as he silently notes her ignorance that 'beggars in India / smile only at white foreigners' (p. 231); in the late poem 'Occasion' it is an Indian journalist who offers a dismal view of a clerk, concluding that India is doomed – 'there's no future for us' – without recognising that his own privilege might tell a different story: 'He offers me another drink. / The servant brings more snacks' (p. 277).

Ezekiel remains aware that his experience too is marked by privilege. He is only able to offer the vernacular 'Very Indian' poems by virtue of his ability also to express himself in the fully mastered form of the standard code. But he refuses to privilege his cosmopolitan cynicism over local belief. In a poem discovered only after his death in 1988, 'The Second Candle', he is struck by his wife showing gratitude for her blessings by lighting two candles for God – one in thanks for her lot and the second for 'a special favour'. Ezekiel's speaker offers no comment, but instead silently stares at the candles and 'wonder[s] at the faith / that deals so simply with its God' (p. 296). This wonder at simplicity is key to Ezekiel's later poems, including the 'Very Indian' sequences. It is an affirmation of the intrinsic value to be found in local cultures, and at times involves a necessary search for an appropriate local language in which to express such respect.

THE LANGUAGE OF THE AFRICAN NOVEL: NGŨGĨ AND ACHEBE

While poetry might appear to be the most direct form in which questions of searching for appropriate language can be raised, the debates around how to find a voice in which postcolonial writers may express their unique situation can also be read within prose writing. Regarding the African novel, these debates have been raised with particular clarity. A central figure here is the Kenyan novelist Ngũgĩ wa Thiong'o. Ngũgĩ began his career writing in English, and indeed studied in Britain, at the University of Leeds, but in 1977 'said farewell to the English language' and wrote all his subsequent plays, novels and short stories in the East African language of Gĩkũyũ.[23] The reasons for this shift, and the significance he sees it having, are most clearly laid out in his 1986 essay 'The Language of African Literature'. In this essay he insists that the issue of language in literary works 'cannot be discussed outside the context of those social forces which have made it both an issue demanding our attention and a problem calling for a resolution'.[24] These 'social forces' cannot, for Ngũgĩ, be meaningfully separated from the legacies of imperialism. He argues that the continuing domination of economics, society and culture in Africa cannot be separated from the question of language. Language is 'the most important vehicle through which [colonial] power fascinated and held the soul a prisoner'.[25] He illustrates this point through reference to his own education, providing a vision of how Macaulay's vision of the transmission of values through the English language played out in 1950s Kenya as a brutal policy of suppression of the local tongue. Children caught speaking Gĩkũyũ at Ngũgĩ's school would be beaten or forced 'to carry a metal placard around the neck with inscriptions such as I AM STUPID or I AM A DONKEY'.[26]

Faced with such a deliberate policy of denigration of African languages, the necessary response is obvious to Ngũgĩ: 'I believe that my writing in Gĩkũyũ language, a Kenyan tongue, an African language, is part and parcel of the anti-imperialist struggles of Kenyan and African peoples.'[27] Only through writing in African languages can an African literature be created; anything else inevitably reveals a slavish inability to shake off the colonial yoke: 'It is the final triumph of a system of domination when the dominated start singing its praises.'[28] Literature in European languages can never be African literature but is at best 'Afro-European', argues Ngũgĩ, even putting his own early work into this category. And while Afro-European literature might contain some remarkable works of art, it nonetheless is defined by, and in turn helps to perpetuate, neo-colonial relationships between Europe and Africa. A literature written in African languages could never be sufficient in dismantling these relationships, but its formation is a necessary first step towards this goal.

Ngũgĩ's argument is often framed as an attack on a view of literature put forward decades before by another important African novelist, the Nigerian Chinua Achebe, who died in 2013. It is worth looking to Achebe's essay to see an alternative to Ngũgĩ's view, before looking at how these issues might be played out in a pair of African novels. In Achebe's essay, 'English and the African Writer', he offers a different and more expansive definition of African literature than Ngũgĩ, seeing it as 'the sum total of all the *national* and *ethnic* languages of Africa'.[29] For Achebe, the ethnic languages are those local ones that are privileged in Ngũgĩ's model, while the national language is often something else: in Nigeria, it is English. He argues that the diversity of languages in Nigeria (including Hausa, Ibo, Yoruba, Effik, Edo, Ijaw and others) mean that it is only through the English language that diverse national subjects can speak to each other. When it comes to communicating

across the continent as a whole, this problem is even more pronounced and only the major world languages (which, because
of the histories of imperialism, means European languages, and
English and French particularly) provide the means for Africans of
various nations and ethnicities to communicate. Achebe does not
suggest that the importance of the English language in Africa is an
intrinsically good thing, describing it rather as something which
'history has forced down our throats'.[30] He also recognises that
there might be a sense of betrayal that haunts those writers who
forego local languages in favour of English. Nonetheless, although
he states that he fully desires the continuation of literature in
ethnic languages, he himself feels he has no choice but to write in
English. However, this language will have to be 'a new English':
'The African writer should aim to use English in a way that brings
out his message best without altering the language to the extent
that its value as a medium of international exchange will be lost.'[31]
This requires a language 'still in full communion with its ancestral
home', as much as it has been 'altered to suit its new African surroundings'.[32] This view is clearly far more conservative than that
of Ngũgĩ, and perhaps also than that expressed by Ashcroft and his
colleagues.

THE PALM-OIL WITH WHICH WORDS ARE EATEN: CHINUA ACHEBE, *THINGS FALL APART*

Conservative though it may seem in relation to some of the others
discussed above, Achebe's view of language does not stop him
offering a version of African experience in a form quite divorced
from a standard understanding of an English literary code. His
Things Fall Apart (1958) is one of the most influential works in
postcolonial literature, not least because it demonstrates the extent
to which novelty can be created in representing a non-European
world, without needing to break fully from the use of European
language. *Things Fall Apart* tells the story of Okonkwo, an important man in the village of Umuofia, an Igbo settlement in what is
now Nigeria. The novel is set during the period of the first sustained contact that the people of Umuofia have with Europeans. As

missionaries and colonial administrators begin to encroach further into the land, Okonkwo leads those who oppose this imposition and eventually kills an Igbo messenger from the white men. Following the shame this murder brings, he hangs himself.

Okonkwo is presented throughout as a brave and strong man, but often crucially out of touch with the values of his own community. He is punished more than once for transgressing Umuofia's laws (eventually being exiled for seven years), but more often he simply seems bemused by some of its practices. In particular, in focusing especially strongly on the masculine values that he so clearly embodies, he fails to recognise that his community might also respect more traditionally 'feminine' beliefs and modes of behaviour. One conversation especially makes this clear. One of the most respected elders of the village, Ndulue, dies, and his wife Ozoemena also passes away on learning of the news. Okonkwo discusses these events with his friends, Ofoedu and Obierika:

> 'It was always said that Ndulue and Ozoemena had one mind,' said Obierika. 'I remember when I was a young boy there was a song about them. He could not do anything without telling her.'
>
> 'I did not know that,' said Okonkwo. 'I thought he was a strong man in his youth.'
>
> 'He was indeed,' said Ofoedu.
>
> Okonkwo shook his head doubtfully.
>
> 'He led Umuofia to war in those days,' said Obierika.[33]

Okonkwo is incapable of recognising that a person might be able to display both manly virtues and a reliance on a woman at the same time. For him, the two must always be separate, and male strength comes precisely through the suppression of any feminine elements.

That Okonkwo's understanding is at odds with the more common wisdom of Umuofia is often suggested through the subtle use of language. Although the novel is written in English, Achebe does not attempt to translate all Igbo words, allowing instead the meanings of the unfamiliar vocabulary to become clear to the non-Igbo-speaking reader through the contexts in which they are employed. However, these contexts remain complicated, to the extent that we can even read Okonkwo seemingly misinterpreting them. We are told early in the novel that his 'whole life was dominated by fear, the fear of failure and of weakness' (p. 10). This aversion to weakness manifests as disgust with his father, a man who never takes a title (to take a title shows that a man is recognised for his achievements in Umuofia). A man without title was known as *agbala*, a word that could also mean 'woman'. However, instead of recognising the link between the two words as contingent and functioning in particular ways for particular reasons, Okonkwo reads them as equivalent and henceforth 'was ruled by one passion – to hate everything that his father had loved. One of those things was gentleness and another was idleness' (p. 11). While being idle is a quality no more prized in Umuofia than anywhere else, Okonkwo fails to see the possible virtues in being gentle. While in some contexts *agbala* may have negative connotations, it is certainly not the case that these are the only meanings attached to the word. We learn later in the novel that Agbala is also the name of the god whose messages are relayed by the priestess Chielo. Okonkwo knows better than to challenge the god but fails to make any link that might upset his simplistic view of male and female relations in Umuofia.

One aspect of Umuofia life that is frequently marked as feminine is the art of storytelling. Noting this link, Okonkwo disdains stories. His son Nwoye recognises this feeling in his father and therefore also rejects such creation stories as his mother might tell as 'for foolish women and children', instead forcing himself to prefer the anecdotes of combat Okonkwo tells (p. 39). Yet the novel shows us that stories are crucial to the society, often in the form of the boiled-down wisdom of proverbs. In proverbs, direct explanation is foregone in favour of examples demonstrated in narrative. Early in the novel we are told that 'among the Igbo the art of conversation is regarded very highly, and proverbs are the palm-oil with which words are eaten' (p. 6). The image here is that a message becomes digestible precisely through its medium; it is the fact that proverbs gesture to embedded local knowledge that can make them so efficacious in facilitating communication within a culture. Proverbs, and stories more generally, contain the heart of a culture's understanding of itself. The form of Achebe's novel, which contains many proverbs and works more generally to introduce the particularities of Umuofia society through the use of episodic stories, reflect this sense that it may be less language that embodies the values of a culture, as Ngũgĩ believes, but rather the use to which it is put, and, specifically, the ways in which stories are told.

Comedy is made of the differences between languages in the novel and the possibilities of misinterpretation: an Ibo interpreter working for the Christians speaks a different dialect from his listeners and therefore 'instead of saying "myself", he always said "my buttocks"' (p. 106). Nonetheless, Achebe does not see the work of translation as necessarily comedic, nor always compromised in its attempts to understand another culture. In the actions of the first white missionary in the region of Umuofia, Mr Brown, we perhaps see a model for the work of translation and communication between cultures. In regular discussions with an Igbo man called Akunna, they discuss their respective religions: 'Neither of them succeeded in converting the other but they learnt more about their different beliefs' (p. 130). In these conversations we can see each man respecting that the ideas of the other are embedded in narratives that as a whole articulate particular understandings of the world. It is when actions and beliefs are divorced from the wider stories that give them meaning that they are reduced, not when they are simply rendered in another language. This splitting of a story from its context is perhaps the final tragedy of *Things Fall Apart*. After Okonkwo's suicide, the British district commissioner considers including him in the book he is writing:

> The story of this man who had killed a messenger and hanged himself would make interesting reading. One could almost write a whole chapter on him. Perhaps not a whole chapter but a reasonable paragraph, at any rate. There was so much else to include, and one must be firm in cutting out details. (pp. 151–2)

As Okonkwo's story gets reduced from a chapter to a paragraph in the proposed book, in recognition of the non-essentialness of 'details', we see precisely what *Things Fall Apart* warns against:

it is not speaking a different language that might divorce people from understanding a local culture, but a failure to recognise how knowledge cannot be easily isolated and that contexts are often best understood as a whole.

ROTTEN ENGLISH: KEN SARO-WIWA, *SOZABOY*

In 1992, a special issue of the journal *Research in African Literatures* revisited the 'Language Question' and published essays from a number of African writers and critics who broadly agreed with Ngũgĩ's stance that African literature could only be written in local languages. One of the few dissenting opinions came from Ken Saro-Wiwa, the Nigerian writer and activist who was to be executed by his country's government three years later. Saro-Wiwa grants Ngũgĩ the right to his opinion but simultaneously rejects any claim that his own decision to use English has resulted in the 'colonisation of the mind' that Ngũgĩ decries: 'I am, I find, as Ogoni as ever. I am enmeshed in Ogoni culture. I eat Ogoni food. I sing Ogoni songs. I dance to Ogoni music.'[34] In a different manner from Achebe, Saro-Wiwa equally insists that the possession and transmission of culture operates through more than just language. However, he has a deeper concern about the implications of Ngũgĩ's insistence on writing in Gĩkũyũ. Within the multi-ethnic states of Africa, the English language is often a key factor in allowing different ethnic groups to communicate with one another. In turning away from this democratic function of English to promote instead the language of a majority ethnic group, Saro-Wiwa questions whether Ngũgĩ 'has thought or cares about the implications of his decision for the minority ethnic groups in Kenya and for the future of Kenya as a multi-ethnic nation or, indeed, as a nation at all'.[35]

In his 1985 novel *Sozaboy*, Saro-Wiwa explores some of the tensions between ethnic groups in Nigeria, but does so in a particularly original and distinct form of English which he labels 'Rotten English'. In an 'Author's Note' to the novel he characterises this as 'a mixture of Nigerian pidgin English, broken English and occasional flashes of good idiomatic English. This language is disordered and disorderly'.[36] In 'The Language of African Literature', Saro-Wiwa suggests that of all varieties of English, he has found 'that which carries best and is most popular is standard English, expressed simply and lucidly'.[37] However, Rotten English's invocation of disorder seems better suited to capture the world rendered in *Sozaboy*. *Sozaboy* is set during the Biafran conflict of 1967–70. The succession of the eastern regions of Nigeria, under the name of Biafra, was driven by manifold reasons. However, a primary factor, and the reason on which international coverage predominantly focused, was the idea that the Igbo, numerically the dominant group in the east, faced discrimination and sometimes violent persecution within Nigeria, which was dominated overall by the Hausa-Fulari and Yoruba groups. For Saro-Wiwa, a member of the minority Ogoni ethnic group, who were mostly located in the Biafra region, the new state was no more a homeland than Nigeria as a whole, and in moving away from a multi-ethnic to a majority model, actually less desirable. He became a supporter of the federalist, anti-secessionist cause.

For Mene, the young Ogoni man who narrates *Sozaboy*, the decision is not so straightforward. While he seems able to articulate a fondness for his town of Dukana (although he often longs for the glamour of Lagos or even Pitakwa – Port Harcourt – to which he often travels in his role as apprentice driver), he never seems to evince any sense of national belonging, either to Nigeria or to Biafra. The different types of belonging that inspire the brutal war are poorly understood by Mene, if at all. This sense of his, at best, partial comprehension of events is particularly emphasised by the Rotten English that provides the novel's distinctive voice.

The novel begins with a sentence that seems incomplete: 'Although, everybody in Dukana was happy at first' (p. 1). The opening conjunction primes the reader to expect a contrast to be drawn but our narrator fails to do this. Instead of introducing details, the hanging grammar offers no more than a sense of foreboding, of unhappiness to come. This lack of detail, in which the facts of the war become obscured by an impressionistic sense of horror and dread, is characteristic of Mene's limited understanding of his situation. After Mene joins the Biafran army he listens to a senior officer describe the enemy:

> I begin to fear this Mr. Enemy you know [. . .] Even the Chief
> Commander General is fearing this man. Why? Even sef, why
> all of us will join hand to kill him. Does he have many heads?
> What is wrong with him? 'E get stronghead? Or did he call
> another man's wife? (p. 78)

The reasons for the war completely escape the young recruit who
can only accept the labelling of an enemy without knowing why, or
even who is meant.

The senior officer in this scene uses 'big big words that I cannot
understand' (p. 78). Repeatedly in the novel the 'big grammar' of
standard English is evoked as possessing a degree of persuasive
power, even when it is incompletely understood. In Mene's dream
of a meeting in Dukana, a dream that will soon seem an accurate
prediction of events, the impact of such language is not diminished
through the fact that it requires translation:

> The man with fine shirt stood up. And begin to talk in English.
> Fine fine English. Big big words. Grammar [. . .] 'Henceforth.
> General mobilisation. All citizens. Able-bodied. Join the mili-
> tary. His Excellency. Powers conferred on us. Volunteer.
> Conscription'. Big big words. Long long grammar. 'Ten
> heads. Vandals. Enemy'. Everybody was silent. Everywhere
> was silent like burial ground. Then they begin to interpret all
> that long grammar plus big big words in Kana. In short words
> what the man is saying is that all those who can fight will join
> army. (p. 47)

Various registers clash here, from the elaborate language of the
orator rendered in fractured form, to the Khana language of the
Ogoni which is named but not shown, and the rotten articulation of
Mene that tries to bring these together. In this syncretism no great
truth is learned but rather only the basic message gets transmitted:
that a war will have to be fought, even if the prospective combat-
ants do not understand why.

Mene joins the army and is proud to take on the new name of
Sozaboy (soldier boy). In his role as soldier he seems to find an
identity with which he can impress the people of Dukana, not least

his new wife, Agnes. However, it is significant that the new name in which he takes such pride is actually one that strips him of his individuality and instead labels him with the same role that so many young men around him are being forced to take on. By the end of the novel, the name seems a curse. After enduring hellish experiences fighting on both sides of the conflict he returns to a wrecked Dukana where he is seen as a ghost who must be destroyed: 'the juju have told us that unless we kill your ghost, everybody in Dukana must die' (p. 180). He is forced to flee his homeland, and give up his adopted name to survive. However, there is no suggestion that he will be able to regain any identity as Mene. Once he has succumbed to the power manifest in 'big, big grammar' or the attraction of a name like Sozaboy, it is not clear that he can go back. At the end of the novel, it is perhaps only the confusions and disorder of his rotten English that allows him any identity at all. The order to be found elsewhere will explicitly oppress him and force him into situations and behaviours that can only result in his destruction.

MONGRELS AND SILENCE: KERI HULME, *THE BONE PEOPLE*

The last literary work to be examined in this chapter on language and voice in postcolonial writing is Keri Hulme's *The Bone People* (1984). The use of language, and the implications it may have, are at the heart of this novel, which includes much dialogue written in Maori (though, like Saro-Wiwa but not Achebe, Hulme provides a glossary at the end of the novel for the benefit of any monoglossic Anglophone readers). The irruptions of Maori language into the text are indicative of a deeper commitment to a Maori ontology and to traditional forms of ordering the world and its representations. In the novel, which tells the story of the gradual coming together of a reclusive woman, Kerewin Holmes, with a mute child, Simon Gillayley, and his often abusive adoptive father Joe, we can see an examination of how the mixture of cultures in Aotearoa New Zealand might be comprehended and managed. Language is at the centre of the process of adaptation.

The Bone People was an immediate success on publication (despite waiting several years for a publisher) but attracted controversy just as quickly, not least when it won the Pegasus Prize, which was to be awarded to a work by a Maori writer. The writer and critic C. K. Stead published one of the most famous attacks, though he is careful throughout to direct his ire at those involved in awarding the prize, rather than at the novelist herself. He questions the criteria of the prize, suggesting that if it was intended to promote and preserve Maori culture, then it should have been open only to Maori language works. Instead, it seems to have been based on a racial criterion, and given that Hulme's claim to Maori ancestry relies on just one Maori grandparent, he questions on what grounds she qualifies. Conceding that the judges may have chosen to consider the novel Maori in terms of its content, he rejects the decision on these grounds also: 'it seems to me that some essential Maori elements in her novel are unconvincing. Her uses of Maori language and mythology strike me as willed, self-conscious, not inevitable, not entirely authentic.'[38]

There are a number of problems with Stead's argument, not least in his suggestion that the writing of Maori identity is only authentic when spontaneous, rather than recognising that it is equally as constructed as any other element of a literary text. But there is a particular issue with his conclusion here – that '*The Bone People* is a novel by a Pakeha [European-descended New Zealander] which has won an award intended for a Maori' – in that it seems to insist on an either/or philosophy of ethnicity at odds with Hulme's intentions as expressed in the novel and elsewhere. In an essay called 'Mauri: an Introduction to Bicultural Poetry in New Zealand', she explicitly admits that 'a sizable number of New Zealanders have both Maori and European ancestry, and a large proportion of these "mongrels" are familiar with both cultures. I am a mongrel myself'.[39] *The Bone People* does not claim to offer the essence of an undiluted Maori identity, but rather engages with precisely this biculturalism or 'mongrelness'.

There is a temptation in reading *The Bone People* to see Joe as an authentic Maori character, Simon as definitively Pakeha and Kerewin (who has similar ancestral roots to Hulme herself) as somewhere between the two, but the text actually directs us to realise that all move along the continuum of mongrelism. Simon, who is known as Haimona by Joe, has a dual name that reflects that of his country, while the continual linkage of him to the Maori trickster-god Maui complicates any sense of pure Europeanness. Meanwhile, Joe himself comprehends that his Maori identity might be as complex as Kerewin's: 'My father's father was English so I'm not yer 100% pure. But I'm Maori. And that's the way I feel too, the way you said, that the Maoritanga [Maori way of being] has got lost in the way I live.'[40] Much of the novel is concerned with how biculturality might play out in Aotearoa New Zealand and how the various elements of its history could be reconciled. A note Kerewin sends to Joe towards the end of the novel seems to suggest that this might best be done through 'commensalism', literally, eating at the same table:

> But if I exist this coming Christ Mass, rejoin me at the Tower eh? O the groaning table of cheer . . . speaking of tables, does commensalism appeal to you as an upright vertebrate? Common quarters wherein we circulate like corpuscles in one blood stream, joining (I won't say like clots) for food and drink and discussion and whatever else we feel like . . . a way to keep unjoy at bay, like those last few weeks before they hauled your corpus away. (p. 464)

The open hospitality of commensal proximity seems to Hulme a way for the people of Aotearoa New Zealand to move forward.

In her essay on bicultural poetry, Hulme suggests that 'mongrel' writings 'owe much to Maori thought and mythology and ways of expression; and *because they are written in English* an equally incalculable debt is owed to taha Pakeha, the side that is European'.[41] Hulme's style in *The Bone People*, in which English prose is threaded through with Maori language and concepts, might seem to capture this mixed heritage, but the novel also presents another image of a language able to respond to the nation's particular history and present. Simon cannot speak but nonetheless has an interesting relation to language and one that perhaps offers the clearest sign of how a successful commensalism might manifest.

After listening to one of Kerewin's overly verbose sentences,

Simon tries to decipher her meaning. The word 'penitential' particularly trips him. He relates the word to 'penitentiary', which he understands to mean jail, though this helps little: 'He kneels for minutes on the end of the bed, trying to dredge up more past conversation that contained the word, but that's the only bit that sounds similar' (p. 47). Simon strives to understand Kerewin's utterance by linking her words to others and trying to pinpoint meaning through the relation. We can read this as perhaps an applied version of Ferdinand de Saussure's observation that words have meaning only in relation to other words, and have no necessary link to the objects and states they signify. Simon goes on to reject language structured in this way later in the novel: 'knowing names is nice, but it don't mean much. Knowing this is a whatever she said is neat, but it don't change it. Names aren't much. The things are' (p. 155). The referential nature of language is here abjured in favour of a more direct relation to the world. This is played out in the 'hand-language' that the mute Simon uses to communicate. Joe tells Kerewin that the boy has rejected 'proper sign language' in favour of his own faster version: 'it's mainly derivation. You know, from an object, or a way of doing things that is ordinary, or from ordinary things, or thing . . . O b, bother' (p. 59). Joe's explanation breaks down, highlighting again the inadequacy of traditional language in coming to terms with the emergence of a newness derived from the immediacy of a particular situation. Hulme's blending of English and Maori in her novel is the main way she chooses to signal biculturalism, but in Simon's innovative and direct (though silent) language, we can perhaps see another way of working through the continual problems postcolonial writers face in developing a new language free from the imperial grip of an old one.

SUMMARY

- The English language can seem primarily the property of the English people, and unsuitable for use in postcolonial contexts.
- The export of the English language, and especially English literature, was seen as a valuable way to inculcate suitable values in colonial peoples.

- In Derek Walcott's poems this history is acknowledged; but he refuses to abandon the language even as he highlights its relation to a brutal past.
- Eavan Boland's poetry frequently draws attention to those aspects of both the past and present that can be obscured by linguistic and literary tradition.
- Ashcroft, Griffiths and Tiffin's *The Empire Writes Back* is a landmark study that identifies postcolonial literature as necessarily engaged in the 'abrogation' and 'appropriation' of standard English.
- In Nissim Ezekiel's 'Very Indian' poems, local variations of English are used to create humour, but also reveal a love and respect of local cultures.
- While Ngũgĩ wa Thiong'o famously rejects writing in English as perpetuating colonial domination, Chinua Achebe insists that a new form of English is possible.
- In Achebe's *Things Fall Apart*, the ways in which stories are told and preserved is seen as more important than the language used.
- Ken Saro-Wiwa's *Sozaboy* uses a 'Rotten English' to suggest the alienation of its narrator from the political situation around him.
- In *The Bone People*, Keri Hulme presents Maori ideas in the English language to evoke biculturalism, but also gestures towards the extra-linguistic as the best way to express this.

NOTES

1. James Joyce, *A Portrait of the Artist as a Young* Man (London: Penguin, [1916] 1992), p. 205.
2. Thomas Babington Macauley, 'Minute on Indian Education, February 2, 1835', in Barbara Harlow and Mia Carter (eds), *Imperialism and Orientalism: a Documentary Sourcebook* (Malden, MA: Blackwell, 1999), pp. 57–8.
3. Ibid., p. 58.
4. Ibid., p. 61.
5. Homi K. Bhabha, *The Location of Culture* (London: Routledge, 1994), p. 89.
6. Gauri Viswanathan, 'Currying Favor: the Politics of British

Educational and Cultural Policy in India, 1813–1854', *Social Text* 19/20 (1988), 103.

7. Derek Walcott, *Selected Poems* (London: Faber and Faber, 2007), p. 7. Further references to this edition are given in the main text.

8. Derek Walcott, *What the Twilight Says: Essays* (London: Faber and Faber, 1998), p. 37.

9. Ibid., p. 9.

10. Eavan Boland, *Collected Poems* (Manchester: Carcanet, 1995), p. 127. Further references to this edition are given in the main text.

11. Eavan Boland, *Object Lessons: the Life of the Woman and the Poet in Our Time* (London: Vintage, [1995] 1996), p. 46.

12. Patrick Pearse, 'I am Ireland' [1914], in David Pierce (ed.), *Irish Writing in the Twentieth Century: a Reader* (Cork: Cork University Press, 2000), p. 260.

13. Bill Ashcroft et al., *The Empire Writes Back*, 2nd edn (London: Routledge, 2002), p. 7.

14. Bill Ashcroft, *Caliban's Voice: the Transformation of English in Post-colonial Literatures* (London: Routledge, 2009), p. 4.

15. Ashcroft et al., *The Empire Writes Back*, p. 8.

16. Ibid., p. 37.

17. Ibid., p. 38.

18. Ibid., p. 38.

19. Nissim Ezekiel, *Collected Poems*, ed. John Thieme, 2nd edn (New Delhi: Oxford University Press, 2005), p. 237. Further references to this edition are given in the main text.

20. Nissim Ezekiel, 'Naipaul's India and Mine' [1965], in Adil Jussawalla (ed.), *New Writing in India* (Harmondsworth: Penguin, 1974), p. 76.

21. Ibid., pp. 88–9.

22. Ibid., p. 77.

23. Ngũgĩ wa Thiong'o, *Decolonising the Mind: the Politics of Language in African Literature* (London: James Currey, 1986), p. xiv.

24. Ibid., p. 4.

25. Ibid., p. 9.

26. Ibid., p. 11.

27. Ibid., p. 28.
28. Ibid., p. 20.
29. Chinua Achebe, 'English and the African Writer', *Transition* 18 (1965), 27.
30. Ibid., p. 28.
31. Ibid., p. 29.
32. Ibid., p. 30.
33. Chinua Achebe, *Things Fall Apart* (London: Penguin, [1958] 2001), p. 50. Further references to this edition are given in the main text.
34. Ken Saro-Wiwa, 'The Language of African Literature: a Writer's Testimony', *Research in African Literatures* 23(1) (1992), 156.
35. Ibid., 156.
36. Ken Saro-Wiwa, *Sozaboy* (New York: Longman, [1985] 1994), p. vii. Further references to this edition are given in the main text.
37. Saro-Wiwa, 'The Language of African Literature', p. 157.
38. C. K. Stead, 'Keri Hulme's *The Bone People* and the Pegasus Award for Maori Literature', *ARIEL: a Review of International English Literature* 16(4) (1985), p. 104.
39. Keri A. L. Hulme, 'Mauri: an Introduction to Bicultural Poetry in New Zealand', in G. Amirthanayagam and S. C. Harrex (eds), *Only Connect: Literary Perspectives East and West* (Adelaide: Centre for Research in the New Literatures in English, 1981), p. 294.
40. Keri Hulme, *The Bone People* (London: Picador, [1984] 2001), p. 76. Further references to this edition are given in the main text.
41. Hulme, 'Mauri', p. 307.

CHAPTER 2

The Need to Belong

The last chapter ended with an address of some of the ways in which Keri Hulme introduces Maori concepts into *The Bone People*. Struggles for recognition of indigenous languages have been an important aspect of the movements for First Nation rights in the last few decades, but by no means the only cause which indigenous peoples such as the Maori in Aotearoa New Zealand, the Aborigines of Australia and Native American and Canadian groups have embraced in the fight to have their understandings of the world granted legal status and their rights honoured on their own terms, not just those of the settler populations who came to dominate these nations. Central to these struggles has been the issue of land. As Sara Upstone observes, the *Oxford English Dictionary*'s definition of a colony includes 'not only a community of settlers, but also "the territory" occupied by that community';[1] the colonial process is often, if not primarily, one of claiming land and the rights to use it for economic gain. Struggles for decolonisation often focused around reclaiming this land, and critiques of contemporary neo-imperialism regularly indict the ways in which Western corporations use and abuse the natural resources of 'less developed' – or politically and economically dependent – countries. For indigenous peoples this can seem a particular issue, in that supposed independence from a colonial power does not seem to have restored their rights to their land, which continues to be withheld from them by other communities within their nations.

FROM *TERRA NULLIUS* TO THE MABO DECISION

A brief examination of a key legal issue of Australian land rights, which involves one of the most famous judgements relating to indigenous sovereignty, will serve to open up some of the ideas this chapter will explore. The British colonisation of Australia in the late eighteenth century, which famously took the form of the transportation of convicts, began after the realisation by the first explorers that the land had little attraction as a trading post. The man most often, erroneously, seen as the 'discoverer' of Australia, Captain James Cook, on noting how little interest the Aborigines had in trading with the British, decided that they had 'no idea of traffic'.[2] As the most widespread definition of common-law property ownership then current was John Locke's formulation that those who did not cultivate the land did not own it, the British government hesitated little before deciding on the policy of transportation.

The British state came to recognise a difference between its colonies established through conquest or accession by treaty on one hand, and by discovery on the other. While Australia was generally perceived as existing in the latter group, this was never formally inscribed in the law of the time. Indeed, as the historian Henry Reynolds points out, many important judicial figures in early colonial Australia believed that the Aborigines' right of 'Native Title' should be respected. It was only later in the nineteenth century, as the settlers came to cultivate much more of the land, often expelling the indigenous inhabitants to do so, that the idea of Australia having existed before colonisation as *terra nullius* or 'empty land' became widespread.[3] The discrimination against indigenous Australians was often justified by invoking their non-presence, particularly until the 1967 referendum, that by a massive majority rescinded section 127 of the 1900 constitution, which had stated that 'in reckoning the numbers of the people of the Commonwealth [. . .] aboriginal natives shall not be counted'.[4] The common law of Australia, which in turn determined the statuary law, acted as if the Aborigines were simply not there.

The 1967 referendum did not, however, guarantee land rights to Aborigines and, in 1972, a group set up a 'tent embassy' outside the national parliament in Canberra, symbolically demonstrating that without land rights they felt they did not belong in Australia. In 1982, Eddie Koiki Mabo, a resident of the Murray Islands in the Torres Strait, led an appeal to the High Court to seek federal government protection against the state of Queensland, claiming that his community could demonstrate unbroken ownership of the land (including the 'construction and maintenance of gardens') and that they therefore had common law ownership of it.[5] The proof of this historical connection was to be found in oral tradition, rather than in written records, but on 3 June 1992, the court found in Mabo's favour. The decision was perhaps not the definitive watershed many considered it to be at the time (mainly because of the manifold particularities of the case, which resisted a general application), but it nonetheless marked a significant moment in which, when two conflicting senses of tradition and belonging were played out, the indigenous people were found to have a stronger case than the settlers.

Issues relating to indigenous communities will be discussed again later in this book, in relation to Thomas King in Chapter 4, and Sally Morgan in Chapter 6. However, this summary of the legacy of *terra nullius* in Australia, and the important interruption that the Mabo verdict can be seen to have made, is intended to allow for a focus on the settler, rather than indigenous, community of Australia. As stated above, white Australia often tried to act is if the Aboriginal people did not exist, despite their obvious presence. Terry Goldie has suggested that this deliberate blindness is one possible response to the anxiety caused among settlers by the existence of a group who might seem to have a stronger claim of ownership:

> The white Canadian [or Australian, he implies] looks at the Indian [or Aborigine]. The Indian is Other and therefore alien. But the Indian is indigenous and therefore cannot be alien. So the Canadian must be alien. But how can the Canadian be alien within Canada?[6]

Goldie labels the processes that attempt to overcome this settler anxiety as 'indigenization': 'a peculiar word [which] suggests the impossible necessity of becoming indigenous'.[7] He is particularly concerned with how this 'impossible necessity' of indigenisation might be seen in settler representations of indigenous people, but he also recognises that it might play out in descriptions of the relationships that settlers may have with their natural environment. For Goldie, these relationships are always marked by the trace of indigenous peoples, even when they are seemingly absent, but the discussion of the attempt to comprehend nature reveals much about the ways in which writers from settler communities may try to enunciate ways in which the land belongs to them (though not necessarily in the exclusive sense challenged by the Mabo decision), and, equally, how they might belong to the land.

IN THE INTERIOR: PATRICK WHITE, *VOSS*

In Paul Carter's important 1987 study, *The Road to Botany Bay*, he looks to the importance of naming the land for the first European explorers in Australia. 'By the act of place-naming,' he famously states, 'space is transformed symbolically into place, that is, a space with a history.'[8] To affix names to a landscape is to give it sense within a narrative, to turn the raw material of the physical world into the building blocks of a national history: 'more effectively than stump-plough or roller, [language] translates the landscape into a familiar arrangement of mental objects, tied together by rules of grammar and syntax'.[9] This sense that a land can be most properly possessed through language plays out in the work of a number of writers, many of whom are concerned to challenge the degree to which this act of capture and display may be achieved.

Patrick White's *Voss* tells the story of the eponymous German explorer who sets out to map the interior of Australia, based largely on the real-life Ludwig Leichhardt who died in the desert in 1848. In an important early scene, Johann Voss discusses the 'meaning' of the expedition with his patron, Mr Bonner, a merchant who represents many of the views of the new Australian colonial bourgeoisie. Voss points out to Bonner that should they 'compare meanings [of the expedition] [. . .] we would arrive perhaps at different conclusions'.[10] The nature of the need to traverse the interior of the continent is already in dispute and, on looking at an unsatisfactory map, Bonner's wish to build on the structures of knowledge already extant is countered by Voss's will to understand the country wholly anew: '"The map?," repeated the German. "I will first make it"' (p. 23). In this conflict of views between the explorer and the merchant, the opposing and yet syncretic values of acquisition and conservatism within the colonial culture of the period are demonstrated. Voss's expedition into the interior will be one into the unknown. The dominant image of the unexplored land that existed in the society from which Voss sets out was that of an uninviting territory, characterised by its desolation, uniformity and harshness. Mr Bonner's daughter sums up this picture with her ideas of 'a lot of blacks, and deserts, and rocks, and skeletons, they say, of men that have died' (p. 28). What Voss must travel into is not just a physical emptiness but a metaphysical one also.

Voss and his party enter the interior with an existing referential system firmly in their minds. Thus, as Voss rides to Sanderson's homestead of 'Rhine Towers' he creates a picture of a fine residence, echoing the German pastoral vision implied by the name. On reaching the actually rather humble place, Voss does not retract the conclusions that the language led him to but rather distorts the place to fit the model: 'It is a castle' (p. 128). His assumptions hold, even if experienced reality must be twisted to fit his prior model. The same thing can be seen in the Yuletide celebration that Judd arranges during the journey. Voss falls to remembering Christmas in Germany and talks of his family, the town streets, the fir trees and the snow. He then compares it with their current festivity; 'It was not altogether different. Except for the snow' (p. 207). The difference between the idyllic scene and the men sitting eating mutton around the campfire in the outback would seem enormous but to Voss the same references must contain both situations.

From its outset the novel explores ideas of speechlessness and the loss of language: Voss is set apart from the society of Sydney because of his German tongue, the beauties of which 'will not bear translation' (p. 81); Bonner's niece Laura tries to keep a diary but finds the blank page 'more expressive' than anything her words could hope to tell (p. 91); and another of Voss's party speaks of how he felt that if he could describe 'with any accuracy some thing [. . .]

then I would be expressing all truth. But I could not' (p. 271). As the expedition proceeds, and they travel further into the inhospitable land, the gap between language and the experience of the world appears to widen. The European referential framework with which they explain their surroundings to themselves begins to falter, as revealed especially in the scene when they must cross a river. When their raft capsizes, the ornithological specimens, which can be seen as the archetypes of ordered classification, are lost (p. 277). Later we find out that all but one of the compasses was also lost and the party is divorced from the certainties of geography that shaped the expedition. In these events we begin to see the forsaking of the European reason that was causing the obfuscation of the experienced world by its strictly delineated scope of expression. With the drowning of the goats – 'the most rational of animals' (p. 211) – we can see not only these animals but also a whole world view 'descending into hell' (p. 277).

From this point in the expedition we see a different outlook beginning to develop. The men now seem to have an altered relation to the land and to their communications regarding it: 'Words that did not belong to them – illuminating, true, naked words – had a habit of coming out' (p. 333). The anomalies that had beset their faculties when trying to address this land have led to a profound change in how they interpret their perceptions and define the world around them. Now, 'objects were the quintessence of themselves' (p. 360); we are shown an abandonment of the culturally defined logic of categorisation in favour of a direct perception that can create a new relation with the country.

The poet Judith Wright argued that it was only through the 'sacrifice' of European self-consciousness that a truly Australian form could come into being.[11] This plays out in *Voss* after the protagonist's death in the desert through the images of Sydney society, where Laura contends that 'perhaps true knowledge only comes of death by torture in the country of the mind' (p. 446). The challenge to traditional modes of reference experienced by Voss's party in the interior has led to the possibility of an 'indigenous' Australian self-awareness. The group of people gathered at the end of the novel, including Laura, the musician Topp, the poet Willie Pringle and the explorer Colonel Hebden, have the opportunity to create an Australian discourse, one that has been freed from much of its colonial heritage and the imposition of a mapping that translates experience into easily possessed forms. Only by accepting that one's consciousness of the world is subject to interruption, decentring and rewriting can one begin to construct a 'new' country that does not suffer from the distortion of having a foreign mode of discourse imposed upon it.

IMMEMORIAL AND RECENT: LES MURRAY

One reviewer of Les Murray's 1996 collection, *Subhuman Redneck Poems*, suggested that the experience of reading it was 'like some venture into the interior, a Vossian epic of effort and observation'.[12] Like *Voss*, Murray's poetry can be seen to advance the cause of a distinct Australian sensibility, though rather than tracing its emergence, as in White's historical novel, this verse is more often concerned to mark its presence in the contemporary and to map the threats that may be ranged against it. Murray's first 'selected poems', published in 1976, was subtitled *The Vernacular Republic*. In this image of a nation whose sovereignty must be considered inseparable from, or entailed by, its idiosyncratic sense of locality, we can detect the crux of Murray's project. His verse traces this national identity, indivisible from the experiences of the Australian people, both indigenous and settler.

'Driving Through Sawmill Towns' (1965) is addressed in the second person and requires the reader to engage with the experience of observing these rural communities within Australia's forests. The poem plays the transience of the driver's vision against the timelessness of the towns. The plural noun in the title contrasts with the present tense verb to suggest that these isolated places, in 'distant valleys', might ultimately have the more substantial presence. While it ends with the observer continuing on their journey, the focus of the poem nonetheless stays with the towns, distinguishing a seasonal change that speaks of ages passing from the brevity of the motorist's view. In this rural Australia, marked by both timelessness and typicality, one can trace elements of what Murray's vernacular republic may consist: a space outside of the fast-moving world of modernity, in which novelty and the immediacy of action are paramount. In 'Driving Through Sawmill Towns' routine and repetition more meaningfully structure experience. In such a world the practices of urban life can seem impossibly distant, as for the woman who

> sometimes [. . .]
> will turn around and gaze
> at the mountains in wonderment,
> looking for a city.[13]

Murray's verse turns to rural Australia most often to find a form of authenticity. It is frequently discovered in habit and stillness. He refutes any idea that the distinctiveness of Australia may be based solely upon its 'newness' as a country (at least for the settler population); instead, his country is ancient and the disjunction between inheritance and experience that so destroyed Voss's party is refused in favour of a sense of continuity.

A later poem, 'The Assimilation of Background' (1990), opens, like 'Driving Through Sawmill Towns', with its observers driving through a rural environment. Here, though, the contrast between modernity and timelessness is explicitly collapsed, as they stop at a farming station, but find no one there. As they return to their car, there is a moment of revelation:

> we saw
> that out on that bare, crusted country
> background and foreground had merged;
> nothing that existed there was background. (p. 337)

While Australia might be seen as a 'crusted country' with a palimpsest of white settler culture imposed on a far older land, Murray refuses the distinction between past and present, and between subject and environment: nothing is background in his republic where people and places have wholly assimilated into a unity. In 'Second Essay on Interest: the Emu' (1983), the distinctive-looking, flightless bird becomes an emblem and metaphor for Australian identity. Questioning how such an odd animal might have evolved, the poet asks 'Are you Early or Late in the history of birds?' (p. 203). The answer, it appears, is both. Murray's version of indigenisation traces the origins of contemporary Australia not only in the ancient land and the practices of the Aboriginal peoples, but also in the cultures developed by the Anglo-Celtic convict-descended settlers: 'My kinships, too, are immemorial and recent, / like my country, which abstracts yours in words' (p. 205). The emu also embodies for Murray some of the major components of what he regards as the most idiosyncratic aspect of Australian identity: its 'brigand sovereignty' or unruliness (p. 204).

Elsewhere, Murray more clearly defines this idiosyncrasy as 'sprawl':

> Sprawl is the quality
> of the man who cut down his Rolls-Royce
> into a farm utility truck, and sprawl
> is what the company lacked when it made repeated efforts
> to buy the vehicle back and repair its image. (p. 183)

'The Quality of Sprawl' (1983) provides examples without definition; a technique which itself seems to correspond to the idea of sprawl. It denotes a disorderliness, a cutting through of pretension and a refusal to privilege appearance over essence. It is bloody-minded, irreverent, inappropriate and ill-fitting: 'like the thirteenth banana in a dozen / or anyway the fourteenth' (p. 183). Murray celebrates sprawl's improvisation and pragmatism as essentially Australian: 'An image of my country. And would that it were more so' (p. 184). Australia can only be possessed, he suggests, by those willing to embrace this looseness. The types of regimentation and categorised understanding which he associates with the colonial era, with contemporary institutional life and with a superficial, urban environment can never truly belong within the timeless and enduring atmosphere of Australia.

Murray's poetry insists that the connection people may have with the land has to be worked for and also that it can be betrayed and lost. In 'The Rollover' (1996) he satirically enacts a role reversal as 'primary producers [. . .] farmers and authors / are going round to watch them evict a banker' (p. 411). Behind the laconic humour rests a serious point that the ethos of contemporary Australia might disenfranchise those groups, both white and Aborigine, who most truly embody the nation. In refusing to respect this connection with the country the emissaries of modern finance risk undoing the process of indigenisation and realienating Australians. In 'View of Sydney, Australia, from Gladesville Road Bridge' (1983) the two Australias are seen together as the poet surveys the city. The high-rise blocks mimicked visually by the column of text in the middle of the poem are linked to images of finance but also to war and destruction. Against this bleak vision for Australia's future, however, ranges the old city of sprawl that more meaningfully connects to both geography and history, both good and bad:

> brewery brick terrace hospital
> horrible workplace; the scale of the tramway era,
> the pea jacket era, the age of the cliff-repeating woolstores.
> South and west lie the treeless suburbs, a mulch of faded flags,
> north and partly east, the built-in paradise forest. (p. 173)

THE TIME OF THE NATION AND THE SPACE OF THE PEOPLE

To move, as I now intend to do, from discussing representations of the need to belong experienced by European-descended Australians to those of West Indians in the Caribbean and Britain in the 1940s and 1950s may seem obscurely motivated or, at best, drawing a tenuous link between very different experiences of settlement. However, I wish to argue that in much postcolonial writing we find tropes of belonging that might seem very different in intention and function but actually operate according to some similar basic ideas. In each case the fundamental questions are those of legitimisation: how a settler community might justify and guarantee its presence and right to belong. While white Australians, a settler community appearing to possess all the power of definition within their national space, might still discover a need to negotiate an anxiety of non-belonging and to reshape their story of the nation accordingly, the West Indians who travelled to post-war

Britain were often disillusioned to discover their exclusion from the nation and relegation to the lowest rungs of society: with the cards stacked against them, their process of coming to own, and belong to, a nation is a very different one. In both cases, though, we find in representations of national belonging a disjunction between ideas of the nation and lived experience within it. While the persistence of ideas of *terra nullius* in Australia perpetuated a refusal to acknowledge the seemingly undeniable presence of indigenous peoples, and, in denying this history, separated the settlers also from the primal history of the land, post-war racism in Britain denied a full humanity to immigrants who, in their proximity, daily demonstrated their necessary kinship as well as the integral role they played in the country. In both cases the idea of the nation desperately needed to be revisited and revised.

National identity has proved to be one of the most persistent lenses through which postcolonial literatures are studied, and this book will return to examining some of these approaches in later chapters. For the moment the focus will be on the very famous definition given by Benedict Anderson in 1983, which described nations as 'imagined communities', and the later expansion of this idea by Homi Bhabha to explain some of the paradoxes at the heart of national belonging. In his influential account of how and why nationalism came to exert such affective and pragmatic power across the world over the last few centuries, Anderson begins by offering 'in an anthropological spirit' a concise definition of the nation: 'it is an imagined political community – and imagined as both inherently limited and sovereign'.[14] Several aspects of this definition are worthy of comment. Firstly, it can seem obvious that nations are seen as communities, but it is important to stress how much they rely on senses of fellow-feeling and comradeship: nations are not the same as states, and cannot be seen solely as the convenient categories through which to manage people politically. Secondly, though, they do *also* exercise this political function; to illustrate Anderson's ascription of their sovereignty we might think of how 'the will of the people' is invoked as a justification of the actions of democratic and autocratic governments alike. Thirdly, nations are limited by their boundaries and work as much by exclusion as inclusion: in understanding the contours of the nation, one always retains a sense of those who belong elsewhere. Finally, and crucially, he notes that nations must be imagined 'because the members of even the smallest nation will never know most of their fellow-members, meet them, or even hear of them, yet in the minds of each lives the image of their communion'.[15] The fact that nations are the product of a collective act of imagination does not make them any less real; like many of the constructs upon which societies are built – money, law, morality – the strength of the communal belief necessary to sustain them actually grants them their particular power.

In his essay 'DissemiNation: Time, Narrative and the Margins of the Modern Nation', first published in 1990, Homi Bhabha complicates this sense of how the nation is imagined by pointing out that invocations of national belonging and identity rely on two different imagined unities of the nation. The first is its unity in time, envisaging a continuity stretching from past to present in which the integrity of the nation is guaranteed precisely by the degree to which it remains authentically the same. In this mode of address, nations are meaningful because they can point to their histories. The second unity is that of space: for an address of the nation to be intelligible, it must assume a body of people who, at any given moment, can be identified as part of the national body; hence the nation demonstrates its continued relevance. In this mode of address, nations are meaningful because they can demonstrate a geographic and demographic completeness. Bhabha names the first instance of imagining the nation as the 'pedagogical' and associates its sense of inheritance with the ideologies of nationalism; the second form of address he calls the 'performative'.[16] As he notes, though, the types of nation imagined through each of these forms will always diverge from each other. The nation today is not the same as it was yesterday, let alone ten, or a hundred years ago. A 'split' always exists between the historical sense of the nation and its present reality. In particular, the presence of groups within the present-day performative nation who are absent from the historical, pedagogical one need to be accounted for. Either the pedagogical imperative may trump the performative, and it be stated that these people do not belong, and should be considered outside the national community, or the performative trumps the pedagogical and the historical continuity of the nation needs to be reimagined to accommodate these new national subjects. In either case, though, the nation must be 'narrated' – conceptions of who belongs, and how, need to be reinforced or modified. It is in this work of reimagining the nation (which might refer either to reiteration or revision of national models – or to elements of both) that we might best bring together the different types of settler identity; both European-descended Australians and West Indian migrants to post-war Britain must live with the tension between the pedagogical and performative nations and negotiate the impact of these on their ability to belong.

CLAIMING THE CITY: SAM SELVON, *THE LONELY LONDONERS*

Tensions between the lived understanding that a nation may have of itself and the realities of lives lived within its borders form a large part of Sam Selvon's *The Lonely Londoners* (1956). The novel follows the adventures of a loose grouping of West Indian immigrants, mostly men, in the London of the early 1950s. At the centre of the novel, both in terms of providing a dominant focalising consciousness, and as the owner of the basement flat where the 'boys' congregate, is Moses Aloetta. He has a position of seniority and authority within the group, largely because he has been in England for longer than most of the others, but the guidance he offers is often marked by his distinct cynicism. If he has picked up wisdom during his sojourn, it is usually centred on knowledge of the structural disadvantages under which these men will labour in Britain, and the futility of trying to challenge this.

Moses's basement serves as a metonym for his greater divorce from experience of public life in Britain. The West Indian migrants are not denied entirely by mainstream British discourse, but as with the famous 1956 *Picture Post* headline 'Thirty Thousand Colour Problems', they are refused individuality.[17] As a whole, they can be seen as a problem in Britain, but there is no space for their individual voices. Instead, the society outside imagines their opinions and then speaks for them:

whatever the newspaper and the radio say in this country, that is the people Bible. Like one time when newspapers say that the West Indians think that the streets of London paved with gold a Jamaican fellar went to the income tax office to find out something and first thing the clerk tell him is, 'You people think the streets of London are paved with gold?' Newspaper and radio rule this country.[18]

Individuality is persistently lost within the flattening enacted by official discourse. Models of being are set up in advance of the arrival of the West Indians and then adhered to. As with the annotation added to their files at the labour exchange – 'J-A, Col': 'that mean you from Jamaica and you black' (p. 28) – the West Indians continually find themselves defined externally.

The novel addresses the effects of these limitations in its portraits of the young men. Although the newly arrived Henry 'Sir Galahad' Oliver is naive regarding what may await him, he inadvertently recognises that his own voice will be hushed by the imposition of a greater narrative that externally defines him: 'I find when I talk smoke coming out my mouth.' Moses's answer confirms the silence imposed on them, but offers a hint of redemption: 'Is so it is in this country [. . .] Sometimes the words freeze and you have to melt it to hear the talk' (p. 15). But the ability to 'melt' the restrictive moulds into which are they fitted is laboriously achieved. In his first excursion into London on his own, Galahad grows so uncertain of his right to belong that he begins to question his very presence: 'A feeling come over him as if he lost everything he have – clothes, shoes, hat – and he start to touch himself here and there as if he in a daze' (p. 24). As their right to belong is questioned, the 'loneliness' of the migrants might manifest in a dangerous effacing of their identity.

Against this invisibility imposed upon them, the West Indians repeatedly assert their presence through small acts that carve out a space of belonging, or, to put it in Bhabha's terms, by performative assertions that question the totality of the pedagogical national vision. The actions of Tanty, an older Jamaican woman, can be seen as just such an assertion. Faced by an English shopkeeper who displays a sign refusing credit to customers, she challenges him as to whether he knows about 'trust': 'Where I come from you take what you want and you pay every Friday.' The shopkeeper responds by saying that he does not offer credit. Tanty later just goes ahead and takes goods, promising to pay at the end of the week. He seems to have no choice but to let her, and then finds that he has 'a list of creditors on his hands. However, every Friday evening religiously they all paying up, and as business going on all right he decide to give in' (p. 66). This is a significant moment not simply because it shows an instance of an Englishman conceding to West Indians' demands; more importantly, the terms under which he would frame the transactions – 'credit' – are refused and instead Tanty imposes her definition of the situation: 'trust'. The West Indians' belonging within the city is not something given by the English, but rather is claimed for themselves.

The novel throughout traces the alternation between the assertion of presence in the city and its deflation on meeting an unyielding sense of national purity. This is perhaps most concisely shown when Galahad dresses for a date. The rituals of dressing are lingered on as he shines his shoes 'until he could see his face in the leather', then laboriously styles his hair 'like a tonsorial specialist', before dressing in a suit of 'the smartest and latest cut'. The preening is an almost aggressive act of display, of establishing himself within the city. However, the first comment he inspires is from a small child: '"Mummy, look at that black man!"' (pp. 73–6). Galahad's crafted act of self-invention is brushed aside in favour of a concentration on the seemingly non-negotiable fact of his race. The novel then recounts how such an incident would previously have led the young man to despair, when the racism he faced led him to insult his own black skin. Now, however, 'Galahad like duck back when rain fall – everything running off' (p. 76). The anecdotal style of the novel, in which chronology is unclear and events from different times are run together, might serve to hide the genuine progression made in such situations. Equally, the pessimism that Moses so clearly articulates in the closing sections of the novel may obscure the book's detailing of how new types of belonging are being forged. The novel itself constitutes a major act of claiming national space – in its capture of London within Selvon's expressive and original vernacular voice it enacts a process of claiming belonging on its own terms, much as Tanty's setting up of the trust system did. Moses's pessimism is important in the book, and serves to disprove any view of the novel as simply a celebration of the lives of West Indians in 1950s London, but this negativity is subtly transcended. On the final page, he imagines writing a book that makes visible the new communities: *The Lonely Londoners* itself is an example of this, a marking of territory and belonging akin to, but profoundly more impactful than, Galahad's self-creation as he dons his suit.

HATING THE PLACE YOU LOVE: JAMES BERRY, *WINDRUSH SONGS*

An interesting echo of Galahad's dressing to make his mark on London can be found in James Berry's 'White Suit and White Shoes' in his 2007 collection *Windrush Songs*. The *SS Empire Windrush* was the ship that carried 492 West Indians from Jamaica to the Tilbury docks outside London, arriving on 21 June 1948 and inaugurating the post-war settlement of people from the Caribbean in London.[19] Berry himself had wished to travel on the *Empire Windrush* but had to wait another few months until he could afford a berth on a later ship, the *SS Orbita*. The poems in *Windrush Songs* serve as a commemoration of this journey taken by Berry, and others like him, as they abandoned their lives in the Caribbean in favour of the uncertainties of a new start in Britain. In the middle section of the collection he traces the thoughts of a number of the migrants as they prepare for their new lives. The narrator of 'White Suit and White Shoes' has a plan for his arrival, based on the outfit he will wear:

> Me goin lan in White Henglan in this
> White suit. Notn else will do [. . .]
> Notice, I dress right for Henglan.
> I must wear notn but White [. . .]
> And skin – the dark betrayer – must go in hidin.[20]

He seems to be playing a dangerous game, naively believing that through his immaculate appearance he might be safe from racism.

Yet the poem ultimately refuses this reading. He concludes by stating that on arrival he will 'get some money' which 'start to pay the debt / that dress me up white – fa Henglan!' (p. 72). At first it may seem that this debt is his own, perhaps built up through the cost of his passage and in purchasing the suit and shoes. But the debtor is not identified and we might rather read it as an obligation owed by 'Henglan' itself, a debt incurred through the legacy of colonialism on which the colonial subject intends to collect. In this light, his choice of clothing may seem more cunning than naive, a determination to redress the balance of history.

Windrush Songs challenges the idea that the West Indians who migrated were ignorant of the difficult situation that might await them in Britain, and that they expected the 'Mother Country' to welcome them with open arms. Of course, views like this could be found among the migrants of this period, one recalling that in the Caribbean, 'we were always British', just as their colonial education had led them to believe.[21] Indeed, this opinion was shared by many British too, and the *Empire Windrush* was greeted at Tilbury with a banner reading 'Welcome Home'. However, not all West Indians subscribed to such an account and, as seen in *The Lonely Londoners*, the idea that they all believed the streets of London were paved with gold was a rank inaccuracy.

Berry sums up the reality of the ambivalent relationship many West Indians had with Britain in his introduction to *Windrush Songs*:

> Despite the aftermath of slavery there was still a respect for England and a sense of belonging. Origins are so important, people need a sense of where they come from [. . .] But England was also the home of the slave masters, and we retained a general distrust of white men. However, England was the nearest thing we had to a mother country; we saw in it some aspects of hope. (p. 10)

In this statement we can discern the dominant attitude to belonging throughout the collection: feeling adrift of belonging anywhere, the migrants settle on 'the nearest thing we had'. To belong nowhere is not an option, and the 'hope' of finding a home drives these people to cross the sea. That they remained unsure of what welcome they would receive is indicated by the story that circulated aboard the *Empire Windrush* that a British warship was ready to sink them at any moment.[22]

The islands they leave are no doubt regarded with affection by some, but the dominant mood is frustration with the endemic poverty in which they are forced to live. The opening poem of the collection refigures the name of the iconic ship as 'Wind-rush', imagining a hurricane that the speaker wishes to see 'batter and mash-up' his island (p. 14). In 'Villagers Talk Frustrations', pastoral images of Caribbean life are overcome by voices that speak of the need to leave an unbearable situation:

> *Man – you can't stay fixed, frightened,*
> *hating a place you love.*
> *You travel on, noh!* (p. 21)

Displaced from an African heritage by the brutalities of the slave trade, these people struggle to see their current location as a meaningful home. For the speaker of 'To Travel this Ship', any sacrifice is worth the chance to experience a 'diffrun sunrise and sundown / in anodda place wid odda ways' (p. 33). The Caribbean fails to offer a home as its history is marked too strongly by rupture; equally the Africa to which they can trace their ancestry fails to provide a workable conception of belonging (the narrator of 'I African They Say' concludes that 'just as Africa sold and abandoned me / I can never consider Africa' (p. 19). Even when the migrants look back fondly on their homelands, belonging is not straightforward: for the narrator of 'Empire Day', what he remembers most clearly are the occasions when as schoolchildren they gathered to celebrate Empire, singing 'Rule Britannia' and waving Union Jacks, 'glowing with all we loyal / virtue to King, Country and Empire' (p. 49).

Belonging is not something that can be uncomplicatedly found on either side of the Atlantic. Instead, it must be fought for, and claimed in whichever ways present themselves. Berry's migrants often reveal themselves as capable of performing this difficult task. In 'Mother Country' the burdens of imperial history are subsumed into a vision of the future that offers to unify the West Indians' fractured belonging and conjoin their British and African parentage. Noting that the 'mother country' had stripped him of his African name and heritage, the speaker proposes making a request of the king: 'that your first grandchild may share / an African name with my first grandchild'. It is a plea for a grand gesture that acknowledges the West Indians' right to call in the debt owed by Britain and thereby to belong there, inaugurating a 'kinship' that 'will ennoble us both' (p. 63). The utopian sentiment that powers this is no doubt unrealistic and doomed to be unfulfilled, but reveals a determination to overcome alienation, and to begin a process of settlement, possessing a part of England and making it a home. The final poem of the collection, 'Hymn to New Day Arriving', contains enough sense of the struggles that await the West Indians to prevent it seeming triumphalist, but it nonetheless resounds with hope: 'New day is a turned-over book page, / new day invigorates with new life' (p. 80). While its final note is a reminder of the ultimate ephemerality or banality of the stories of the few hundred people on the *Empire Windrush*, this is yet an ordinariness that contains a history of the labour that has gone into belonging, and is the reward that then can be reaped.

NEW BEGINNINGS AND RESPONSIBILITIES: J. M. COETZEE, *DISGRACE*

'For a man of his age, fifty-two, divorced, he has, to his mind, solved the problem of sex rather well.'[23] The opening line of J. M. Coetzee's *Disgrace* introduces us to David Lurie, a university professor who would specialise in Romantic literature, though is forced instead to teach communication studies at the fictional Cape Technical University in Cape Town, South Africa. Immediately we can detect Lurie's self-assurance and confidence in his mastery of his situation. In the opening chapters he demonstrates further his sense of entitlement, beginning an affair with a student in which he clearly capitalises on his power over her. After a few awkward sexual encounters, including one which, despite Lurie's characterisation of it as 'not rape, not quite that' (p. 25), cannot really be meaningfully construed otherwise, a complaint is raised against him and he is soon dismissed from his employment.

The novel is set in 1997, in the middle of the hearings of the South African Truth and Reconciliation Committee (TRC), which sought to uncover and address human rights violations during the apartheid era of racial separation. One feature of the TRC was that perpetrators of violence could claim amnesty from prosecution in return for full and complete confessions of their crimes (849 people had been granted such amnesty by the time the amnesty committee was dissolved in 2001). The disciplinary committee that Lurie is required to face at the university somewhat resembles the TRC in this respect, and he considers the demand to confess made of him unacceptable. At one point he is asked to prove the sincerity of his regret, which is too much for him: 'That is preposterous. That is beyond the scope of the law [. . .] Let us go back to playing it by the book. I plead guilty. That is as far as I am prepared to go' (p. 55). The TRC was designed to help build a foundation upon which the new South African state could be built. Given the painful history of apartheid, it was felt that a significant act of clearing space was needed in order to start anew. At Lurie's hearing it appears that such an act at a personal level is beyond him.

Disgrace's attention to the desires and drives of individuals (especially those of Lurie himself) ensures that we should not read the novel too easily as allegory, but the extent of change taking place in South Africa during its first decade of democracy equally makes it unwise to read without taking some of this political and social context into account. In fact, we might read *Disgrace* as a novel in which both broad questions about belonging in the new South Africa and the ethics of individual sexual, familial and con-vivial relationships are explored.

After his disgrace in Cape Town, Lurie travels to the rural Eastern Cape, where his daughter Lucy has established a small-holding. He feels alien in the rural environment, and expresses surprise at how well his daughter has adapted: 'Curious that he and her mother, cityfolk, intellectuals, should have produced this throwback, this sturdy young settler. But perhaps it was not they who produced her: perhaps history had the larger share' (p. 61). His sentiments here are interesting: he describes Lucy as a settler, linking her strongly to the white (usually Afrikaner) farmers who first spread out from the Cape Colony to claim the rest of South Africa. In Coetzee's study of the pastoral literature that memorialises this settlement, he suggests that the settlers were seeking 'a dialogue with Africa, a reciprocity with Africa, that will allow [them] an identity better than that of visitor, stranger, transient'.[24] We might then read Lucy as a 'throwback' to this attempt to own and belong to Africa. However, the settler tradition was also based on a disavowal of the presence of the indigenous people and an aggressive colonialism. Lucy clearly rejects this, not only through the interdependence she shares with her Xhosa neighbour, Petrus, but also in her refusal to accept Lurie's definition of her property: 'Stop calling it *the farm*, David. This is not a farm, it's just a piece of land where I grow things – we both know that' (p. 200). If her connection with the land is to be established, it must be without this historical baggage.

The status of Lucy's claims to belonging is redefined in the assault at the centre of the novel, when the property is invaded by three black men and she is multiply raped. Lurie, who is locked in a toilet for the duration of the attack, and then burned with methylated spirits, feels powerless in not being able to help her during the attack and this is exacerbated when Lucy refuses to tell the police investigating the invasion about the rape. Lurie accuses her of acting in this way because of the continuing shadow of apartheid – 'Do you hope you can expiate the crimes of the past by suffering in the present?' – but Lucy rejects this, suggesting that thinking in terms of such abstractions is unhelpful (p. 112). Later, Lurie tries to understand the rapists as driven by 'history speaking through them', but this does little to help him and Lucy understand the 'personal' violence of the attack (p. 156). The violence done to her is never presented as something that can adequately be understood or put to rest. Instead, Lucy eventually seems to accept Petrus's insistence that the rape must be seen as 'history', and no further justice sought, but does so in a way that simultaneously forces future responsibility onto her neighbour. She is pregnant as a result of the rape and insists that Petrus must act as the child's family. A new code of relationships must be established in which belonging or owning land cannot be divorced from the ways in which we belong also to other people. Lucy accepts that her solution may be humiliating in that it involves giving much up, but argues that 'perhaps that is a good point to start from again [. . .] With nothing. No cards, no weapons, no property, no rights, no dignity': as David observes, 'Like a dog' (p. 205).

Lurie too seems stripped of all he had possessed, though he does not accept it in the same way as Lucy does. Instead, he perhaps learns less what it means to surrender oneself to others' moral duty and more what it might mean to take up moral responsibility for others. When he first arrives in the countryside, Lucy advises him to volunteer at a centre which euthanises stray and unwanted dogs. When she first suggests it, he is unsure: 'it sounds like someone trying to make reparation for past misdeeds', and therefore corresponds to the notion of public recantation and pleading for forgiveness that he rejects (p. 77). However, as Lucy points out, his motives matter little to the animals and he ultimately finds himself regularly taking vanloads of dead dogs to feed into an incinerator in support of 'his idea of the world, a world in which men do not use shovels to beat corpses into a more convenient shape for processing' (p. 146). The novel ends with Lurie giving up a dog to be put down, despite having formed an attachment to it. Here, belonging is re-envisaged as the responsibility one has to another (even a non-human other). *Disgrace* implies that these are the key relationships that must be explored before any other sense of postcolonial belonging can be established.

SUMMARY

- The practice and legacies of colonialism are inextricably bound up with the idea of land, ownership and belonging.
- In the Mabo case, we see a clear contrast between different ways of justifying a group's ownership of land.
- Patrick White's *Voss* explores the need for European settlers to abandon their ways of thinking in order wholly to belong in Australia.
- In Les Murray's poetry an authentic Australianness, predicated

on a connection to the ancient land, is seen as under threat from the modern world of institutional order.

- Building on Benedict Anderson's idea that nations are 'imagined', Homi Bhabha identifies a necessary tension between the historical ('pedagogical') and geographical ('performative') unities of all nations.
- Sam Selvon's *The Lonely Londoners* documents the small acts through which West Indian settlers assert their presence in the city.
- In James Berry's *Windrush Songs*, it is shown that any act of belonging can only be forged through struggle.
- Placing responsibility to others at the centre of belonging, J. M. Coetzee's *Disgrace* explores how white South Africans might renegotiate their relation to their nation after the end of apartheid.

NOTES

1. Sara Upstone, *Spatial Politics in the Postcolonial Novel* (Farnham: Ashgate, 2009), p. 4.
2. Quoted in Alice Brittan, 'Australasia', in John McLeod (ed.), *The Routledge Companion to Postcolonial Studies* (London: Routledge, 2007), p. 72.
3. Henry Reynolds, 'Native Title and Pastoral Leases', in M. A. Stephenson and Suri Ratnapala (eds), *Mabo: a Judicial Revolution: the Aboriginal Land Rights Decision and its Impact on Australian Law* (St Lucia: University of Queensland Press, 1993), pp. 119–31.
4. Quoted in John Rickard, *Australia: a Cultural History*, 2nd edn (London: Longman, 1996), p. 232.
5. David Mercer, 'Terra Nullius, Aboriginal Sovereignty and Land Rights in Australia: the Debate Continues', *Political Geography* 12(4) (1993), p. 315.
6. Terry Goldie, *Fear and Temptation: the Image of the Indigene in Canadian, Australian, and New Zealand Literatures* (Kingston: McGill-Queen's University Press, 1989), p. 12.
7. Ibid., p. 13.

8. Paul Carter, *The Road to Botany Bay: an Essay in Spatial History* (London: Faber and Faber, 1987), p. xxiv.

9. Ibid., p. 64.

10. Patrick White, *Voss* (Harmondsworth: Penguin, [1957] 1981), p. 20. Further references to this edition are given in the main text.

11. Judith Wright, 'The Upside-Down Hut', in John Barnes (ed.), *The Writer in Australia: a Collection of Literary Documents, 1856–1964* (Melbourne: Oxford University Press, 1969), p. 335.

12. John Greening, quoted in Steven Matthews, *Les Murray* (Manchester: Manchester University Press, 2001), p. 154.

13. Les Murray, *Collected Poems* (Manchester: Carcanet, 1998), p. 11. Further references to this edition are given in the main text.

14. Benedict Anderson, *Imagined Communities: Reflections on the Origin and Spread of Nationalism*, revised edn (London: Verso, 2006), pp. 5–6.

15. Ibid., p. 6.

16. Homi K. Bhabha, *The Location of Culture* (London: Routledge, 1994), pp. 145–8.

17. Stuart Hall, 'Reconstruction Work: Images of Post-war Black Settlement', *Ten 8*(16) (1984), pp. 2–9.

18. Sam Selvon, *The Lonely Londoners* (London: Penguin, [1956] 2006), p. 2. Further references to this edition are given in the main text.

19. Matthew Mead has challenged the usually accepted figure of 492, suggesting that 531 or 532 might be more accurate. See Matthew Mead, '*Empire Windrush*: the Cultural Memory of an Imaginary Arrival', *Journal of Postcolonial Writing* 45(2) (2009), 137–49.

20. James Berry, *Windrush Songs* (Tarset: Bloodaxe, 2007), p. 71. Further references to this edition are given in the main text.

21. Mike Phillips and Trevor Phillips, *Windrush: the Irresistible Rise of Multi-racial Britain* (London: Harper Collins, 1998), p. 12.

22. Ibid., p. 64.

23. J. M. Coetzee, *Disgrace* (London: Secker and Warburg, 1999),

p. 1. Further references to this edition are given in the main text.

24. J. M. Coetzee, *White Writing: on the Culture of Letters in South Africa* (New Haven, CT: Yale University Press, 1988), p. 8.

CHAPTER 3

Coming of Age, Coming into Difference

The figure of the child often seems a central one in post-colonial literature, and stories of childhood and of coming into maturity are frequent. Of course, at least since the Romantic era of the late eighteenth and early nineteenth centuries, the representation of children has been important in much literature in English. Children are often used to embody a sense of innocence, untouched by the corrupting effects of society. The child is also often marked by a sense of timelessness; while adults are always situated firmly in time, with their attitudes and actions determined by the social forces around them, children can seem further from such pressures, closer to a state of nature and thus an authentic sense of essential humanity. Against the petty concerns and divisions of the experienced world of adults, children can be written as offering a bathetic deflation of pomp, connecting instead with a truer sense of how the world is, or how it should be.

Against this, though, we can place an alternative and equally commonplace tradition: that of coming of age. In these representations the child or young person is seen less as in a state of innocence as one of ignorance. Social awkwardness or ineptitude hinders their chances of achieving happiness or fulfilment and they can only find resolution by coming to a full understanding of their society and reconciling themselves to the place they will occupy within it: in short, by becoming a functioning adult. The key site in which this theme is explored is the *bildungsroman*, or novel of formation, a genre in which we follow a character into adulthood and trace the decisions they must take in order to develop into the position of maturity that can guarantee them happiness, or at least contentment, within their milieu.

In postcolonial writing, there may be further reasons why tales of children and young people seem so significant. The archetypes of the child as essentially innocent, and of needing to be reconciled with the world to flourish, are woven around other important tropes and images of what childhood may mean. Firstly, there is the persistence of ideas of the colonised world as essentially immature and incapable of looking after itself. The definitive expression of this may be Kipling's image of 'sullen peoples, / Half devil and half child', on whose behalf the 'White Man's burden' of paternalistic imperialism must be shouldered,[1] but it continues in such habits as speaking of 'less-developed countries', imputing a degree of immaturity and belatedness to those parts of the world which supposedly need assistance from more fully grown nations. Secondly, decolonisation and the process of nation-building that succeeds it are often marked by a rhetoric of youthfulness, imagining the postcolonial nation as a child growing into its place in the world. Of course, such imagery is problematic not only because it risks denying the long histories of societies in which the colonial era was ultimately only a relatively short period of time, but also in that it may imply the colonial power as an (absent) parent, determining and perhaps controlling the fate of its offspring. Despite these problems, images of childhood and maturity often allow for a working through of issues of autonomy and national self-realisation. Yet in the postcolonial novel, as much as in any other, the allegorical figure of the child as an embodiment of newness can be balanced against the material struggles of the *bildungsroman*: while the former might seem to eschew the vagaries of experience in favour of symbolic readings, the latter insists on some kind of reconciliation with social norms.

NATIONAL ALLEGORY

In thinking about the child in postcolonial literature functioning as an allegory for societies coming to terms with postcolonial existence, it is useful briefly to consider Fredric Jameson's controversial arguments about 'national allegory'. In a 1986 article, Jameson made the bold claim that:

> All third-world texts are necessarily [. . .] allegorical, and in a very specific way: they are to be read as what I will call *national allegories* [. . .] *the story of the private individual destiny is always an allegory of the embattled situation of the public third-world culture and society.*[2]

It is important to note that Jameson is not, as in the present discussion, dealing only with stories focused around children and that his category of 'third-world literature' is not wholly congruent with the definition of postcolonial literature that informs the present study. Jameson's category is by no means limited to Anglophone literatures, and would exclude several of the 'Western' nations included in my definition (such as Australia and Canada); he instead focuses on those locations outside of the capitalist/communist dichotomy of Cold War politics. Nonetheless, there are significant areas of overlap and his claim has become an important point of reference within postcolonial literary studies. At the heart of his argument is the suggestion that the literature of the capitalist West evinces a pronounced split between the personal and the political, and that it is ultimately poorly able to include the latter, focusing instead on individual psychological dramas. In contrast, he argues, 'all of this is denied to third-world culture, which must be situational and materialist despite itself [. . .] where the telling of the individual story and the individual experience cannot but ultimately involve the whole laborious telling of the experience of the collectivity itself'.[3] What may *seem* to be novels about third-world individuals must, for Jameson, instead be read as documenting the national struggles of their homelands.

There are undoubtedly problems with Jameson's argument, not least in its sweeping nature, which seems to set out a clear and unbridgeable distinction between 'Western' and 'third-world' texts. As Aijaz Ahmad points out in one of the most famous critiques of Jameson's essay: 'we live not in three worlds but in one [and] this world includes the experience of colonialism and imperialism on both sides of Jameson's global divide'.[4] To split literatures so radically from one another involves an unconvincing postulation of a natural separation between them that is difficult logically to sustain. Yet to reject the simplistic generalisations of the model does not require entirely abandoning Jameson's basic idea that texts from different parts of the world may relate to their contexts in diverse ways. Imre Szeman summarises Jameson's account of these relations by suggesting that the third-world text 'necessarily and directly speaks to and of the overdetermined situation of the struggles for national independence and cultural autonomy in the context of imperialism and its aftermath'; removing the insistence on necessity here, and instead speaking of a tendency, refusing the unhelpful totalisation inherent in Jameson's model but preserving its sense that there may be important differences at work here.[5]

Another flaw in Jameson's argument lies in his determination that third-world writers create national allegories 'despite themselves'. Again, while it seems reasonable to suggest that certain political, economic and cultural conditions might encourage particular literary modes, it is quite another to strip agency from writers in this way and risks forfeiting the opportunity to explore how the creation of national allegory may be a very deliberate strategy, and sometimes even knowingly constructed with an eye on irony. In Salman Rushdie's *Midnight's Children*, the central trope of the child as national allegory often verges on parody, with the novel's opening lines overstating the connections between protagonist and nation in order to complicate any simple equations of text and context:

> I was born in the city of Bombay . . . once upon a time. No, that won't do, there's no getting away from the date: I was born in Doctor Narlikar's Nursing Home on August 15th, 1947. And the time? The time matters, too. On the stroke of midnight, as a matter of fact. Clock-hands joined palms in respectful greeting as I came. Oh, spell it out, spell it out:

at the precise instant of India's arrival at independence, I tumbled forth into the world.[6]

Rather than envisaging national allegory as a mode that the third-world writer must invariably produce, we can instead view it as one possible strategy, or element of storytelling, that might allow them to explore diverse political *and* individual predicaments. When found in the postcolonial novel of childhood and adolescence, it may be just one way of exploring the materiality of the cultures in which individuals are formed.

A SHADOW OF THE NATION: RODDY DOYLE, *A STAR CALLED HENRY*

Roddy Doyle's *A Star Called Henry* (1999) uses many of the tropes of *Midnight's Children* in placing the tale of a young man's coming to maturity within a key moment of national history, and allowing his actions to help shape the course of the broader story of the nation. Set during the Irish struggles against British colonial rule, the novel perhaps does not fit neatly into Jameson's criteria for a third-world text, but does nonetheless demonstrate how post-colonial texts can employ the device of national allegory as part of their techniques for exploring the history and culture of newly independent nations.

A Star Called Henry engages directly with the romantic mythology of Irish decolonisation, featuring such national heroes as James Connolly, Michael Collins and Eamon de Valera, but the novel is determined always to undercut the simplistic stories of nationalism and instead uses its hero, Henry Smart, to provide an alternative account of the inception of the new state. While nationalist accounts rely on a sanctified version of Ireland, Henry seems to embody a suppressed other of the nation, revealing some of the alternative possibilities that are closed down in the call for a homogeneous version of the country. From the opening of the book, the protagonist is marked by a duality between his material circumstances and the impossible ideals of others: he is not his parents' first child called Henry and his mother often looks up to the star that she insists the first Henry, who died as a baby, has become. Henry is therefore always required to assert his identity against prior claims to it. From his infancy, 'I was the other Henry. The shadow. The imposter.'[7] Henry's existence always seems in danger of being overwhelmed by stories outside of himself, and his fight to assert his autonomous agency as he grows is often one pitched against the forces that would relegate him back to the shadows.

Born in the first years of the twentieth century, Henry comes of age as the movement for Irish independence reaches its zenith, finding himself a teenager bearing arms in the ill-fated occupation of the Dublin General Post Office during the Easter Rising of 1916. Yet despite his location at the heart of events, Henry's nationalism seems little driven by love of his country and the concept seems at first entirely alien to him. As a five-year-old boy in 1907, he's caught up in the crowd watching the procession of the visiting King Edward VII. His reaction is spontaneous and heartfelt: 'Fuck off!' he shouts (p. 51). The older narrator looks back on why he had this reaction as a child and rejects the idea that it had anything to do with incipient national feeling: 'Was I a tiny Fenian? A Sinn Feiner? Not at all. I didn't even know I was Irish' (p. 52). His reaction in some ways is more simple: on seeing the 'fat man' and his 'floozy' he recognises immediately that they were not raised in extreme poverty and that they belong to a different world from him. His outburst is driven by a negative anger at the deprivation in which he and his family and neighbours must live, rather than by a positive vision of Irish liberation. His full adoption of the nationalist cause comes after the death of his much-loved little brother from tuberculosis, when he sees Arthur Griffith and Countess Markievicz burning the Union flag. The cause becomes for Henry a channel for frustration born of poverty.

During the GPO occupation, Doyle depicts the tension between the different movements united in the Rising, with Henry firmly allied to Connolly's socialist cause, and scornful of the others. Even here, though, he is less driven by a utopian vision of the future than by anger at the inequalities of the present and a need to assert himself personally against them. When the British soldiers attack, Henry does not fire at them but instead takes aim at the shops to which he had always been denied access:

I fired at Noblett's window, and the cakes and creams jumped out of their stands. O'Farrell's. The glass fell onto the tobacco and cigars [. . .] A bullet for Dunne & Co., and their hats danced in the glass. One for the All-Ireland Servants Registry Office – there'd be none of that shite in the new republic. And Cable and Co., and more and more shoes. (p. 105)

Henry's destruction is methodical and deliberate; it is an assertion of his individuality and determination not to be cowed into subservience. In 1916, it is precisely this autonomy that is worth fighting for.

However, following the crushing of the Rising and execution or dispersal of its leaders, Henry seems to drift for a while from politics. When he returns, it is because of the inveiglement of Jack Dalton, who convinces him that ballads are being sung about him in English jails. Until this point, Henry has flourished through refusing to allow himself to be defined by others and insisting on his individuality; now, his vanity determines that he accepts the picture Jack describes and by the end of this process of flattery he is prepared 'to fall dead for a version of Ireland that had little or nothing to do with the Ireland I'd gone out to die for the last time' (p. 171). If Henry as a child represents some of the ferocious energy created by the repression and injustice of colonial rule, then his adolescent compromises, which fit him far more pliantly into nationalist narratives, can be read as a capitulation to the idea of national community. As the novel demonstrates, however, this is a dangerous maturity for Henry to accept, as he risks losing the individuality for which he has fought so strongly.

Alfie Gandon, later O'Gandúin, is the shadow figure who most directly contrasts with Henry. While Henry's nationalism is powered by a hatred of injustice, Gandon uses the movement to further his own shady business interests. Henry slowly discovers that many of the murders he carried out during the War of Independence were in fact to ease the taking of power by Gandon and men like him, and to help build the new country in which Henry has no stake: 'never had, never will' (p. 327). Henry kills Gandon, but the conservative nationalism he represents remains dominant and Henry realises he will have to leave the country or be killed himself. Although he loses his country, Henry seems finally to have reached an adulthood in which his autonomy is reclaimed. He is now a husband and father and even in exile can insist on his individuality. The last words of the novel are Henry's name as he reasserts himself over the pernicious national narratives that sought to disenfranchise him in the name of Irish independence.

IN TWO MINORITIES: SHYAM SELVADURAI, *FUNNY BOY*

The coming of age story told in Shyam Selvadurai's *Funny Boy* (1994) ends, like *A Star Called Henry*, with the protagonist leaving his country, fearing for his life if he stays. Arjun 'Arjie' Chelvaratnam is the younger son of a middle-class Sri Lankan family who are forced to emigrate to Canada during the anti-Tamil riots in Colombo in 1983. As with Doyle's novel, *Funny Boy* explores the development of a protagonist who seems not to belong fully within the dominant stories his nation tells of itself; but Arjie's status is made complicated by two factors: his ethnicity, and also his sexuality.

The novel begins with recounting the 'spend-the-days' at which Arjie and his cousins stay all day Sunday at their grandmother's house. In the games that take place, the children divide along gender lines, though Arjie always plays with the girls. His favourite game is 'bride-bride', in which he plays the bride, dressed in a white sari and wearing lipstick and rouge. Just a few pages into this first episode of the novel, Selvadurai's narrator interrupts to anticipate the later exile from Sri Lanka. He links this departure to the loss of childhood and to entering 'the precarious waters of adult life'.[8] The process of maturity that will eventually be marked by his leaving begins for Arjie on these spend-the-days and it is not the difference caused by being part of the Tamil minority that first begins his estrangement (even if that will be why he eventually must leave) but the way in which he occupies a gender role forbidden to him.

When Arjie dresses as a bride, 'I was able to leave the constraints of myself and ascend into another, more brilliant, more beautiful self' (p. 4). The person he becomes is portrayed as a fuller and more complete human being. It is not then within the act of transvestism that Arjie becomes alienated; rather, his distance begins when others pass judgement on the seven-year-old boy's desires. The catalyst here is his cousin Tanuja, 'Her Fatness'. Jealous of Arjie's dominance of the girls' games, she verbally attacks him, trying to draw attention to the unacceptability of his difference. She calls Arjie 'pansy', 'faggot' and 'sissy', but although the children recognise these words as insults, they do not understand what they mean, and therefore dismiss them. It is only when Arjie appears in drag before the adults of the family, and they express concerns that he might be 'funny', that he truly starts to recognise his isolation: 'The word "funny" as I understood it meant either humorous or strange, as in the expression, "that's funny". Neither of these fitted the sense in which my father had used the word' (p. 17). The uncanny use of the word, in which its familiarity seems somehow suspended, captures the sense of adriftness experienced as Arjie grows older: he must learn new categorisations and values and, in doing so, discover that these may exclude him.

Arjie is no longer able to play comfortably with the girls. As he gets older it becomes clear that he could never be accepted into the collectivity guaranteed by femininity. At the same time he is not only excluded from the camaraderie of his male cousins but does not wish to integrate with them anyway. Absent is any possibility of a gay community, where he might find affirmation and reciprocation of his desires. Homosexuality exists outside of language in his community, in that disavowed space created through the novel use of 'funny'. Arjie's development must take place without the tools of self-description that might help him to orientate himself. Lacking such a vocabulary also denies him other types of belonging. As Selvadurai has written elsewhere, 'The pure sense of being Sri Lankan was based on rigid heterosexual and gender roles [. . .] By being gay, was I no longer Sri Lankan?'[9] Once it becomes clear that a crucial part of who he is cannot be articulated within the extant cultural vocabularies of Sri Lanka, it becomes questionable whether he can belong to the nation at all.

Of course, Arjie's intellectual and emotional growth also involves coming to realise his difference as a Tamil living in the majority Sinhalese Sri Lanka. Unlike homosexuality, this minority identity is very clearly demarcated within the national vocabulary. In his youth, Arjie is able to discount the importance of the ethnic divide, believing that his mother's sister, Radha, will be able to marry the Sinhalese Anil. However, it becomes clear that this is not the case: Radha is attacked and injured by Sinhalese militants and no longer wishes to pursue her relationship. Arjie's maturity consists in part in realising the depth of the divide between the ethnic groups.

Towards the end of the novel it seems that Arjie is able to challenge each form of personal reduction that his minority statuses force upon him. In the sexual relationship he begins with his school friend Shehan, he finds at least a nascent sense of a communal space where he can express his sexuality. His strength of feeling for Shehan also leads him to challenge the ways in which his ethnic belonging is supposed to determine his actions. Selected to read a poem at prize-giving by the headmaster of his school, who wishes to impress a minister and ensure that Tamils continue to be entitled to attend the institution, Arjie deliberately mangles the words in protest at the headmaster's brutal treatment of Shehan. Rather than standing up for his increasingly persecuted ethnic minority, as he is expected to, Arjie instead makes a gesture of solidarity with the only person he knows who shares his sexuality.

However, this seeming ascription of higher value to his chosen gay 'community' over an ethnic unity that is largely imposed upon Tamils is undercut by the closing scenes of the book. While the first five chapters are written with the hindsight of the adult narrator contemplating his childhood, the final chapter moves into the present tense of diary entries as the family is forced from its home by the rioting. As when the attack on Radha stripped Arjie of his romantic notions of inter-ethnic relations, so does the brutality of these few days seem to require that he recognises the binding power of ethnicity, even if he would rather not be characterised in this way. Leaving Sri Lanka also means leaving his lover, and understanding for the first time that 'Shehan was Sinhalese and I was not' (p. 302). While part of growing up for Arjie is exercising his agency in disrupting the prize-giving, another stage is the recognition that some social structures, while patently unjust, are beyond the strength of the individual to challenge.

NATURAL AND ETHICAL BEHAVIOUR: SHANI MOOTOO, *CEREUS BLOOMS AT NIGHT*

Much of *Funny Boy* is concerned with Arjie's attempts to insist on his humanity against the discourses of ethnic and racial prejudices that would deny it. In Shani Mootoo's *Cereus Blooms at Night* (1996), the category of the human is itself placed under interrogation. Ambrose Mohanty returns from his education in the Shivering Northern Wetlands (Mootoo's fictional land that seems very like Britain) to the island of Lantanacamara (which is similar to the Trinidad in which Mootoo was raised). He reveals that he soon abandoned the theological education for which he had been sent away and instead studied entomology. He explains his reasons to the girl he wishes to woo, Mala Ramchandin:

> At the heart of theology [. . .] is the assumption that humans are by far superior to the rest of all of nature, and that's why we are the inheritors of the earth. Arrogant, isn't it? What's more, not all humans are part of this [. . .] Some of us are considered to be much lesser than others – especially if we are not Wetlandish or European or full-blooded white.[10]

Ambrose points to the assumption of human domination over nature as making possible hierarchies within humanity such as racial discrimination. A more productive way of viewing the world seems to be required in order to abandon such notions of superiority and thus neutralise such relations of power.

The plot of *Cereus Blooms at Night* goes back to the childhood of Chandin Ramchandin, Mala's father, who suffers under the distinctions of humanity that Ambrose observes. Chandin is taken in by a Wetlandish missionary and encouraged to develop as a Christian, with a view to guiding and teaching the people of his colony. He is impressed by the 'smarter-looking, smarter-acting Reverend's religion, and there soon came a time when to his parents' dismay, he no longer visited' and he instead slavishly mimics European dress and behaviour (p. 30). Raised within the Reverend's home, he develops an attraction to the daughter of the house, Lavinia, but is told that this is an inappropriate relationship, as he is like a brother to her. However, when Lavinia gets engaged to her cousin Chandin recognises that the unnaturalness of their match in the Reverend's eyes had more to do with racial difference than familial relations. In response, Chandin immediately marries Sarah, 'a woman from his background' (p. 45), and they soon have two daughters. However, when Lavinia returns from her failed engagement she and Sarah begin a sexual affair, eventually abandoning Chandin and the girls. In his anger and increasing instability, Chandin begins sexually abusing his daughters, especially Mala, on a nightly basis.

In juxtaposing these types of sexual relation all considered unnatural by Lantanacamaran society (miscegenation, lesbianism and violent incest), *Cereus Blooms at Night* challenges the idea that conformity to a model of nature offers any clear ethical compass. For the novel's main internal narrator, the male nurse Tyler, Chandin's story complicates the task of trying to understand his own homosexuality:

> I was preoccupied with trying to understand what was natural and what perverse, and who said so and why. Chandin Ramchandin played a part in confusing me about these roles, for it was a long time before I could differentiate between his perversion and what others called mine. (pp. 47–8)

Tyler needs to understand which rules to follow and thus how eventually to achieve a settled adulthood, even though he is already over thirty. The process is finally made possible when he is made the sole carer of Mala Ramchandin, now an old woman and resident of a nursing home.

Tyler's superior informs him that the elderly residents are 'all like children' (p. 13), but this seems particularly true of Mala. She has reverted to a pre-linguistic state and communicates mostly through mimicking the calls of animals and birds. She seems to have embraced a second childhood that is also a rejection of humanity; her connection with the natural world even extends to the smell of her body, 'an aroma resembling rich vegetable compost' (p. 11). We learn that Mala murdered her abuser father and lived alone with his decaying body in her house for many years, surrounded by animals, birds and insects. Through this connection with nature she is able to help Tyler in an unexpected way: she steals the uniform of a female nurse from a washing line and gives it to him to wear. When Tyler first dons it, he is uncomfortable, 'not a man and not ever able to be a woman, suspended nameless in the limbo state between existence and nonexistence', but Mala's silent acceptance encourages him to realise that the space outside of names may be a valuable one, providing a respite from the social rules that 'manacle nature'. Ultimately, Tyler feels 'extremely ordinary' in the feminine clothing, able for the first time, thanks to Mala, to inhabit an identity usually suppressed by the mores of Lantanacamara (pp. 77–8).

Tyler's parallel in the book, and ultimately his romantic consort, is Ambrose's son Otoh. Born a girl, Ambrosia, he soon begins to live as a boy, convincing the community so thoroughly 'that even the nurse and doctor who attended the birth, on seeing him later, marvelled at their carelessness in having declared him a girl'. His name is a shortening of his original nickname Otoh-boto, itself an acronym of 'on the one hand . . . but on the other', gesturing at his 'ability to imagine many sides of a dilemma (and if it weren't already a dilemma, of turning it into one) and the vexing inability to make up his mind' (p. 110). This embrace of ambivalence and uncertainty sets Otoh apart from the discriminating certainties of the island, and perhaps makes him better able to understand Tyler's transgression of usual gender boundaries.

Otoh's other important characteristic is his ability to care. When Ambrose returned from the Shivering Northern Wetlands, he proved unable to protect Mala from Chandin and fled from her. In guilt, he regularly leaves food outside her house, but as he increasingly begins to give up the world, spending most of his time asleep, his son Otoh is required to perform this errand in his stead. Otoh feels this gesture is insufficient and looks to make a deeper connection, 'to meet her and apologize for him and say that even though he was my father I wasn't a coward like him and that I would take care of her' (p. 124). It is his intervention that eventually liberates Mala from the house and into the care of Tyler, where she can begin to lay her demons.

While Chandin seems driven into becoming a monster by the strict divisions of a colonial and sexually repressive society, Mala and Ambrose, as a younger generation, seem forced to suffer for this as they each withdraw from adult life: Mala into her silence and isolation; Ambrose into his interminable slumbers. Yet Tyler's and Otoh's generation seems able to begin to trace a third way, which neither capitulates to the destructiveness of conforming to dangerous codes of 'natural' behaviour, nor entails complete abjuration of this undesirable world. Instead, through becoming comfortable with indeterminacy, and through being motivated always by the desire to care for others, they start to map a model of adulthood within which they might flourish.

TRAPPED: TSITSI DANGAREMBGA, *NERVOUS CONDITIONS*

Tsitsi Dangarembga's *Nervous Conditions* (1988), set in 1960s Rhodesia, takes its title from Jean-Paul Sartre's 'Preface' to Frantz Fanon's *The Wretched of the Earth* (1961). Sartre's preface discusses the colonised elites, those selected to receive an education in European values, even as they are denied the rights fully to participate in European privilege. He writes of how these 'white-washed' young people were unable to think or say anything for themselves and instead only 'echoed' the knowledge and ideals they had absorbed: 'From Paris, from London, from Amsterdam we would utter the words "Parthenon! Brotherhood!" and somewhere in Africa or Asia lips would open '. . . thenon! . . . therhood!'[11] This mimicry is exceptionally damaging for those who practise it; it turns them into the 'natives', who are necessarily always of less value than the fully human Europeans. Crucially, in Sartre's reading of Fanon, this is a process in which neither the Europeans nor their others can be exempted from responsibility: 'The status of "native" is a nervous condition introduced and maintained by the settler among colonized people *with their consent*.'[12]

The suggestion that mimicry is a form of damaging neurosis plays out across several characters in Dangarembga's novel. Central is Babamukura, a school headmaster and the character closest to Sartre's figure of the European-educated native. Babamukura dominates his extended family, with the imprimatur of his foreign education bolstering his authority. His triumphant return is heralded by his brother who declares:

> Do you see him? Our returning prince. Do you see him? Observe him well. He has returned. Our father and benefactor has returned appeased, having devoured English letters with a ferocious appetite! Did you think degrees were indigestible? If so, look at my brother. He has digested them![13]

In Jeremiah's praise, the image is of Babamukura consuming and incorporating European knowledge, rather than the other way around, but the novel increasingly challenges this idea, and examines whether consumption is only a one-way process.

Babamukura seems keen to reproduce his success more widely and arranges for his nephew Nhamo to move in with him and his family and attend the mission school. When Nhamo returns after his first year, the changes in the boy are apparent. Not only is he 'fit and muscular', but also seems to have skin 'several tones lighter in complexion than it used to be' (p. 52). Crucially, though, he acts as if he has forgotten his mother tongue, Shona. It emerges that this particular change is mostly affected, but his wish to imply that he can now only communicate in English reveals much of his desire to assimilate European norms. When he suddenly takes ill and dies at the mission, his mother reacts to the news as if his actual passing was only a further aspect of the process started through his education, which equally destroyed crucial parts of him: 'First you took his tongue so that he could not speak to me and now you have taken everything, taken everything for good' (p. 54).

The death of Nhamo allows Tambudzai, his sister and the novel's narrator, to take up the place at the mission school in his stead. Like her brother, she seems actively to desire the changes this shift in location will bring about – 'At Babamukura's I expected to find another self, a clean, well-groomed, genteel self who could not have been bred, could not have survived, on the homestead' (pp. 58–9) – but she is soon disconcerted by these changes when Anna, the servant at the mission house, begins to treat her deferentially (pp. 84–5). Tambudzai begins to realise that while she desires changes, for herself and for those around her, she cannot always control what these are. Like the women of her family, who have been 'battered' into accepting 'myths' of womanhood as their authentic selves (p. 140), and then feel compelled to inhabit and reinforce these positions, Tambudzai is increasingly conditioned to behave in certain ways, even when it seems she is freely making choices. This comes to a head when Babamukura requires her to participate in the wedding of her parents, an event she considers an embarrassing sham. She is unable to tell him so, as the values he represents have become so ingrained in her:

> My vagueness and my reverence for my uncle, what he was, what he had achieved, what he represented and therefore what he wanted, had stunted the growth of my faculty of criticism, sapped the energy that in childhood I had used to define my own position. (p. 167)

Tambudzai's counterpart in the novel is Babamukura's daughter Nyasha. Herself largely raised in England, and far more distant from traditional Shona life than her father, having genuinely lost the language, she is nonetheless deeply critical of the processes of colonial education, bemoaning that 'it's bad enough [. . .] when a country gets colonised, but when the people do as well! That's the end, really, that's the end' (p. 150). Nyasha is fascinated by the historical circumstances of colonialism and determined to understand and therefore challenge the current order: 'you had to know the facts if you were ever going to find the solutions' (p. 95). She even attacks the popular view of her father as a great benefactor, instead insisting on analysing him as 'a historical artefact' and arguing that he is compelled by his circumstances to behave the way he does (pp. 161–2).

However, although Nyasha's reading and constant intellectual enquiry seem to generate sharp insights into the society around her, it is not clear that this acuity is beneficial to her. After Tambudzai leaves for the Young Ladies College of the Sacred Heart, Nyasha is isolated at school, due to her inarticulacy in Shona. Her self-awareness becomes particularly problematic: while she is able to criticise the impact of colonial ideology on her father, she does not fail to recognise its presence in her own life. When she writes to Tambudzai that she intends to begin a diet 'to discipline my body and occupy my mind', the verbs suggest punishment and besiegement, rather than control and contemplation (p. 201). She develops severe eating disorders, refusing food in a reversal of the way in which Babamukura was seen as devouring European knowledge. Eventually, she has a violent fit, tearing her history book with her teeth, and ranting that 'They've trapped us!' (p. 205). Nyasha may be able to diagnose the neuroses of the colonial condition, but is not able to identify a cure and instead 'the self is disassociated, and the patient heads for madness'.[14]

Tambudzai seems equally at risk of profound alienation, and unlikely to grow into adulthood without suffering similar problems. Indeed, while she reads the fates of Nhamo and Nyasha as warnings, she is inclined to ignore them: 'I told myself I was a much more sensible person than Nyasha, because I knew what could or couldn't be done.' However, the novel ends by suggesting that despite her repression of these omens, a 'seed' was planted by the experiences, which gives Tambudzai the ability ultimately to see beyond 'Sacred Heart and what it represented as a sunrise on my horizon' (p. 208). A new consciousness is required for models of adulthood that are not compromised in the same way as Babamukura's. Experiences like those of Nyasha, which appear entirely destructive for her, can at least be mined to allow Tambudzai greater resources for developing her own personality.

INHERITANCE AND ACCIDENTS: ZADIE SMITH, *WHITE TEETH*

The stories of the children and young adults of Zadie Smith's *White Teeth* (2000) cannot be separated from those of their parents. The novel is vitally concerned with inheritance, and with how a particular relationship to history might be transmitted across generations. Although often read as a novel about multiculturalism, it rarely represents the sense of community around which multiculturalist philosophies articulate, but instead reads individuals primarily as members of families, forced by these networks of belonging into existence within specific historical moments and dynamics across time. The titles of the first three sections of the book are each preceded by a pair of dates, tying the novel's present into a long history. While the first date of each pair indicates the year in which that part of the novel is predominantly set (1974, 1984, 1990), the second (1945, 1857, 1907) leads far deeper into what the central metaphor designates the 'root canals' of the characters: those historical circumstances that lie as unseen determinants of contemporary conditions and individuals. The novel's epigraph suggests that 'What's past is prologue', and therefore that to understand any contemporary story we must always account for the historical circumstances that led to this point.

This relation to history is given particular importance in the 'century of strangers',[15] in which the great demographic upheavals of mass migration have set geography against history, carrying people many thousands of miles from where their family's story has until then been located. For Alsana Iqbal, this dislocation is inseparable from loss and the threat of annihilation. Her sense of losing identity through a divorce from history is felt particularly in the fears she has for her son, Millat:

> [she] would regularly wake up in a puddle of her own sweat after a night visited by visions of Millat (genetically *BB* where *B* stands for Bengali-ness) marrying someone called Sarah (aa where 'a' stands for Aryan), resulting in a child called Michael (*B*a), who in turn marries somebody called Lucy (aa), leaving Alsana with a legacy of unrecognizable great-grandchildren (Aaaaaaa!), their Bengali-ness thoroughly diluted, genotype hidden by phenotype. (p. 282)

One of the key questions of *White Teeth* is to what extent the traces of history that shape contemporary lives should be embraced in order to give those lives full meaning and, if they are abandoned, what else might remain to shore up a sense of identity.

The four main adolescents in the novel – the twins Millat and Magid Iqbal, Irie Jones and Joshua Chalfen – are forced to make decisions about how they are to define themselves in terms of their affiliations. Thy each look to defy their parents as part of this process: Joshua rebels against his genetic researcher father by joining an extreme animal rights group; and the two sons of the struggling Muslim Samad Iqbal take opposing paths to one another, with Magid embracing a secular rationalism as militant as the Islamist group Millat joins. However, it is Irie's development that the novel addresses in greatest detail. For her, defying her parents does not mean rejecting all elements of her inheritance, and she instead turns to her maternal grandmother and through her to the Jamaican side of her ancestry. However, it becomes clear that the vision Irie has of Jamaica is far less historical than idealised. She builds a myth of belonging to a place she has never visited, short-circuiting the actual messy business of time passing, to connect with an imagined place of pure experience, untainted by history, 'where things simply *were*'. The attraction is to the 'magical fantasy word' of 'homeland', which 'sounded like a beginning. The beginningest of beginnings. Like the first morning of Eden and the day after apocalypse. A blank page' (p. 345).

Much of Irie's coming to maturity in the novel comes in learning to reject the comfort of this return to an idea of homeland. Against the purity of the imagined past is always set the random busyness of everyday life and the unsettlement of fixed ideas this entails. Samad complains to Irie about the predicaments of migration, trapped between a land in which migrants are often unwelcome and one to which return is impossible. Eventually, 'I come to believe that everything is an *accident*' (p. 349). Yet while this suggestion seems like the bleakest possible fate to Samad, to Irie it implies paradise: in welcoming the accidental, the burdens of historical determination might be avoided. In the outburst Irie eventually directs at the older generation, it is their clinging to history that is most fully attacked: outside her family's circle, she insists, people do not care about the past, 'because it *doesn't fucking matter*' (p. 440).

While the disruptions of migration and multiculture irrevocably change the lives of settled and settler populations alike, narratives other than national belonging are nonetheless relied upon to shore up personal and social identity against the threat of uncertainty and the anxiety that may come from living in a land of accidents. While the consolations of political certainty are explored in Smith's representations of the FATE animal rights group, far more of *White Teeth* examines particularly how two certain metanarratives are drawn upon to understand the world: religious thought and scientific belief. Within the novel these are each seen as reductive and tending to fundamentalisms in which other possibilities for conceptualising existence are closed down.

The insistence on fundamentals is in some ways an insistence on stasis, whether manifest in Marcus Chalfen's desire to remove the unexpected through the genetic programming of a mouse, or in Samad's dismissal of the idea that the children of migrants might relate differently to their circumstances: '"Don't speak to me of second generation! One generation! Indivisible! Eternal!"' (p. 250). Against this, history forces us to concede that 'multiplicity is no illusion' (p. 486). The novel ends with both religious and scientific convictions seemingly defeated by the forces of chance embodied in the coin-flipping Archie Jones foiling Millat's attempted assassination of Marcus, and instead inadvertently freeing the genetically-modified Futuremouse™.

At the end of the penultimate chapter, however, a slightly different conclusion is reached. Here Smith seems to question whether multiplicity is as achievable, or as desirable, as it might seem elsewhere in the novel. She recognises that difference itself is subject to commodification and therefore may be subject to a stasis just as determining as any other marker of social or communal identity. The imagined respondents to a branding survey that asks them to imagine 'a new British room, a space for Britain, Britishness, space of Britain, British industrial space cultural space space' ultimately reject the insistence on locating and commodifying the materiality of identity and instead make a plea for space without content or context: 'the answer to every questionnaire nothing nothing space please just space nothing please nothing space' (p. 443). The truncated prose and retreat into silence here jars in a novel so notable throughout for its verbosity. The suggestion is not so much of something that cannot be articulated but of something without existence at all. Ultimately, the only alternative to taking up an identity that fits within the expectations of society may involve the destructive act of self-immolation, and leaving oneself with no selfhood at all.

SUMMARY

- Postcolonial literature has frequently found in the figure of the child a way to trace not only the conflicts faced by individuals but also those waged across their societies.
- Frederic Jameson's claim that all third-world literature is necessarily national allegory has been widely criticised, but may provide a way to understand the specific means by which social contexts are articulated in these texts.
- In Roddy Doyle's *A Star Called Henry* the national narrative is seen as a tempting but dangerous way to define one's self.
- The two minority statuses caused by ethnicity and sexuality in Shyam Selvadurai's *Funny Boy* are rendered very differently in national discourse, and each requires specific forms of agency in response.
- Shani Mootoo's *Cereus Blooms at Night* challenges the social categories of the natural and instead sees its character striving for ethical forms of adult behaviour.
- The internalised colonial ideas that beset the characters of Tsitsi Dangarembga's *Nervous Conditions* prove destructive even when they are consciously apprehended.
- Zadie Smith's *White Teeth* explores whether history necessarily determines the present or whether a new generation can instead form identities based on contingency and chance.

NOTES

1. Rudyard Kipling, 'The White Man's Burden' [1899], in Rudyard Kipling, *Selected Poems*, ed. Peter Keating (London: Penguin, 1993), p. 82.
2. Fredric Jameson, 'Third-world Literature in the Era of Multinational Capitalism', *Social Text* 15 (1986), p. 69.
3. Ibid., pp. 85–6.
4. Aijaz Ahmad, *In Theory: Nations, Classes, Literature* (London: Verso, 1992), p. 103.
5. Imre Szeman, *Zones of Instability: Literature, Postcolonialism*

and the Nation (Baltimore: Johns Hopkins University Press, 2003), p. 85.

6. Salman Rushdie, *Midnight's Children* (London: Vintage, [1981] 1995), p. 3.

7. Roddy Doyle, *A Star Called Henry* (London: Vintage, [1999] 2000), p. 33. Further references to this edition are given in the main text.

8. Shyam Selvadurai, *Funny Boy* (London: Vintage, [1994] 1995), p. 5. Further references to this edition are given in the main text.

9. Shyam Selvadurai, 'Introduction', in Shyam Selvadurai (ed.), *Storywallah: Short Fiction from South Asian Writers* (New York: Houghton Mifflin, 2004), p. 4.

10. Shani Mootoo, *Cereus Blooms at Night* (London: Granta, [1996] 1999), p. 198. Further references to this edition are given in the main text.

11. Jean-Paul Sartre, 'Preface', in Frantz Fanon, *The Wretched of the Earth*, trans. Constance Farringdon (London: Penguin, [1961] 1990), p. 7.

12. Ibid., p. 17.

13. Tsitsi Dangarembga, *Nervous Conditions* (Banbury: Ayebia Clarke, [1988] 2004), p. 36. Further references to this edition are given in the main text.

14. Sartre, 'Preface', p. 17.

15. Zadie Smith, *White Teeth* (London: Hamish Hamilton, 2000), p. 281. Further references to this edition are given in the main text.

CHAPTER 4

Communities, Values, Transgressions

Smith's *White Teeth* seeks to map the challenges faced by individuals growing into their identity. The individual's search for identity seems a dominant idea in contemporary culture, but it is an idea that quickly becomes resistant to simple explanation when subject to analysis. While identity can sometimes be perceived as that which makes us unique, an idiosyncratic selfhood that distinguishes us from all others, it is rarely the desire to discover one's difference that fires the search for identity. As the word itself suggests, identity is predicated on sameness, on the finding of shared characteristics, attitudes or practices with another or others. In fact, identity politics is rarely about the promotion of individual diversity, but far more often involves the affirmation of a particular mode of communal unity.

Yet identity perhaps always begins from difference: when one's communal values are those of the majority, or are widely accepted to be the norm, there is rarely a need to assert this as an identity. Rather, identity functions as a mode of coming together for those excluded from the normalising majority position. It is recognition of the exclusion from full belonging of women, queer people and black people from dominant social ideas, for example, which gives rise to female, queer and black identities. If corresponding male, straight and white identities then become apparent, this is in reaction to the development of the identity of the minority or disempowered group. Until the challenge to univocal ways of conceiving the world is made through the affirmation of the subordinated identity, there is no need for the dominant identity to see itself as such; instead, its viewpoint can purely be described as the normal or natural way of the world.

Finding identity then, is often less about the individual's intrinsic self-actualisation than their establishment of lines of affiliation with a group or community. It is in the mutually enabling bonds of the communal that a space of succour and growth might be found. However, while communities can offer support to the individual who feels alienated from the dominant currents of society, they may not always do so in ways that allow individuals wholly to flourish. Smith bemoans the danger of community coming to crush individuality in her discussion of 'that impossible injunction "keep it real"', which she sees as originally intended to foster unification within the community of black people working to establish an identity distinct from, and able to resist subordination by, dominant whiteness: 'We were going to unify the concept of Blackness in order to strengthen it. Instead we confined and restricted it.'[1] This need to establish a unified world view to foster communal resilience ultimately 'made Blackness a quality each individual black person was constantly in danger of losing'.[2] For Smith, the simplification and reduction this promotes can make maintaining the community as negative a process as that marginalisation which led to the call for community in the first place.

The popular understanding of community is often dominated by the type of distinction famously explored by the German political thinker Ferdinand Tönnies in the late nineteenth century. Tönnies identified two distinct 'relationships based on positive mutual affirmation' operating among human beings. Groups are constituted by one or other of these ties. The key difference is that the social connections can be understood 'either as having real organic life, and that is the essence of *Community* [*Gemeinschaft*]; or else as a purely mechanical construction, existing in the mind, and that is what we think of as *Society* [*Gesellschaft*]'.[3] This contrast, between the naturally occurring connections of community, and the artificially constructed ones of society, continues to animate discussions of community, which is frequently seen as a more healthy form of human association, predating the anonymous and dehumanising social transactions that characterise modernity.

One of the characteristic features of such invocations of community is the suggestion that it has either been lost, or is imminently threatened with destruction. Its archetype is the village, a collection of familial groups small enough for everyone to know each other and self-sufficient enough to have only limited contact with the world outside. Yet this definition of community seems exceptionally limited. Indeed, as the concept only seems to have been formulated in opposition to the far more numerous and fluid associations of society, it can at times take on the character of the type of impossible construction upon which nostalgia is sustained. The figure of the knowable community functions as a fiction to critique the actual relationships of the world. This is not to deny the continuing existence of small rural settlements, or the existential importance of their compact closeness to those who live within them, but to recognise that constituting these as the ideal or only form of community is a significant ideological manoeuvre. Rather than identifying these associations as the lost or threatened 'true' community, they might instead be understood as instances that embody the *function* of community particularly effectively. If community is understood as function or practice, instead of simply as one particular mode of association, then other types of communal structure jostle for space alongside the village archetype.

An influential reimagining of community was carried out by Anthony Cohen in his 1985 study *The Symbolic Construction of Community*. For Cohen, there is no particular mode of association that necessarily corresponds to community, although some modes of living allow more easily for the development of community than others. Community, rather, is seen as a 'boundary-expressing symbol', marking out the ways in which members of groups differentiate from other groups. To be a member of a community is to exist within 'a cluster of symbolic and ideological map references' which serve to 'socially orient' the individual.[4] Crucially for Cohen, these symbols held in common can be interpreted differently by different members of the community, and their meanings may indeed change over time; their primary function, however, is always to differentiate one particular community from another.

While postcolonial literature is certainly not always innocent of the nostalgia of romanticising the rural knowable community, it has also allowed for the examination of the symbolic delineation of community. As Smith's example above shows, the symbols of community can frequently be employed to contest marginalisation; but the policing of the boundary always runs the risks of enacting a marginalisation or subordination within the group, and a failing to adapt to changing external circumstances.

LEARNING TO LISTEN: NADINE GORDIMER, *BURGER'S DAUGHTER*

The eponymous heroine of Nadine Gordimer's *Burger's Daughter* (1979), Rosemarie 'Rosa' Burger, is identified in the title of the novel by her relationship to her father Lionel Burger, a white anti-apartheid campaigner, who Gordimer mostly modelled on the real South African activist Abram 'Bram' Fischer (1908–1975).[5] In the same way as this distancing title, the novel's opening section equally views Rosa from the outside, showing how other people locate her within their networks of understanding. For a passer-by, looking at the crowd of visitors outside the prison where Rosa's mother is being held, she is just a schoolgirl who 'must have someone inside'; for the others in the crowd, however, she is notable as Burger's daughter, and an anonymous voice insists '*she was an example to us all of the way a detainee's family should behave*'.[6] Yet when Rosa's voice first interrupts this third person opening, it is to question the way in which these modes of identification function: '*When they saw me outside the prison, what did they see?*' (p. 7).

Burger's Daughter is partly Gordimer's attempt to explore the consciousness of the 'segment' of South African society to which she herself belonged, one which she describes in her essay 'Living in the Interregnum' (1981) as those white people preoccupied 'neither by plans to run away from nor merely by ways to survive physically and economically in the black state that is coming', but who instead want to be a constructive part of it.[7] In Rosa, who is a generation younger than her creator, Gordimer is able to dramatise the particular difficulties of belonging to this community and the strains that must be faced in trying to offer a coherent opposition to apartheid when, as a white person, one has been formed within and by the privilege this status grants.

In the first parts of the book, in which the young Rosa has to cope with the imprisonment and death of both her parents, she lives for a time with Conrad, a postgraduate student who nihilistically rejects any kind of political commitment. He acts as a temptation and devil's advocate for her, constantly attacking the type of upbringing she had and suggesting that the political commitment of the Burgers led them to neglect important and necessary aspects of fulfilled human life:

> What'd you celebrate in your house? The occasions when somebody got off, not guilty, in a political trial [. . .] There was a mass protest or a march, a strike [. . .] These were the occasions you were taught [. . .] were the real ones, not your own private kicks and poor little ingrown miseries. (p. 47)

Conrad offers Rosa the alluring idea of focusing on herself as an individual, of choosing not to locate herself always in the brutal political landscape of her nation.

Gordimer writes elsewhere that 'all that is and has been written by South Africans is profoundly influenced, at the deepest and least controllable level of consciousness, by the politics of race'.[8] The centrality of race to all aspects of life in apartheid-era South Africa means that it is not just writers who bear this deep inscription on their consciousness. When at a party held at a black friend's house, Rosa reflects on the use of the term 'place', rather than 'house' or 'home' to describe where one lives, a usage she says began with black people and spread to whites: 'A "place", somewhere to belong, but also something that establishes one's lot and sets aside much to which one doesn't belong' (p. 147). At the most basic level of locating oneself in the world, the divisions of apartheid must be acknowledged.

It is ultimately not Conrad's urging for her to abandon this awareness of political determination in favour of focusing on herself that leads to Rosa's crisis of community, so much as an attack on the type of resistance her parents offered to their society's racial hegemony. The mid-1970s saw the rise of the Black Consciousness Movement in South Africa, a group that, among other things, rejected the idea that white people could help the cause of black liberation. At the party Rosa attends, this view is powerfully put forward: 'Whites, whatever you are, it doesn't matter. It's no difference. You can tell them – Afrikaners, liberal, Communists. We don't accept anything from anybody. We take. D'yu understand? We take for ourselves' (p. 155). It seems that it is this critique that leads Rosa to wish to leave Africa. She visits Brandt Vermeulen, a prominent Afrikaner whose cosmopolitan tastes do not seem to hamper his support for apartheid, to try to obtain the passport she has been denied as the child of political activists. Vermeulen speaks sadly of her father, seeing his resistance to white supremacist ideals as a case of betraying 'his people' (p. 187). It is this idea that she will always belong to a white community, forever marked by its privilege, that Rosa seems to hear from both black opponents and white supporters of apartheid. Faced with this, she feels unable 'to live in Lionel's country' (p. 213); while he felt able meaningfully to fight against segregation, her sense of being compromised by the colour of her skin is too much and she flees to Europe.

In Europe she feels without personality at all for a time, because she cannot be identified as part of a community. However, she soon finds herself at a party in London where her celebrity as 'Burger's daughter' seems to return, and which she does not seem to reject until she meets a man who as a little boy had lived with her at her parents' house. The fact that she is only able to call him by his patronising nickname, 'Baasie' (little boss) and does not know his African name, Zwelinzima Vulindlela, angers him. He later telephones and criticises her father's work, and her own furthering of it by trading on his name, as simply white self-interest, mocking her for thinking 'you aren't white and I'm not black' (p. 330). The way in which at the party her individuality is subsumed by her father's politics, followed by the Black Consciousness-style attack on her racial privilege, seems to mirror in miniature the narrative of the earlier sections of the book, but while it had before led her to leave South Africa, on this occasion it inspires her to return. She likens Baasie's views to those of Vermeulen: each saw her whiteness as indicating she is like every other white person. She contrasts this with the lesson she has now finally learned from her parents who 'never limited [them]selves to being like anyone else' (p. 343). She does not have to deny her whiteness and what it entails in a segregated society, but may rather acknowledge it and then look for ways to go beyond its restrictions.

On her return to South Africa Rosa does not attempt to take up a leading political role, but instead accepts a position as a physiotherapist in a black children's hospital, trying to ease suffering a little. In her essays of this period, Gordimer often quotes the black South African poet Mongane Wally Serote:

> White people are white people
> They must learn to listen.
> Black people are black people
> They must learn to talk.[9]

In withdrawing from any attempt to lead the struggle against apartheid, and instead simply looking to support the struggle by black people for their own liberation, Rosa seems to achieve a degree of 'white consciousness' which is about this imperative to listen rather than talk. Towards the end of the novel, the most directly political statement (in its concision contrasting strongly with Lionel Burger's one-hour-and-forty-five-minute courtroom statement of his position) comes from the Soweto Students Representative Council, whose real-life statement of resistance is reproduced in full in Gordimer's novel.[10] Like Rosa, Gordimer seems committed to listening to, rather than helping to form, black South Africans' political resistance.

Rosa is arrested for political subversion and detained without charge in the closing chapters of the novel. It is left ambiguous whether she is guilty of any of the activities in which she is suspected of being involved. In the prison, she finds an ironically mixed community, as segregation between black, white and 'coloured' people is only loosely enforced (pp. 366–7). More importantly, though, she has found a way of acknowledging her status as part of a white community without having to accept either apartheid or a paternalist attitude to black struggles for liberation.

AVOIDING HISTORICAL PITFALLS: THOMAS KING,
TRUTH AND BRIGHT WATER

While Gordimer's novel traces the struggles of a young person to find a way to acknowledge their community and background without replicating its destructive values, Thomas King's *Truth and Bright Water* (1999) shows a whole community unsure of who they are either in the past or in the present, searching for ways to understand themselves but also struggling to fight against the deprived circumstances in which they live. Truth and Bright Water are the names of two settlements, the former a town in the United States, and the latter a Native American reservation across the border in Canada. The novel, throughout, is marked by splitting, doublings and mirrorings, and the notion of boundaries and whether they can be crossed, is frequently central.

In his 2005 study *The Truth about Stories*, King discusses the US Indian Arts and Craft Act, and the Canadian Bill C-31 amendment to the Indian Act of that country. Each of these pieces of legislation sought to establish a legal basis for determining who was to be classed as 'Indian'. For the US, the key criterion was membership of a recognised tribe; in Canada the classification relied more on having a 'pure' Indian ancestry. In each case, King notes that 'unlike most other ethnic groups, we have two identities, a cultural identity and a legal identity'.[11] This complicated overlapping of communities has a number of effects, and is reflective of a deeper problem with the way the North American nation states deal with their Native populations. The Native is allowed either to exist solely within tradition and remain apart from mainstream culture and politics or to forego their claim to indigeneity and become like all other American citizens.

In *Truth and Bright Water* the Native people seem not to see the national boundary that separates the town from the reservation as in any way impenetrable, and regularly cross the line. For King, himself raised in the US and a naturalised Canadian, the boundary is simply a convenient dichotomy, which bears little relation to the actual meaning of the land, and certainly does not match the ways in which Native bands before colonisation would have understood their surroundings. Nonetheless, the river that constitutes the divide is a genuine obstacle and difficult for the locals to cross. A bridge was designed to span the divide, and partially built, but the project failed and it was never finished. That failure indicates the neglect on the part of those in power to provide the means for the Native community to connect with each other, and with North American society more generally.

The legally recognised identity of the Natives on the reservation, and of those who have moved into the town, allows them to trade upon their 'Indianness', and sell the romantic image of the Indian to tourists, especially those from Europe. Tradition and kitsch are wilfully blended together in the hope of shifting merchandise:

> Beaded belt buckles, acrylic paintings of the mountains, drawings of old-time Indians on horseback, deer-horn knives, bone chokers, T-shirts that say things like 'Indian and Proud', and 'Indian Affairs Are the Best'. And all of it, according to the signs that everyone puts up, is 'authentic' and 'traditional'.[12]

Forced into the mode of having to accept a marginalised cultural identity, the Native community tries its best to capitalise on it, though rarely with success, as the structures of the modern nation states in which they live are so weighted against them. The reservation's chief, Franklin, tries to establish a camping resort to attract visitors to the wilderness, but a faulty septic tank leaves the site haunted by a bad smell, 'musty like bad breath or a lingering fart' (p. 107). The name of the resort, Happy Trails, is a corruption of the name given to the genocidal clearances that forced Native Americans west in the early years of the nineteenth century, the Trail of Tears. It seems that the brutal facts of this history continue to haunt the contemporary Native community, and to scotch their efforts to change their situation.

The legacy of the Trail of Tears finds another echo in the name of the character whose return to Truth inspires much of the novel's narrative, Monroe Swimmer. James Monroe, US president from 1817 to 1825, was one of the architects of the Native clearances. In pairing this name with Swimmer, which suggests the animals that dived beneath the water to collect the earth that was to form the world in many Native creation myths, King signals the desire of this man to overturn historical suffering and create a new world for the Native population.[13] Swimmer had found celebrity as a 'famous Indian artist', due to the fact that 'he landed in Toronto just as being an Indian was becoming chic' (p. 28). However, his art took him in a different direction from the reproduction of typical symbols of Indianness, such as those sold at Bright Water. Instead, he became a restorer of paintings, specialising in nineteenth-century landscapes. These paintings symbolise a mainstream North American view of the countryside and 'all look alike. Craggy mountains, foreboding trees, sublime valleys with wild rivers running through them' (p. 138). Yet, in handling these works, Swimmer became convinced that under the paint were the images of Indian villages, erased by the act of white people imaginatively claiming the landscape as their own. He paints the Indians 'back' into the paintings, to reclaim the land for its original owners.

Back in Truth, Swimmer tries to take this act of reassertion through artifice further. He paints the church building which represents the persistent efforts of colonisation in such a way that it becomes indistinguishable from the prairie that surrounds it, and tries to repopulate the land with buffalo by using wire models of the animals to lure them back. In his most significant symbolic act, he has stolen the bones of Native children from the museums in which they were stored and performed ceremonies to return them to the land to which they belong.

While the novel never condemns Monroe Swimmer's recuperative acts, it is questioned to what degree this attempt to heal historical trauma can be sufficient to address the problems of contemporary Native communities. The narrator's cousin, Lum, seems to suffer particularly as a Native in North America. After having lost his mother at a young age, he is regularly beaten by his father, Franklin, and is unable to move on, given the chronic unemployment the young people of his community face. He comes to identify with the bones of the lost children and, after watching Swimmer ceremonially throw a skull from the broken bridge, he dives from it. His dive in some ways echoes that of the animals which created the world, though incompletely as he fails to resurface and is instead killed. The retreat into focusing only on the sins of history seems to offer little productive hope for the future.

However, the potential for redemption may lie in the character who mirrors Lum, the narrator Tecumseh, whose name is shared with a great chief who fought to unify Indian tribes in the face of the clearances. While Lum seems to represent a destructive clearing of the past, Tecumseh contains the seeds of the complementary instinct to rebuild. Swimmer tries to recruit him as a 'minstrel', asking the teenager to record the artist's 'great deeds', though Tecumseh remains sceptical about the 'trick[s] you do with paint' (p. 203). Instead, the narrative he provides in the novel seems more determinedly banal, chronicling the actual daily experiences of the Natives. He can seem oblivious to the weight of history that surrounds him: a girl turns up at Happy Trails calling herself Rebecca Neugin, who seems to be the ghost of her namesake who left a famous first-person account of the suffering of the Trail of Tears, but Tecumseh appears entirely unaware of the association. Nonetheless, this does not necessarily serve to divorce his story from those of the past. King has praised 'associational' writing about Native communities, which recognises that codes and values drawn from long histories continue to shape contemporary life.[14] As Tecumseh's grandmother puts it, there is 'more to a story than just the words' (p. 232). The history that Swimmer wants to recreate is already present in Tecumseh's ordering of the world; it just needs to be recognised.

The novel's other Monroe is the Hollywood star Marilyn Monroe. Lucy Rabbit is determined to look like Marilyn, and insistent that the star herself was of Indian heritage (and that so too was Elvis Presley, the other great 1950s idol). Here, the presence of Native people in American culture is seemingly taken to implausible extremes, but Lucy's improbable claims refuse the dwelling in the past that seems imposed by the fabrication of the authentic Indian through commercial exploitation, and only partly overcome in Swimmer's simulated redress of historical injustice. Her insistence speaks instead of finding a place for the Native community in modern North American society, rather than just that of the past, much as Tecumseh's own narrative does.

MOTES IN THE EYE OF HISTORY: DIASPORA SPACE

In the two novels looked at so far in this chapter we can see individuals and communities who challenge straightforward ideas of
the nation. Chapter 2 introduced Benedict Anderson's influential
conception of the nation as an 'imagined community', a grouping
of people who do not need to know each other to feel confident that
they meaningfully belong with each other. In their different ways,
both Rosa Burger of *Burger's Daughter* and Tecumseh in *Truth
and Bright Water* upset the imagined communities to which they
belong. Rosa is unable to subscribe to the segregationist agenda
demanded of her as a white South African, but neither does she
imagine that she can simply ally herself with the black community
in its struggle against apartheid. A unique type of community
within the national space must be imagined. Tecumseh is posi-
tioned very differently from Rosa within the power structures of
the nations between which he moves. Yet, even as an indigenous or
'First Nation' subject, the novel suggests that he would do badly
to retreat only to 'his' community, defined in reductive terms.
Modern nations need to recognise the diversity within them and
communities must be constituted at different levels to fulfil different, equally important, functions.

One type of community that has received particular attention
within postcolonial studies is that of diaspora. Diasporic communities are those formed by migration, made up of people who inhabit
lands other than those from which they are imagined to originate.
The very idea of community in these cases provides much of the
symbolic focus upon which their unity depends. The term traditionally referred to the displaced Jewish people, though is now
commonly used in referring to the African diaspora, the Indian
diaspora, the Irish diaspora and so on. Robin Cohen has provided a
detailed list of features that may be found within a diasporic community, though he notes that these aspects may be stressed to different degrees in different diasporas:

(1) dispersal from an original homeland, often traumatically;
(2) alternatively, the expansion from a homeland in search of
work, in pursuit of trade or to further colonial ambitions; (3)

a collective memory and myth about the homeland; (4) an ide-
alisation of the supposed ancestral home; (5) a return movement; (6) a strong ethnic group consciousness sustained over
a long time; (7) a troubled relationship with host societies; (8)
a sense of solidarity with co-ethnic members in other countries; and (9) the possibility of a distinctive creative, enriching
life in tolerant host countries.[15]

Diasporic communities therefore live within and across the boundaries of modern nations, and complicate the national urge for
homogeneity. In Homi Bhabha's words, they are 'the mote[s] in
the eye of history, its blind spot that will not let the nationalist
gaze settle centrally'.[16] It is important to note that while migration
is an essential precursor for diaspora, this need not be a recent
movement of people. Indeed, it is possible for generations to pass
without any of the diasporic community residing in their place
of origin. This can lead to a considerable divergence between the
homeland idealised by the diaspora and the actual circumstances
of that place in the present-day. Even the first-generation migrant
is subject to such a discrepancy as the world left behind is built
through memory and desire in the light of retrospect and distance.
Salman Rushdie discusses how this plays out for people like him,
who long left behind the nations in which they were born: 'we will
not be capable of reclaiming precisely the thing that was lost [. . .]
we will, in short, create fictions, not actual cities or villages, but
invisible ones, imaginary homelands, Indias of the mind'.[17]

   Yet these 'imaginary homelands' are no less significant in
structuring the lives of the diasporic community purely because
they are fictional. Rather, the work of sustaining the myth can
become the element that draws people together and enables the
sense of identity through community. Diasporic communities are
not hermetically sealed off from the wider societies in which they
live. The work of preserving their difference does not preclude
engagement with the world outside, and this inevitably leads them
to change. The gap between the lost homeland and the diasporic
subject grows not just because the homeland undergoes historical change, but also because the dispersed community adapts and
evolves to its new location. Avtar Brah points out that this is not a

one-way interaction and the host society too will undergo changes in harbouring these communities, and it needs also to be noted that 'border crossings do not occur only across the dominant/ dominated dichotomy, but that, equally, there is traffic within cultural formations of the subordinated groups'.[18] Brah names this pattern of overlapping and interconnecting influences 'diaspora space'. It certainly should not be seen as simply consisting of a flattening of difference, and any change is often fiercely resisted, within both host and diasporic communities. Diasporic space is frequently the site of conflict and the changes it fosters in brokering diverse forces of community and tradition are not always positive for the individuals who must inhabit it.

HOW NEWNESS ENTERS THE WORLD: SALMAN RUSHDIE, *THE SATANIC VERSES*

Salman Rushdie's *The Satanic Verses* has often been seen as a definitive exploration of diaspora space, and of the transformations that might happen within it. His description of the novel formulates its intention in precisely this way:

> *Melange*, hotchpotch, a bit of this and a bit of that is *how newness enters the world*, and I have tried to embrace it. *The Satanic Verses* is for change-by-fusion, change by conjoining. It is a love song to our mongrel selves.[19]

For Rushdie, when people and cultures come together in diaspora space new and exciting modes of being become possible – modes that perhaps draw from older senses of cultural identity but which reimagine, translate and transcend these to reach towards the new.

The novel is centred on the story of two Indian men, Saladin Chamcha and Gibreel Farishta, who in its opening pages fall from an exploding aircraft into the English Channel just off Hastings. Miraculously unharmed, they then have to negotiate ways to belong in an England that refuses the normal laws of reality and instead contains elements of the magical and impossible. The two men have very different personalities and react to the changes they begin to undergo in very different ways.

Saladin has lived in England since childhood and made it his mission 'to become the thing his father was-not-could-never-be, that is, a goodandproper Englishman'.[20] He rejects his familial and national history instead to become English, in line with the limited vision he has of that identity. His England is a land of 'cricket, the Houses of Parliament, the Queen [. . .] warm beer, mince pies, common sense' (p. 175). It is a caricature of the nation, but one that he wants to embody. He cultivates an accent, and even a facial expression, that connotes this imagined national narrative. However, despite the absurdity of Saladin's desire, there is pathos in that, despite his embrace of a myth of English superiority, he is still not allowed to fit in. His fame as an actor is solely achieved through his work on the radio as 'the Man of a Thousand Voices' and through his heavily disguised appearance on a children's television show. His friend Zeeny sums his situation up: '"they pay you to imitate them, as long as they don't have to look at you"' (p. 60). As much as his father who is embarrassingly 'Indian', Saladin can never be the 'goodandproper Englishman' he wishes to be (p. 43). The identity he wishes to buy into will not accept him because of his perceived difference. In contrast, Gibreel is also an actor, but in India. Famous for his roles in 'theological' films portraying various Hindu deities, the Muslim Gibreel seems able to thrive in working with diverse national stories without unsettling his sense of self, and he is adored for his talent.

However, with the explosion of the aircraft, both men are forced to reassess their strategies of belonging, not least because they each begin to experience bizarre physical changes. Saladin's body becomes goat-like and devilish, his penis 'greatly enlarged and embarrassingly erect' (p. 157). He becomes an icon of evil, a representation of sinfulness and of unconstrained sexuality. Arrested by immigration officials, he is beaten and abused and taken to a Detention Centre, where he meets other immigrants who have also undergone disturbing physical changes. Another inmate of the centre explains to Saladin why these changes have taken place: '"they describe us [. . .] That's all. They have the power of description and we succumb to the pictures they construct"' (p. 166). The immigrants have arrived in a country where alterity is frightening to the settled population, and people who are not seen to belong to the narrative of a pure community are instead consigned to one that constructs them as beasts, demonic, threatening and grotesque.

Gibreel, meanwhile, takes on the features of his angelic namesake, developing a noticeable halo. However, he is adrift in Britain, not only apart from his homeland but also suffering from a loss of religious faith. He reacts by searching for certainties, and by trying to bend this new place to his will. His strategy for survival is to impose himself on the foreign country, and make it his own. 'He had the city in his pocket' – the London *A to Z* – and he wants to possess the material city in the same way (p. 156). He is determined to dominate the city, to map it in his mind as fixedly as has been done in the pages of the street plan. His wish to freeze the world, to understand it by capturing it as in a picture, refuses to allow that the city, and the nation, might always be changing and becoming something new. His rejection of ambiguity and flux strengthens his belief in himself as the archangel, and he feels that 'he was losing the last traces of his humanity' (p. 336). Rushdie suggests that refusal to accept change, and welcome newness into the world, is less than fully human.

Gibreel heads for destruction and eventually takes his own life, but Saladin reaches a happy ending by the close of the novel. Despite consistently fighting to reject the changes that happen to him, he nonetheless begins to perceive ways of understanding change differently. The marginalised diasporic communities of London come to celebrate his devil-like image and, in appropriating it for their own purposes, nurture an identity of resistance to the racism that would construe them as inferior. Saladin comes to realise that the assimilation he attempted in becoming the 'goodandproper Englishman' was as much a facet of an exclusionary ideology as the transfiguration he undergoes while under arrest. The self must instead be translated and becomes something continuous with, but different from, that which it was before. This hybrid identity is not just separate from the dominant identity, not just outside of the prevailing and marginalising ethos, but formed explicitly in opposition to it.

Despite the fantastic elements of the novel, Rushdie is concerned to demonstrate that his allegories have a meaningful political import within the contested materiality of diaspora space. Following the fire that forms the novel's climax, a character reminds us that 'what has happened [. . .] is a socio-political phenomenon. Let's not fall into the trap of some mysticism. We're talking about history: and an event in the history of Britain' (p. 468). Saladin seems dismissive throughout of the idea of the diasporic community having a valuable identity, but attends a political meeting late in the book where a speech seems to have a profound effect on him, so much so he has to leave the room: 'we shall be changed; African, Caribbean, Indian, Pakistani, Bangladeshi, Cypriot, Chinese, we are other than what we would have been if we had not crossed the oceans [. . .] we have been made again: but I say that we shall also be the ones to remake this society, to shape it from the bottom to the top' (p. 404).

Saladin Chamcha is able to return to India and to reassume his proper name Salahuddin Chamchawala at the end of the novel, not because he rejects British culture, but rather because he reaches an understanding that culture is fluid, heterogeneous and open to influence and change, in India as much as Britain. The crucial element in his coming to this realisation is his participation in a diasporic community, recognising that while he on his own could be easily labelled and marginalised, a community together has strength of identity sufficient to formulate its own values. Gibreel, on the other hand, was tied to an idea that values had to be unchanging and therefore retreated into isolation from others. *The Satanic Verses*'s love song to mongrel selves is importantly structured around a sense that positive cultural change does not happen for individuals, apart from the communities in which they are embedded; it needs to be imagined, and enacted, collectively.

THE RUSHDIE AFFAIR AND THE *UMMA*

The Satanic Verses is infamous across the world less for the way in which it examines how diasporic communities might adapt both themselves and their host societies, than in relation to the events that followed its publication. Large sections of the novel deal with the disturbing dreams that begin to haunt Gibreel and contribute to his breakdown. In these dreams we see the struggles of a prophet named Mahound in a city called Jahilia. The relation to the Prophet Muhammad in Mecca and the early history of Islam is clear. A Muslim politician in India, Syed Shahabuddin, publicly raised the idea that the novel was therefore extremely insulting to Muslims, and thanks to his campaign the book was banned in India. The events of the 'Rushdie Affair' soon escalated, with large-scale demonstrations against the book held in Bradford and London, and they reached a climax of sorts on 14 February 1989 when the Ayatollah Khomeini, spiritual leader of Iran, issued a call for 'all the intrepid Muslims in the world' to execute the author and publishers of the book.[21] Rushdie was forced immediately to go into hiding, protected by the British Secret Services, where he remained for several years.

In the novel, Islam is criticised as a demanding and rigid idea, contributing in large part to Gibreel's breakdown, but it is rarely assessed as a form of community in its own right. In fact, Rushdie seems critical of the idea that such a community may exist. He is critical of nationalist sentiments and keen to shown how diasporic space might force nations to refigure themselves, but the nation as the basic communal unit of modern social life remains key to his ideas. He expands on this in some detail in an essay first written in 1985, and revised during the *Satanic Verses* controversy. He builds on aspects of Benedict Anderson's arguments about the way in which the religious conception of time (in which everything is experienced in its totality by the creator and in which the passing of time is simply an illusion experienced by mortals) has ceded to the secular ideal of linearity and one event following another, linked through space in national stories. For Rushdie, 'our sense of the world is now clock-ridden' and the predominance of the nation-state has voided any space for a meaningful assertion of the religious idea of unity in time: 'When religion enters the political arena today, then, it does so as an event in linear time; that is, as a part of the world of the nation-state, and not a rejection of it.'[22] Later in the essay he suggests that Khomeini's revolution in Iran can only be understood through the lens of the politics of the nation, and that the same might even be true of the early years of Islamic Mecca.

However, many other writers on the topic are reluctant to assume that the religious community of believing Muslims, the *umma*, can best be understood through recourse to the idea of nations and nationalism. For Ernest Gellner, an important theorist of nationalism, there was a key difference between the European use of the national idea to counteract the loss of what Tönnies called *Gemeinschaft* and the emergence of 'fundamentalism' in the Islamic world, by which term Gellner refers to a complete trust in Quranic instruction. He sees each as a manifestation of 'the victory of a standardised high culture in mobile anonymous societies' but formed in completely different ways.[23] Not all scholars would agree that fundamentalism is the only way to conceive of the transnational structure of the *umma*, but several agree that the idea is fundamentally opposed to a philosophy of the nation. S. Sayyid describes the *umma* as a diaspora, though first by significantly challenging the traditional conception of diaspora. In Cohen's taxonomy above, the idea of homeland is central to diaspora, both in terms of the original trauma of dispersal and as a focus to which the diasporic subject can look back. For Sayyid, though, the most salient feature of diaspora is its function as 'anti-nation', complicating 'the relationship between the political and national'.[24] He sees the *umma* as precisely such a formation, allowing a space for political community which has nothing to do with the nation. The remainder of this chapter will focus on two novels that seem to explore this idea but will argue that in the first the community afforded within the *umma* seems resolutely non-political, and that in the second a suggestion of non-national political community is offered, but that this is ultimately formed around ideas other than transnational Islam.

FAITH WITH AND WITHOUT AGENCY: LEILA ABOULELA, *MINARET*

Leila Aboulela's *Minaret* (2005) tells the story of Najwa, who was raised in a prominent family in Sudan, but is forced by political events into exile in London. It explores how she moves from the secular and Westernised life she lived in a nominally Muslim society to her embrace of pious Islam in a secular one. The novel moves between two stories, each covering different periods in her life: the first, from 1984 to 1991, details the privileged life she lived in Khartoum and the difference she experiences on moving to London; the second covers a shorter period between 2003 and 2004 and shows her now deeply religious and wearing hijab clothing. She begins a stunted love affair with Tamer, the brother of the woman who employs her to mind a young child. These two stories are presented alternately throughout the book and each come to conclusion at its climax, though the achievement she seems to have made at the conclusion of the earlier period is made more complicated by the story told in the latter.

The lives Najwa and her twin brother live in Khartoum are structured largely around their consumption of Western consumer goods and culture, involving a string of parties where they listen to pop music. In her tight skirts and make-up, she is occasionally made uncomfortable by the provincial young women at her university who wear traditional Islamic dress, becoming self-conscious about how her life differs from the devout version to which her nation supposedly subscribes. However, more disturbing are the speeches she hears from Anwar, a left-wing student to whom she develops an attraction. He lambasts her about the discrepancies of wealth that exist in the country and how her politician father benefits from this. The sheltered life she lives that feels so immune to critique is shattered when the government in which her father serves is overthrown in a coup and he is arrested. The rest of the family flee to London, where they learn of his execution: 'the earth we were standing on split open and we tumbled down and that tumbling had no end, it seemed to have no end, as if we would fall and fall for eternity [. . .] As if this was our punishment'.[25]

When the novel resumes in 1989, this 'punishment' seems to have continued: Najwa's mother has died, and her brother's drug habit has eventually resulted in his imprisonment. Now living in straitened circumstances, she learns that the government in Sudan has fallen again, this time to an Islamist military coup, and that Anwar too is now in London. She resumes her relationship with him, seemingly in the hope that this might reduce her sense of isolation. It appears at first that the disdain which with he had previously regarded her privilege is now less important – 'here no one knows our background, no one knows whose daughter you are, no one knows my politics' – and that they can now be equals (p. 157). Yet the promise of community in a strange land that he offers is never complete and he continues occasionally to mock her and her family. In fact, it appears that she regards this punishment for what her father did and how her family benefited from it as a necessary scourging, one that may allow entry into, or even itself be, meaningful shared experience. Even as she acknowledges that he would have told her father's story to others, she rewards him by buying him an expensive computer from what remains of her money (pp. 169–70).

It becomes apparent, however, that she will never truly belong with him, and even after they have intercourse, he jokes that he would never accept her father's blood running through his children's veins (p. 233). The final spur that causes her to leave is the realisation that, holed up in his flat, they have missed the beginning of Ramadan. As fasting was one of the few religious activities in which she would participate in Sudan, she feels she has lost something important. Anwar's dismissive comment that in Khartoum the fast was only given meaning by its status as a 'community activity' seems to offer her inspiration, and she goes to the mosque for the first time in years (p. 231).

The warm reception Najwa receives at the mosque, at last giving her a sense of meaningful community, and her subsequent decision to begin wearing hijab, constitute the climax of the novel's earlier narrative. Wearing a headscarf she feels 'invisible' and free, having made a decision to reject completely the destructive life she had lived in Khartoum and continued through her relationship with Anwar in London. Aboulela has commented on this use of the idea of invisibility, insisting that she means it 'in a entirely positive way', to suggest that Najwa need no longer be defined through her exposing herself to the judgement of men.[26]

In the later period of the novel, Najwa is now entirely comfortable with wearing hijab, and within the transnational, multi-racial community of women with whom she prays at the Regent's Park mosque. This appears to be precisely the redemptive sense of *umma* she needs to escape her past. Yet, she is still somehow incomplete.

In an important scene at an Eid party, the women all appear with their usual modest clothing. There is a sense that their religion brings them together, but once they remove the 'uniform' of the hijab, they remain individuals, revealing the diverse ways in which one might be a good Muslim. However, when Najwa appears without her coverings, she worries that she looks 'intriguing, with secrets I don't want to share' (p. 186). She remains secretive, and ashamed of her past. Her desire for invisibility appears directed not only to the world outside, but to those within the *umma* also.

Tamer appears to be the only person with whom she is willing to share the story of her past life. He shares her dislike of 'Westernised' ways and also, in his rejection of politics as being necessarily relevant to Muslims, offers a strong contrast to Anwar. However, she struggles fully to commit to sharing the love he has for her. She accepts the payout to leave him from his mother almost with relief, after listening to a lesson at the mosque that suggested the sinfulness of children disobeying their parents. She is able to travel to Mecca to do hajj and also wrangles a promise that his parents will allow him to change his university course to something that better reflects his interests in Islamic culture. It seems that her individual cravings have been sublimated in favour of the correct Islamic solution. This is certainly how Aboulela describes the ending of the book: 'She relies on God and her faith'.[27] Yet while the earlier story concluded with Najwa making a bold choice to put her trust in religion, this later decision seems more of a capitulation to the will of others. In an extension of the way in which the version of Islam to which Najwa and Tamer subscribe has no space for politics, it seems here also to deny any agency to the novel's heroine. The final chapter, in which she does not seem pleased by the outcome of events, but rather continues to be tortured by her family's past, contains the suggestion (particularly in its final word of 'guilt'), that she is actually continuing the work of punishing herself that had formed her relationship with Anwar. The sense of finding strength through the community of Islam when she took up wearing hijab is oddly replaced in the concluding pages with a vision of Najwa as helpless and without the resources to address it.

NOSTALGIA AND RESISTANCE: MOHSIN HAMID, *THE RELUCTANT FUNDAMENTALIST*

The title of Mohsin Hamid's *The Reluctant Fundamentalist* (2007) invokes the idea of fundamentalist Islam, and the shadow of terrorist acts carried out by those who believe they are acting for a Muslim cause haunts the book. The novel consists of a monologue given by a bearded Pakistani man to a nervous American in a Lahore marketplace, and is clearly shaped by the repercussions of the attacks on the World Trade Center in 2001, and particularly by the US response to this, in the form of the 'War on Terror'. But the title ultimately is deceiving: although the narrator, Changez, is a Muslim, and may have connections to acts of violence (the novel is deliberately ambiguous about this throughout), it does not seem that his religion is especially significant in guiding his life, and he certainly appears distant from the violent interpretation of the faith that inspired the 9/11 attackers.

Rather, the fundamentals to which he is asked to return are the financial data of the firms which he is asked to value for Underwood Samson, the prestigious company that recruits him straight from Princeton University. An immigrant from Pakistan, Changez excels in the American financial world, finishing first above his colleagues in the regular appraisals made by his employer. He seems to embody the ideal of the successful migrant, but nonetheless worries sometimes about whether he has 'a stable *core*' that might structure his identity.[28] His sense of floating without ballast is particularly clear in his relationship with Erica. As an American woman, Erica (like Underwood Samson – note the significant initials), partly acts as an allegory for the United States that Changez wants to embrace. While she seems fond of him, their relationship is stunted and they are physically unable to consummate their relationship. They are only finally able to have intercourse when he pretends to be her deceased former boyfriend, Chris. Following orgasm, Changez feels 'at once both *satiated* and *ashamed*' (p. 106). This sense of having one's needs fulfilled, but only at great cost, seems to resonate throughout the relationship he has with America.

It comes to a head when he travels with the company to the Philippines and is distressed by the way in which the young

Americans exercise their dominance 'as members of the officer class of global business' (p. 65). In a key moment, he looks at one of his colleagues and thinks 'you are so foreign' and that he instead shares 'a sort of Third World sensibility' with the Manilans around him (p. 67). He does not belong with the Americans, but on the side of the oppressed. This takes its most shocking form on the night of his departure when he watches the collapse of the Twin Towers on television and smiles: 'despicable as it may sound, my initial reaction was to be remarkably pleased'. However, his pleasure is explicitly that 'someone had so visibly brought America to her knees', and involves no reference to Islam (p. 72). He turns against the fundamentalism of US global power, rather than towards an Islamic one.

Changez comments to his American listener at one point that an understanding of recent history 'allows us to put the present into much better perspective' (p. 45). The novel insists on a historicised understanding of violence against America but it also shows how the spectres of history rise up within America as it seeks to rally itself after the 9/11 attacks. The trauma of the event seems to harm further Erica's delicate mental state, and she retreats more deeply into the 'nostalgia' of imagining Chris to still be alive. Similarly, Changez sees the nation as a whole retreating into a nostalgia in reaction to this attack from outside: 'Living in New York was suddenly like living in a film about the Second World War [. . .] What your fellow countrymen longed for was unclear to me [. . .] but that they were scrabbling to don the costumes of another era was apparent' (p. 115). Erica and Chris's love is described as being 'a religion that would not accept me as a convert' (p. 114), and the national retreat to a mythic history seems also to contain both this sense of exclusion and the emotive power of religious belief.

Hamid has spoken of how, in the reaction to the events of September 2001, there has been a promotion of 'Western preconceptions about Islam, or about people from the Muslim world that they belong to something that is anachronistic, which is from the past'.[29] In *The Reluctant Fundamentalist*, this sense of an ideology from another era is instead imposed upon American imperial power. After a Chilean publisher describes Changez as a 'janissary' – a formerly-Christian soldier fighting for the Ottoman Empire 'to erase their own civilisations' (p. 152) – the young Pakistani is inclined to recognise 'how traditional your empire appeared' and to identify the social structures of contemporary America as those of far older brutal regimes (p. 157).

In contrast to this, Changez's opposition can seem defiantly modern. His choice to begin wearing a beard is not done in pious recognition of the Quranic requirement for modesty, but rather so that he does not 'blend in with the army of clean-shaven youngsters who were my co-workers' (p. 130). His identity increasingly is based on resistance to the narratives that had previously attracted him to America. His return to Pakistan, where he finds employment as a radical lecturer, is partly a nationalist redress to the global capitalist narratives he now identifies as so harmful, but the community he finds is not the traditional national body (the demise of which is traced in the novel's early chapters when he talks of how the traditional social order in Pakistan is decaying, with little sense of what might replace it), but a coming together of people in reaction to the spread and callousness of American global power. Whether Changez is or is not involved in acts of violence is left ambiguous at the end of the novel, but it is clear that the community he finally finds outside of America is not fired by a fundamentalist retreat to Islam, but rather through reaction to the fundamentalism of US-led capitalism and exploitation of the rest of the world.

SUMMARY

- As with many other marginalised groups, postcolonial subjects have frequently found resistant identities through turning to notions of community, but community can often work to restrict individuals as much as offer them a space to flourish.
- Nadine Gordimer's *Burger's Daughter* explores the struggle of a white South African to assert values distinct from those of her racially privileged community.
- Thomas King's *Truth and Bright Water* shows the attractions of defining indigenous community as based in either authenticity or a history of suffering, but rejects both as a satisfactory way forward.

- Diasporas formed by the migration and settlement of people with a shared idea of a homeland can be seen as specific, transnational communities.
- Salman Rushdie offers a powerful defence of the need for flexibility from both diasporic migrants and host societies in *The Satanic Verses*.
- The community of believing Muslims known as the *umma* shares some features with diaspora, but does not need a homeland to unite its transnational members.
- In *Minaret*, Leila Aboulela shows a woman finding in the *umma* in Britain a sense of community she has lost forever in her home nation.
- The community found by Changez in Mohsin Hamid's *The Reluctant Fundamentalist* has actually nothing to do with the *umma*, but is forged instead in the resistance to US-style globalised capitalism.

NOTES

1. Zadie Smith, *Changing My Mind: Occasional Essays* (New York: Penguin, 2009), pp. 141–2.
2. Ibid., p. 142.
3. Ferdinand Tönnies, *Community and Civil Society* [1887], ed. Jose Harris, trans. Jose Harris and Margaret Hollis (Cambridge: Cambridge University Press, 2001), p. 17.
4. Anthony P. Cohen, *The Symbolic Construction of Community* (Chichester: Ellis Horwood; Tavistock, 1985), p. 57.
5. For details of Fischer's life see Stephen Clingman, *Bram Fischer: Afrikaner Revolutionary* (Amherst: University of Massachusetts Press; David Philip Publishers, 1998).
6. Nadine Gordimer, *Burger's Daughter* (London: Bloomsbury, [1979] 2000), pp. 3, 6. Further references to this edition are given in the main text.
7. Nadine Gordimer, *Telling Tales: Writing and Living 1950–2008* (London: Bloomsbury, 2010), p. 376.
8. Ibid., p. 235.
9. Mongane Wally Serote, 'Ofay-Watcher, Throbs-Phase'

[1972], in John Reed and Clive Wake (eds), *A New Book of African Verse* (London: Heinemann, 1984), p. 91. Quoted in Gordimer, *Telling Tales*, pp. 217, 256–7, 282, 379.

10. As possession of this document was considered a criminal offence, Gordimer's decision to reproduce it led to the immediate banning of *Burger's Daughter* in South Africa.

11. Thomas King, *The Truth about Stories: a Native Narrative* (Minneapolis: University of Minnesota Press, 2005), p. 149.

12. Thomas King, *Truth and Bright Water* (Toronto: Harper Collins, 1999), p. 221. Further references to this edition are given in the main text.

13. King, *The Truth about Stories*, pp. 10–20.

14. Thomas King, 'Godzilla vs Post-Colonial', *World Literature Written in English* 30(2) (1990), 14.

15. Robin Cohen, *Global Diasporas: an Introduction* (London: UCL Press, 1997), p. 180.

16. Homi K. Bhabha, *The Location of Culture* (London: Routledge, 1994), p. 168.

17. Salman Rushdie, *Imaginary Homelands: Essays and Criticism, 1981–1991* (London: Granta in association with New York; Viking, 1991), p. 10.

18. Avtah Brah, *Cartographies of Diaspora: Contesting Identities* (London: Routledge, 1996), p. 209.

19. Rushdie, *Imaginary Homelands*, p. 394.

20. Salman Rushdie, *The Satanic Verses* (London: Viking, 1988), p. 43. Further references to this edition are given in the main text.

21. Lisa Appignanesi and Sara Maitland, *The Rushdie File* (London: Institute of Contemporary Arts, 1990), p. 68.

22. Rushdie, *Imaginary Homelands*, p. 382.

23. Ernest Gellner, *Nationalism* (London: Phoenix, 1998), p. 84.

24. S. Sayyid, 'Beyond Westphalia: Nations and Diasporas – the Case of the Muslim *Umma*', in Barnor Hesse (ed.), *Un/settled Multiculturalisms: Diasporas, Entanglements, Transruptions* (London: Zed, 2000), p. 43.

25. Leila Aboulela, *Minaret* (London: Bloomsbury, 2006), p. 61. Further references to this edition are given in the main text.

26. Claire Chambers, 'An Interview with Leila Aboulela', *Contemporary Women's Writing* 3(1) (2009), 92.
27. Ibid., p. 99.
28. Mohsin Hamid, *The Reluctant Fundamentalist* (London: Hamish Hamilton, 2007), p. 148. Further references to this edition are given in the main text.
29. Amina Yaqin, 'Mohsin Hamid in Conversation', *Wasafiri* 23(2) (2008), 46.

CHAPTER 5

War Zones

The Reluctant Fundamentalist's Changez sets himself up against the pervasive forces of contemporary global capitalism, the current imperialism through which the world's wealthy dominate the rest of the planet. In stepping out from the space opened for him within the privileged community of American finance, he seeks instead a place of resistance, to fight against a system that promotes and perpetuates planetary inequality. Part way through Michael Hardt and Antonio Negri's extremely influential study *Empire* (2000), which analyses the ways in which the managed inequalities of contemporary globalisation reproduce relationships of a previous Imperial era, they stop to reflect on the possibility of resistance:

> The first question of political philosophy today is not if or even why there will be resistance and rebellion, but rather how to determine the enemy against which to rebel. Indeed, often the inability to identify the enemy is what leads the will to resistance around in such paradoxical circles. The identification of the enemy, however, is no small task given that exploitation tends no longer to have a specific place and that we are immersed in a system of power so deep and complex that we can no longer determine specific difference or measure.[1]

In colonial societies the enemy often seems easily identifiable – the colonising power as an occupying force inevitably inspires the colonised people to rise up against them and fight for independence. In the postcolonial era, the source of oppression is often not so easily recognised and may be identified with internal enemies as frequently as those without.

Tamara Sivanandan writes that 'most of the territories under European colonial domination achieved independence only after prolonged struggle' and notes that, more often than not, this involved elements of armed resistance. Forged in violence, then, 'most of the new nation states achieved independence in a spirit of heady expectancy'.[2] This feeling of expectation seems tied to the violence that brought about liberation: there is a sense that the degree of struggle and sacrifice undergone demands the formation of a new, equitable order. It also means that a degree of violence as a norm persists within many of the postcolonial nations formed at that moment of independence. A significant cohort of the first generation of postcolonial leaders were military men or at least had been involved in guerrilla fighting (and a number of contemporary statesmen still have this kind of personal history). It has frequently been the case that postcolonial nations have proved as ready to resort to violence in policing their own people or against rival states as any colonial power had been (many of which continue to profit from this state of affairs through lucrative contracts to supply arms). Indeed, the experience of many postcolonial subjects has been that of living in a war zone, a space where violence can structure all aspects of everyday life.

FRANTZ FANON AND THE CLEANSING POWER OF VIOLENCE

Early in Frantz Fanon's *The Wretched of the Earth* (1961), a book that explores particularly the anticolonial struggle in the French North African colony of Algeria, he writes that 'the naked truth of decolonisation evokes for us the searing bullets and bloodstained knives which emanate from it'.[3] The influence of Fanon's book is perhaps unmatched in the postcolonial world and its analysis of the colonial situation and the nature of the fight for independence have not only proved invaluable for others seeking to theorise the types of conflict it explores, but also operated as something like a handbook for the emerging generation of postcolonial leaders in Africa and more widely, who frequently used (and often abused) his insights into how a nation might free itself from political, military and psychological domination by a colonial power. Violence is often at the centre of Fanon's discussion; he sees it as an essential element of national liberation.

For Fanon, colonial societies act as a very particular kind of social arena, and create unique subjects within them. The 'settler' and the 'native' (Fanon's terms) come into being because of the particular forms of power relations at work in the colony and each of their existences is crucially predicated on the fact of the other's: the settler defines the native (negatively) and in doing so creates the hierarchy that gives his own role its meaning. Decolonisation, therefore, is nothing less than 'the terrible creation of new men', as the native becomes something other through the process of freeing himself (p. 28). Fanon's key insight is that this birth of a new '"species" of men' does not simply happen at the same time as national independence but is made possible through the material – violent – process of decolonisation itself (p. 27). He writes that 'at the level of individuals, violence is a cleansing force', arguing that the act of turning on and routing the former oppressor is a crucial means of asserting humanity for the oppressed (p. 74). Yet, violence cannot only be assessed in terms of its positive effects on the individual and it retains social functions that can persist long after the initial autonomous gesture of defending one's selfhood.

Fanon describes the colonial society as functioning in large part through the imposition of stereotypes of the native that involve their total degradation: 'He is, let us dare to admit, the enemy of Values, and in this sense he is the absolute evil' (p. 32). Establishing this moral hierarchy provides the settler with the justification for the political domination that constitutes colonial relations in all its forms, from missionary Christianity to the use of DDT pesticides: 'the recession of yellow fever and the advance of evangelization form part of the same balance sheet' (p. 32). The colonial world operates according to a Manichean logic, sharply divided between ideas of good and evil, and with the 'absolute evil' of the native comes the rationale for their subordination in all things.

Yet this Manichean logic contains within it the seeds of its own destruction. Fanon argues that it persists in an inverted fashion throughout the period of decolonisation and that 'to the theory of the "absolute evil of the native" the theory of the "absolute evil of the settler" replies' (p. 73). As the colonised people rise up, they apply the concept of absolute difference upon which colonial domination relied, and can easily develop a policy of no tolerance or mercy for the former masters.

Fanon provides an interesting example of how this inversion of Manicheanism works out in relation to violence. During the early stages of decolonisation, he notes one can often witness a pattern of 'terror, counter-terror, violence, counter-violence'; each time the anticolonial forces try to assert their power, they are met with reprisals and punishment, often not just on the perpetrators but on the community more broadly. They may then respond themselves with more killing, which provokes further retaliation. However, Fanon notes, the settlers' violence in response to the threat made upon them is never proportional and always outstrips the original offence, 'for machine-gunning from aeroplanes and bombardment from the fleet go far beyond in horror and magnitude any answer the natives can make' (p. 70). Here the extent to which the natives are seen as less than human comes most vividly to the fore as their huge losses are considered equivalent to or lesser than the much smaller casualties suffered by the settlers. Fanon suggests that the natives in part accept this skewed equation, but that they do so by insisting on a bloody parity: that they must also take no account of how many settlers may die in the course of decolonisation. They respond to their dehumanisation under colonisation with a corresponding dehumanising of the colonisers, which offers a *carte blanche* for inflicting excessive violence in return.

Despite arguing that colonial violence necessarily fosters a compensatory violence among the colonised, Fanon is ultimately optimistic, or even utopian, about the eventual outcome of decolonisation forged in this way, arguing that the violence of national liberation actually benefits the colonised people through 'investing their characters with positive and creative qualities' (p. 73).

Working *together* as part of an armed struggle creates a unity that allows for a strong nation, necessarily democratic and refusing to accept any individual who sets themselves up as a 'liberator'.

However, as noted above, while the exercise of violence may have a particular cathartic effect on an individual, it may not play out socially in quite the way Fanon hopes. Postcolonial Africa has in fact had no shortage of leaders setting themselves up as national liberators, and national unity has frequently failed long to outlast the expulsion of the colonisers. At one point in his analysis, Fanon suggests that early stages of an anticolonial uprising may actually manifest in violence between natives, as their frustration meets with a feeling of impotence when faced with the power of the settler. It is only when the true source of this alienation and true enemy is identified as the settler that violence can begin to work its positive effects. However, despite the work of decolonisation, many former colonial peoples found that their situation had not improved, and the enemy was often more difficult to recognise as local elites colluded with international forces even when decrying them at home. The combination of heady expectations disappointed, and a habit of violence inculcated through the necessary struggles of decolonisation, could have terrible effects.

GHOSTS FROM THE FUTURE: V. S. NAIPAUL, *A BEND IN THE RIVER*

One of the most powerful novels to trace the effects of European imperialism in Africa, Joseph Conrad's *Heart of Darkness* (1902), sees Charlie Marlow travelling in a steamer up an unnamed river to find the rogue ivory agent Kurtz. The bleak, forbidding and primeval African bush seems at first to be the titular place of darkness, but when Marlow finds Kurtz we realise that the real darkness may be that of European colonialism itself, embodied by the brutal agent who has built his own empire of terror in the heart of the jungle. *Heart of Darkness* is an indictment of the colonial mindset, a reminder that the oft-proclaimed goal of bringing civilisation to the 'dark places of the Earth' is often in practice the opposite, a vicious process of domination and exploitation.[4]

Although unnamed in the novel, the river up which Marlow travels is clearly the Congo, and the land he moves through is the Belgian colony of the same name, which Conrad himself had travelled through some years before. By 1975, the independent Congo had been renamed Zaire, and V. S. Naipaul's essay of that year, 'A New King for the Congo', about the postcolonial nation, and especially its leader, Mobutu Seso Seko, undercuts some of the atmosphere of Conrad's novel by trying to establish history more clearly, for example by pointing out that the river would not have been the prehistoric place conjured up in Conrad's descriptions, but was served by eleven steamers at that time.[5] *A Bend in the River*, Naipaul's 1979 novel that explores the situation in Zaire (though, as in *Heart of Darkness*, the country is left unnamed), can also be seen as a corrective response to Conrad. While Conrad's vision was of the terrible truth about European imperialism, Naipaul delivers an equally bleak vision of the postcolonial nation, just as corrupted by greed, and just as likely to attempt to hide this under rhetoric of noble improvement. In his 1975 essay, Naipaul explicitly likens Mobutu to Leopold II, the despotic ruler of the Belgian Congo, and suggests a clear line of inheritance between them.[6] In *A Bend in the River* this sense of repetition is heightened further and a sense of an eternal permanence of violence in Africa is evoked.

The novel continually works to upset any simple linearity of time, not just through its occasional use of prolepsis, which ensures we know always that the story's unhappy ending is inevitable, but also by blurring the boundaries between past and present. This is especially clear when the narrator, Salim, looks at the collection of African masks kept by the Belgian priest Father Huismans. The masks look as if they could be hundreds or even thousands of years old, but he realises that some of them had been made no more than a year or two before.[7] The ancient refuses to pass away and allow the passage of the present. On arriving in the town on the bend in the river that is the setting for most of the novel (unnamed but based on Kisangani, formerly Stanleyville), Salim is equally disconcerted by modern buildings destroyed during the conflicts that had followed national independence. Faced with this dereliction of a recent dream of progress, 'you felt like a ghost, not from the past, but from the future [. . .] You were in a place where the future had come and gone' (p. 33).

The idea of progress is central to the novel, as the Mobutu-like president, known only as 'the Big Man' looks to develop the new African nation. The utopianism of postcolonial planning manifests in bold projects for modernising the land, not least in the construction of the new Domain near Salim's town, 'a miracle that would astound the rest of the world' (p. 110). Yet it becomes clear that no one is sure quite what the Domain should be used for, and it begins to become derelict even before it is finished. The president's desire to be seen as creating modern Africa is frustrated by the fact that no clear model exists for doing this, and that so much of modernity is inseparably associated with the Western powers that had so recently ruled in Africa. Eventually, both the president and the insurgency that rises against him talk instead of the need to 'go back to the beginning' (pp. 12, 293). Progress becomes inverted and Africa can seemingly only move forward by discovering its age-old traditions. But, like those masks whose age was undeterminable, the 'ancient' traditions can as easily be a fabrication produced in the present.

Salim is a Muslim of Indian descent, raised in an East African family who had lived on the coast for generations. He is a hybrid figure, part of Africa and yet in other ways separate from it: he frequently describes his community as 'people of Africa', distinct from the Africans themselves (p. 17). His move to the unnamed central African state displaces him further, but allows him to avoid the violence against 'foreigners' such as himself that breaks out in his homeland. However, in his new land also his status is precarious, and his trading business is eventually nationalised and taken away from him. The diverse community of expatriates living in the town on the bend in the river eventually fail to fit within the president's vision of a new Africa, and are thereby disenfranchised. Salim tells the reader of his habit of distancing himself from situations and seeing them as if from the outside (p. 22), but this does not seem to save him from sharing the fate of his community: he is not an outsider to the degree that he is seen by others, or even as he sees himself, but crucially tied to the fate of this new nation. The nationalisation seems at first to have logic about it, which arises from ethnic chauvinism and tribalism, but it becomes clear that even this is insufficient to understand the violence that erupts. Ferdinand, the 'boy from the bush' who rises through the post-colonial education system to become the region's commissioner explains to Salim: 'You mustn't think it's bad just for you. It's bad for everybody [. . .] We're all going to hell, and every man knows this in his bones. We're being killed. Nothing has any meaning' (p. 291). The horror of the situation is finally articulated by Salim's servant Metty: 'They're going to kill all the masters and all the servants [. . .] They're going to kill and kill' (p. 293).

The violence that threatens on a national scale seems indivisible from that which happens more locally, like the bar fights Salim sees where 'what looked like a drunken pushing and shoving, a brawl with slaps, turn[s] to methodised murder, as though the first wound and the first spurt of blood had made the victim something less than a man, and compelled the wounder to take the act of destruction to the end' (p. 63). Violence increasingly seems to become its own end. The president's method of dealing with rebellions is to come down with reprisals as frequently on his men as on the rebels, further dislocating any sense of community, and inculcating a climate of fear through making allegiance impossible. Asking about Pierre Mulele, who led a rebellion against Mobutu, Naipaul is told in Zaire that nobody knew the purpose of the killings he ordered: 'He was against *everything*.'[8] When progress is seen as possible only through a return to an imagined past, then destruction is inevitable. As the past remains always inaccessible, it is hard to see where this destruction can end.

A Bend in the River, then, offers the message back to Conrad's indictment of European colonialism that the heart of darkness can be found as easily in postcolonial Africans. This is not a simple lament for European colonial civilisation, as Britain, Canada and the United States are shown in the novel as equally morally bankrupt, but rather a deeper pessimism about the dream of civilisation at all. A constant trope in the novel is that of the water hyacinths that have appeared in the river and grown out of control, choking up the waterway. They serve as reminder of the encroachment of nature, parallel-ing Naipaul's bleak vision of violent human nature always acting to destroy any dreams of civilisation and progress we may cultivate.

TRUE NATIONALISM: TAHMIMA ANAM, *A GOLDEN AGE*

While *A Bend in the River* takes as its focus the cycle in which war is perpetuated and violence and destruction repeated, Tahmima Anam's *A Golden Age* (2007), set during the 1971 war that secured the independence of Bangladesh, instead seems to explore the ability of war to create. The title can seem oddly positive for a novel that deals with military occupation, torture and genocide. The evocation of Rabindranath Tagore's song 'My Golden Bengal' (1905), which eventually became the national anthem of the new state of Bangladesh, reveals that the achievement of autonomous nationhood is a prize that makes the suffering understandable, and even bearable. Yet nationalism is indirectly discovered in the novel, belatedly coming into focus for its heroine as a consequence of more directly personal ties.

The 1948 Partition of India created the state of Pakistan, divided into two 'wings' either side of India. East Pakistan, the more populous of the pair, in turn was formed by the splitting of the state of Bengal, leading (as in so much of India) to the displacement of millions, as Hindus moved to the Indian side of the border, and Muslims to Pakistan. Relations between the two wings of Pakistan, however, soon became tense as Bengalis came to resent the concentration of political power in West Pakistan and the fact that profits from the jute industry in the eastern wing were siphoned to support the development of its western counterpart. The Awami League, under the leadership of Sheikh Mujibur Rahman, fought for increasing autonomy for East Pakistan. In the 1970 elections, the League won 160 of 162 seats in East Pakistan, and demanded full autonomy within the nation. The central government responded by arresting Mujib and banning his organisation, which in turn led to a full declaration of independence and Pakistani occupation of the new state of Bangladesh. The civil war that followed was particularly brutal and included a programme of genocide carried out against the Hindu population of the seceding wing. By the end of 1971, however, support from India (where a refugee army of secessionists had been built) ensured the success of the rebels and the new nation was born.

A Golden Age is mostly set in Dhaka in 1971, though contains flashbacks to the earlier life of its heroine Rehana Hague. Rehana has a complicated relationship with Bangladeshi nationalism, even as her student children, Sohail and Maya, embrace it with passion. A Calcutta-born Urdu-speaker, she does not feel a necessary linguistic or geographical connection to her land and finds that the 'hard, precise words' of nationalist discourse 'did not capture [her] ambiguous feelings about the country she had adopted'.[9] Anam has suggested that she chose Rehana as the focus of the novel precisely because of her 'dispassionate view of the revolution', and the novel is the tale of her journey to nationalism.[10]

The opening of the novel, set in 1959, introduces Rehana's personal crisis. Her husband, Iqbal, dies from a sudden heart attack and a judge rules her unable to care for Sohail and Maya, instead entrusting them to the care of Iqbal's brother and sister-in-law, Faiz and Parveen, in Lahore in the west wing. The novel contains a frontispiece map of South Asia with a line marking the passage of PIA flight 010, the aeroplane that takes Rehana's children away. This visual inscription of the personal tragedy onto the political landscape signals how these two levels are to be brought together in the novel. Parveen tries to reassure Rehana that the adoption is only temporary and will end when she recovers, and Rehana makes a significant link in reflecting that this characterises her bereft condition 'as though it were an illness, something curable, like what was happening to the country' (p. 7). Faiz and Parveen are not only the couple who take away the children but also represent the condescending elites of West Pakistan: their patronising removal of the children parallels the way in which the west wing of Pakistan patronises and dismisses the east, for its 'own good'. The analogy between Rehana's struggle for her children, and Bangladesh's fight for independence, begins to be established.

The novel's prologue also tells the story of a day trip taken when Iqbal was still alive. Although he was due to ride a train with his wife and children, he instead worries about mishaps and settles on the 'safe' solution of driving in his car alongside the train containing his family. Safety here is therefore only guaranteed at the cost of an absurd separation. While Rehana is frequently tempted by this kind of safety, the desire to live 'ordinary, unexceptional lives' (p. 50), she ultimately recognises that some compromises are unacceptable and some battles have to be fought. Following the departure of her children, she fights her way out of poverty to reclaim them by building a house in the grounds of her bungalow and, we learn later in the novel, by stealing to fund its construction. Again, the analogy to the national situation seems clear – her need to build a place that belongs to her mirrors the pride in Bengali culture that is growing around her, while her theft suggests that at times of crisis a conventional morality cannot always hold.

A Golden Age does not allow the relationships between familial love and national loyalty to remain only at the level of analogy. Rehana is increasingly drawn into political action, but initially only through wanting to please her politically-active children, ten years returned from Lahore. She harbours in her home first medicine for the rebels, then arms, and finally a wounded major who needs to be hidden from the occupying army. In carrying out these actions, however, she begins to question whether in fact she acts only for her children's sake and that 'perhaps she really was doing it for the benefit of the country' (p. 111). The major has no doubt about it: when she reveals her doubts to him whether she is a nationalist at all, he insists that her love for her home, and her children's home, precisely make her a 'true nationalist' (p. 142).

However, Rehana's full epiphany only comes on leaving Dhaka to join Maya at a refugee camp in Calcutta. There she is initially disgusted by the poverty and abjection of these displaced people, but ultimately comes to find a way to care for them and to recognise that the violence carried out against her country is precisely violence against the familial love she holds so dear. The occupying soldiers' cruelty towards families, the murdering of sons and raping of daughters, is a crime not only against the nation, but against the familial bonds she sees as so important. The family is not just analogically related to the nation then, but a part of the same kind of shared love. Her eventually abandoning of Faiz to his fate in a Bangladeshi prison is the result of his violation of that bond of love. The fact that he remains her brother-in-law cannot mitigate the magnitude of his crime against the force that makes families meaningful.

In an article on the contemporary political crises in Bangladesh,

Anam recalls Walter Benjamin's claim that a state of emergency is always also a place for the emergence of the new, and she reflects that 1971 can seem a crucible for novel possibilities.[11] Certainly this is how Maya sees it, describing how exciting the war is for demonstrating 'a whole nation, coming together' (p. 101), and later stating that in a war, 'we can do whatever we want' (p. 206). However, the novel as a whole seems less certain about the uncritical celebration of war and sounds a more careful note. Despite the linking of familial and national affection, the novel's two central love stories each end unhappily, split along the division between the personal and political: Sohail eventually repudiates his love for the girl next door, Silvi, because of her reactionary political views, while Rehana allows the major, a nationalist hero she has come to love, to sacrifice himself in order to save Sohail. Despite the 'golden' emergence of Bangladesh, the coming together of individual and national goals is not rendered as a permanent achievement and a note of caution is sounded when Rehana visits her husband's grave at the close of the novel and realises that 'we have to try to find ways to exist in a country without war' (p. 273). While the war made the country possible, and showed her how to love it, the solutions cannot be relied on to be permanent.

A BAN ON WREATHS: AGHA SHAHID ALI, *THE COUNTRY WITHOUT A POST OFFICE*

The war between India and Pakistan that broke out around Bangladesh's secession was followed by the Simla Agreement of 1972, which stated the urge on both sides to find solutions to problems through traditional diplomatic means, rather than through recourse to armed conflict. It was of particular relevance in regard to the region of Kashmir in the north-east of the Indian state. A predominantly Muslim region with a Hindu ruler at the time of Partition, it was expected to become part of Pakistan but instead mostly transferred to India. Each nation has since claimed rightful ownership of the part of the region administered by the other. The Simla Agreement committed both parties to peaceful resolution of the conflict but in no way constituted an agreement over national borders. The Indian-administered region in particular has seen continual civic unrest, with separatist groups, often though not always supported by Pakistan, clashing with the Indian Army. One controversial incident in this ongoing turmoil took place in 1995 in Chrar-e-Sharif at the Shrine of Sheikh Noor-ud-Din, a Sufi saint held in great regard by many Muslims and Hindus. After separatist militants sheltered there from the Indian Army this sacred site was largely destroyed by fire. Each side blamed the other for the tragedy.

The burning of the shrine is the focus of the poem 'I Dream I am the Only Passenger on Flight 423 to Srinagar' in the 1997 collection *The Country Without a Post Office* by Agha Shahid Ali, who was raised chiefly in Kashmir and Delhi, but based for most of his adult life in the United States. In the poem he travels in the titular aeroplane to arrive just as the shrine is destroyed. The saint himself appears on the flight to lament the destruction and that 'It is too late for threads at Chrar-e-Sharif.'[12] In a note to another poem in the collection, Ali reveals the custom 'for both Muslims and Hindus to go to Sufi shrines and make a wish there by tying a thread' (p. 94). In 'I Dream . . .' the saint demands of the narrator to 'ask all – Muslim and Brahmin – if their wishes came true'. If each side claims to love Kashmir, the poem asks, why do they collude in its destruction?

Before the saint appears to the narrator, he listens on the aeroplane to a *ghazal* sung by one of the form's great performers, Begum Akhtar. The *ghazal*, a poetic form which originated in Arabia in the seventh century, was held particularly dear by Ali, who edited a collection of English-language assays at the form in 2000. The word *ghazal* translates from the Persian as 'an address to the beloved', and while *The Country Without a Post Office* contains some of Ali's most famous uses of the form, the idea of an address to that which is loved could meaningfully cover every poem in the collection. The beloved object is Kashmir itself. Ali worries, however, that his love for the country may in some ways be as destructive as that proclaimed by the nation-states that fight over it. He reveals at the end of one of the *ghazals* in the collection ('The only language of loss . . .') that the meaning of his name, Shahid, is 'beloved'. In lauding his beloved homeland, Ali remains always aware of the danger of a selfish, inward-turned desire. In 'Farewell' his personal and intimate vision of Kashmir may be seen as a bulwark against the dangerous nationalist myths that threaten to consume the territory – 'My memory is again in the way of your history' – but also as risking a self-absorption that forgets the actual fate of the land: 'Your history gets in the way of my memory' (pp. 21–2). Much of *The Country Without a Post Office* consists of Ali's negotiation of this bind.

For the titular figure of 'The Correspondent', Kashmir is just another war zone, tragic in much the same way as the Sarajevo he has visited just before. The images of suffering he captures can be turned into easily consumable scenes, and indeed he is under pressure to 'revamp / his stories, reincarnadine / their gloss' (p. 55). Against the reality of suffering in Kashmir – 'the reports are true, and without song' (p. 16) – what role can a poet have? The beginnings of the answer Ali finds are given by the second meaning he reveals for the name Shahid: it means 'witness' in Arabic. The idea of this poet who lives on the other side of the world acting as witness to the day-to-day hardships of Kashmir can seem problematic, but Ali is careful to delineate more clearly what the role of the witness should be. In 'Ghazal' ('Where are you . . .') he goes so far as to reject the name Shahid. The *ghazal* form relies on couplets, the second line of each containing always the same refrain (the *radif*), preceded immediately by the rhyme (the *qafia*).[13] In this *ghazal*, the *radif* is the single word 'tonight', which is preceded in most of the couplets by *qafia* words that pepper Ali's laments for Kashmir: 'farewell', 'expel', 'Hell'. However, the final couplet offers an interesting turn in its renaming of the speaker: 'And I, Shahid, only am escaped to tell thee – / God sobs in my arms. Call me Ishmael.' The words of lament have led us to Melville's famous opening line, but more importantly to the name of the son of Abraham, who accepts his role as part of a sacrifice.[14]

Ali's desire in *The Country Without a Post Office* is to be more than just a passive witness and instead try to live the suffering of Kashmir along with its residents. In the title poem, the odd status of Kashmir, claimed by two countries, but seemingly loved by neither, is noted in the piles of letters that have gone nowhere.

The stamps of these letters have been cancelled but the seals have 'no nation named on them' (p. 49). No one appears to want to claim the stories that the Kashmiris have sent out into the world. Eventually the narrator reads the letters. His response is not to wish to offer any commentary, or even to add his pleas to the stories in the letters, but rather only to voice the fact that they exist:

> It's raining as I write this. I have no prayer.
> It's just a shout, held in, It's Us! It's Us!
> whose letters are like cries that break like bodies
> in prisons. (p. 51)

The final response to taking on these stories of Kashmir is the wish 'to live forever'. In that way his role as the witness who is also a sacrifice can be prolonged.

In one of the many returns to Kashmir in dreams that take place in the collection, a driver who meets the narrator offers him a bouquet to mark a death: 'There's a ban on wreaths!' (p. 27). Mourning is not a luxury open to him, as he must work instead to relate the troubled stories, even if this seems impossible. In 'At the Museum', a poem that can seem rather divorced from the rest of the collection, he describes the 4500-year-old statue of a servant girl found in Punjab. While recognising the incongruity of a monument to so lowly a figure, Ali nonetheless is 'grateful' for its existence. While the poet is unable to live forever, there remains perhaps a space for his work to continue to record the struggle of otherwise forgotten people, in defiance of those powerful forces that instead want to impose their own narratives.

STATES OF EXCEPTION, BIOPOLITICS AND NECROPOLITICS

Since 1990, the Indian state of Jammu and Kashmir has been subject to the provisions of the Armed Forces (Special Powers) Act (AFSPA). Originally passed in 1958 to enable the Indian government to crush a secessionist rebellion in Nagaland in the far north-east of the country, the AFSPA legislation allows for individual Indian states (and since 1972 the central government) to suspend the normal rule of law in 'disturbed' areas and grants the army exceptional powers. The provisions of the Act include allowing for the armed forces legitimately to open fire on any gathering of more than five people and to destroy any structure where absconders wanted for any offence may be staging armed attacks. These powers (which may well have led to the destruction of the shrine at Chrar-e-Sharif) are far in excess of those normally granted to the Indian Army and therefore remain controversial, seen by many as ensuring that Kashmiris are denied the usual freedoms of belonging to a democratic state. Such 'states of exception' as they are called by the philosopher Giorgio Agamben (following the mid-twentieth-century thinker Carl Schmitt) are not confined to India, and the withdrawal at times of 'emergency' of human rights otherwise considered fundamental to a state's constitutional validity has been a widespread phenomenon throughout the postcolonial world (and this does not exclude the 'West' – the American prison at Guantanamo Bay in Cuba is the site of perhaps the twenty-first century's most famous state of exception).

For Agamben, the function of the state of exception is to enforce a division between two conceptions of life: the first that of 'bare life', our biological, animal existence; and the second the idea of the 'good life', our political existence or our participation in society that enables us to enjoy the full benefits of our humanity. The human being who suffers under the state of exception is not just stripped of particular rights, but is seen to lose, in Hannah Arendt's phrase, 'the right to have rights' at all.[15] He or she becomes '*homo sacer*', the person who can be killed but not murdered, as that essential part of their humanity is taken away.[16]

Agamben follows Schmitt in suggesting the sovereign (that person or persons is seen to have the legitimate right to wield ultimate power within a territory) can be identified precisely because of their ability to invoke a state of exception and suspend constitutional guarantees.[17] This extraordinary power to pronounce upon the status of people's humanity and to make individual human bodies less than human persons constitutes part of what is known as the 'biopolitical' order; the ways in which what may seem our inalienable rights to be counted as human and treated accordingly are in fact subject to particular political decisions. One of Agamben's greatest concerns is that the withdrawal of political rights and thereby full humanity is increasingly becoming less the exception than the norm and that 'all politics becomes the exception'.[18]

Part of Agamben's aim is to challenge some of the definitions of the biopolitical formulated by the thinker with whom the concept is perhaps most associated, Michel Foucault. Agamben's model insists on the distinction between bare and social life being a feature of the earliest age of political association, whereas Foucault located the age of biopolitics as a comparatively recent formulation. For Foucault, one of the key stimuli for the emergence of biopolitics was the shift from the feudal order to modernity, as the sovereign was no longer an individual monarch but a government entrusted with acting for the people as a whole. Sovereignty, in his view, therefore shifted from being a right to kill with impunity to being constituted by the need to help the populace live: 'It is as managers of life and survival, of bodies and the race, that so many regimes have been able to wage so many wars,' he argues.[19] This legitimacy based on protecting the lives of their people, Foucault argues, is matched by a concomitant need to control those lives, in a basic biological sense. This control takes two forms: the control of the individual human body (whether through the workplace, the prison, the asylum or more diversely across society) and the management of the 'species body' of the people as a whole (through control of health, reproduction and so on).[20] War, incarceration and other assaults upon individual bodies are seen as the means to keep the sovereign body of the people flourishing. In this way, aggressive nationalism and racism flourish: 'the death of the other, the death of the bad race, of the inferior race (or the degenerate, or the abnormal) is something that will make life in general healthier: healthier and purer'.[21]

One of the key figures in extending the notion of biopolitics to colonial and postcolonial societies is the Cameroonian Achille Mbembe. In his influential essay 'Necropolitics' (2003), he challenges the notion that the type of biopolitical regulation Foucault describes is adequate to understand how colonial and postcolonial relations function. In attempting to explain both the reduced conditions in which so many postcolonial subjects are forced to live, and the ease with which it seems possible for them to be killed, he combines both Agamben's notion of the withdrawal of political life and Foucault's sense of a regulatory regime through which life is managed. He intends for his concepts of 'necropolitics and necropower to account for [. . .] the creation of *death-worlds*, new and unique forms of social existence in which vast populations are subjected to conditions of life conferring upon them the status of the living dead'.[22] The necropolitical order requires that these populations who live in the state of bare life need to be regulated no less than those whose survival functions to legitimate sovereign power. His key historical example of this tight regulation of the less than human is the slave plantation economy of the Americas; for more recent examples he turns to apartheid South Africa and to the extreme demarcation of spatial freedom that Israel imposes upon the Palestinian people.

Mbembe's invocation of a necropolitical order also has interesting implications for our understanding of war and armed conflict. He notes firstly that in the contemporary era it is often a mistake to assume that sovereign powers alone have a monopoly on legitimated violence, and that the vast majority of armies on the African continent (and increasingly widely) are 'composed of citizen soldiers, child soldiers, mercenaries, and privateers'.[23] Given this parcelling out of sovereignty in the form of the right to decide who lives and who should die, 'the logic of survival' increasingly becomes a determining factor in people's behaviour: 'one's horror at the sight of death turns into satisfaction that it is someone else who is dead [. . .] And each enemy killed makes the survivor feel more secure'.[24] Alongside this, however, we also see 'the logic of martyrdom' which explains for Mbembe the actions of an archetypal contemporary figure, the suicide bomber. Destroying oneself to kill one's enemies seems inexplicable within the logic of survival, but if it is viewed as removing from them the power over one's death by taking one's body which has been reduced to the state of bare life and turning it into a weapon (to 'metal', as Mbembe puts it) then death itself can be a way of transcending the restriction of necropolitics.[25]

A DUTY TO STAY ALIVE: CHRIS ABANI, 'BUFFALO WOMEN'

Chris Abani's 2006 collection *Hands Washing Water* contains a sequence of twelve poems under the title of 'Buffalo Women'. They take the form of letters, and, as the poet explains in a detailed note, they chart

> the correspondence between Henrietta and her girlfriend Jane, a gay couple living together in the California area during the [American] Civil War. Henrietta/Henri is a recently emancipated slave, and Jane is a white woman from the South. Such relationships did exist at the time and it was not uncommon during the Civil War for women to pretend to be men in order to enlist to fight [. . .] Troops were segregated, with all-black corps having white officers. However, in 'Buffalo Woman' [sic] Henri is the only soldier of color in an all-white company.[26]

The sequence offers a startling reflection on biopolitics, necropolitics and the readiness with which categories of humanity can fluctuate at times of war. As a young man Abani was imprisoned, tortured and sentenced to death in Nigeria. Several of his works deal with brutality and violence in the land of his birth, notably including his 2009 novel *Song for Night* which chronicles the experience of a child soldier.[27] 'Buffalo Women' can seem entirely divorced from this in terms of both time and place. However, in a talk Abani gave for the TED organisation in 2007, he revealed how a process of transposition may be at work here, relating how one of his schoolteachers negotiated the ban on speaking of the Biafran War by instead instructing his Nigerian charges on the history of the Holocaust – 'the story is fluid, and it belongs to nobody'.[28] 'Buffalo Women' can in the same way serve as an exploration of violence and the curtailment of humanity that can resonate in many contexts.

In one sense 'Buffalo Women' is a story of passing, of acting as someone whom one is not: Henri is (at least) triply marginalised because of her gender, her race and her sexuality, but is able to circumvent these restrictions through successfully performing as a soldier. The poems increasingly serve to reveal this transformation as a problematic and dangerous process. In some ways the deception can seem playful, and Abani himself toys with his reader by keeping back the final revelation of Henri's gender until the last word of the sequence (though most readers would have deciphered the many clues by this point). In Jane's early letters at least the deception can figure as comedy, when despite warning of the danger that her and Henri's relationship might be seen as 'witchcraft', she still amusedly reports that 'Rev. Pickering spoke highly of your manhood' (p. 35). The incongruity of this praise may not lie only in the fact of Henri's woman's body but also in the colour of her skin: for a white man to praise a black soldier in this way is notable for its incongruity. Yet this blurring of the fixity of the categories between which Henri moves does not remain comic. In her first letter Jane uses a code to refer to Henri's vulva by calling it her 'mortal wound' (p. 33): the body is from the start beginning to be associated with the violent sphere in which Henri will move.

In Henri's letters, the blurring of categories becomes yet more tainted with images of violence; she describes early on how the bloodlust seems to drive soldiers on in this war 'relentless as my old master's cracker drove me'. At the end of this letter she apologises for 'let[ting] this vulgar life / into the more gentle innocence of yours' (pp. 31–2). It is not entirely clear if the vulgarity is intended to refer to the mention of war's violence, or to her history as a slave, or even to her new masculine self. The destabilisation of fixity in Henri's letters increasingly takes a dark turn. She begins her second letter by noting that

> Flesh is a curious thing. To the eye
> it does appear seamless in that thinking stronger
> than any metal. (p. 34)

The reader might expect afterwards a reflection on how her performance has allowed her to deny the fleshly constraints of gender (Jane's previous letter ends by indicating that she has sent cloths for the secretive swaddling of Henri's breasts). However, flesh is literally permeated here, as Henri describes its reaction to being torn open with a bayonet, and goes on to reveal that she has carried out her first killing – 'And I loved it'. The act of killing a (presumably white) Confederate soldier has furnished her with a 'wholesome, profound' feeling (p. 34). Her marginality as a black woman is perhaps most powerfully rejected in the assertion of self that comes from killing another person.

Jane is disturbed by this letter, but is perhaps intended to be reassured by Henri's following despatch, which tells of her stripping naked to bathe and then masturbating while imagining herself back with her lover. She reflects how she 'would like to reveal the truth of us, of myself' (p. 37). This sense then can seem a return to her 'authentic' body and to the intimate relationship that constitutes her home. The violent transformation suggested in her previous letter is rescinded and it is suggested that any change will be purely temporary. However, this is the last of her letters to which we see a reply from Jane, and that reply in turn is not received until Henri pens her final message. We understand that the five letters she writes in between these are never received by Jane, which Henri ultimately appreciates, for they recount a disturbing turn in events.

In Henri's fourth letter, the seventh of the sequence, she returns to the joy she feels in killing, not this time 'with the justice of a sword' but by battering the enemy to death with the butt of her rifle. Again she feels 'alive, so alive' but can still stop to reflect that 'I am afraid of what I am becoming, Jane' (pp. 39–40). This question of becoming increasingly troubles the poem. Previously she had suffered under the social label with which she had been categorised; by becoming a soldier and fighting alongside white men she had become something immune from that previous degradation, but the processes of transformation have not stopped. In her next letters she describes how the platoon has been cut off by adverse weather in a landscape that seems physically marked by reminders of brutal mortality, 'the horizon [. . .] filled with splintered trees grinning / like teeth in a skull' (p. 41). 'Something malevolent' is brewing among the soldiers and they are described as being like butterflies in chrysalises at a point of metamorphosis. The shocking nature of that change is what Henri must always keep from Jane and everybody else.

As the platoon slowly starves to death in the snowy wastes, the soldiers begin to denigrate their older and sick comrades, labelling them 'crones' and thereby rescinding their rights to participate in the privilege of virile masculinity. The captain tries to rally his troops by insisting that 'it was our duty to stay alive'. However, by this point, the imperative for the healthy troops to stay alive can be translated into the denial of that right to those they have labelled as worth less than themselves. When they murder a 'crone' in the eleventh and penultimate letter, the man is referred to as 'it', and then as a 'pig' and a 'bag of bones'. This determined stripping of humanity from their victim makes it possible for the other soldiers then to cook his flesh and 'while the crone dripped fat into the fire, / we mimicked the noises it made before dying'. The final line of the letter – 'And so we have become' – suggests that whatever they have now been transformed into cannot have a name: even as it was made possible by the refusal of humanity to others, it has perhaps compromised their own humanity beyond description (pp. 47–9).

The final letter reframes the terrible events in the stories Jane eventually hears into a seemingly impressive human achievement: 'our resourcefulness allowed us to find food / during the winter months' (p. 50). The decision has clearly been made never to speak of what happened. Henri seems to wish to return for good to her 'true' body, which is now validated from outside by 'the doctor whose lust weighed my breasts before discharging me' (p. 50). Henri refers to Jane as her 'redemption', but it remains unclear whether redemption or return to her previous mode of humanity is possible for Henri after the transformations that war has wrought on her.

GIVING YOUR LIFE FOR THE TRUTH: MICHAEL ONDAATJE, *ANIL'S GHOST*

Michael Ondaatje's 2000 novel *Anil's Ghost* is in part an exploration of how literature might address conflict, and of what it might do in the face of the extreme trauma of war. It deals with Sri Lanka in the 1980s and 1990s when the government was dealing brutally with violent campaigns staged not only by Tamil guerrillas in the south but also by the Marxist group the JVP. Ondaatje (Sri Lankan by birth, but a long-time Canadian citizen) has insisted that he wanted to resist any pressure to offer an explanation of the conflict – 'it isn't a statement about the war, as though this is the "true and only story"' – and instead that he wanted only to explore a limited set of individual 'unhistorical, unofficial' lives.[29] Wary of how the West can so easily simplify and distort accounts of foreign wars – 'truth broken in suitable pieces and used [. . .] alongside irrelevant photographs',[30] he has instead written of the work as motivated by 'a responsibility to diverse voices', each of which deserves 'the deepest intricacy'.[31] The result, in Margaret Scanlan's words, is an unusual novel about terrorism: 'It reproduces no political rhetoric, adjudicates no political claims, projects no political solutions [. . .] We understand early that we will find no master narratives, no organic psychologies, no resolution and no moral.'[32]

Yet Ondaatje's claim to be focused only on the individual worlds of his characters can seem a little disingenuous, as the major figures in the book each can be seen to embody a strategy for dealing with war. Between them, different responses to conflict are offered, and to some degree subject to evaluation. The eponymous Anil is a forensic scientist, searching for the undeniable empirical truth; against this we can place the archaeologist who searches for deeper historical explanations (at first this role seems to be taken by Sarath, but it is actually Palipana, his mentor, who embodies it most clearly); Gamini offers the figure of a doctor, concerned only with the process of healing; while Ananda, the drunken crafts-man, introduces the idea of representing, rather than unearthing and identifying, the truth. Each character has their own method for dealing with the war and the novel shows that each strategy may have its uses. In a subtlety that stops these characters being only representatives of types, Ondaatje also shows that these means of addressing trauma may not be wholly separate from one another.

Anil returns to the Sri Lanka of her youth after prolonged stays in England and North America, which she considers to have provided her with some moral 'distance' on the country (p. 11). She is there to carry out a United Nations investigation into the government's suspected human rights abuses. She is paired with Sarath, a local archaeologist, who leads her to the skeleton they name Sailor, a recently-killed body found in a restricted government-protected site. Anil becomes determined to find out Sailor's real name, and the manner of his death, believing that to do so would offer proof of the government's crimes and provide an 'opportunity' for justice (p. 52). Her belief is that the individual body can act as a metonym for the wider acts of state terror: '*One village can speak for many villages. One victim can speak for many victims*' (p. 176). Yet despite this driving urge, she nonetheless entertains fears at times that her report to Geneva might remain without 'meaning' (p. 55). In fact, even after she and Sarath discover Sailor's real name – Ruwan Kumara – she continues to refer to the body by its nickname.

The novel's suggestion that the empirical truth may not be the only, or most reliable, type of truth available is reinforced by the story of the archaeologist Palipana's disgrace. At the end of a respected career he lost credibility when it was revealed that his recent 'discovery' explaining 'the political tides of royal eddies of the island in the sixth century' was based on runes that did not actually exist (p. 81). The novel goes on to explain that Palipana believed his trick actually to be a revelation of deeper truths: expertly familiar with the particularities of the local archaeology, his fabrications were in fact 'the hidden histories, intentionally lost, that altered the perspective and knowledge of earlier times. It was how one hid or wrote the truth when it was necessary to lie' (p. 105). The idea of hiding and writing as equivalent acts suggests a type of truth that shies from the empirical and is revealed indirectly through other means. Something similar happens when Anil and Sarath commission Ananda to build a reconstruction of Sailor's head. Instead of actually recreating how the dead man appeared in life, he crafts a peaceful face, 'comfortable with itself', that represents 'what he wants of the dead' (p. 184). Ananda creates this face that is not Sailor's to help him cope with the loss of his wife, one of Sri Lanka's many disappeared. However, when the head is placed in a village in a hopeless attempt to elicit identification, a drummer comes to play next to it, giving the artificial figure of the placid dead man a ceremonial status, and encouraging a process of communal mourning, suggesting again that there may exist truths more important at times than the merely material.

Sarath's brother, the doctor Gamini, has no time for the type of deception Palipana practised, sarcastically exclaiming 'Wonderful! To study history as if it were a body' (p. 193). For him, the only truth is that of the body and he has learned to reject any statement of belief in favour of a focus solely on the imperative to care for the wounded and the sick (p. 119). He is equally dismissive of Anil's mission to name Sailor – '*What would you do with a name?*' (p. 252). Addicted to the drugs he takes to help him through his marathon shifts at Accident Services Hospital in Colombo (nicknamed Gunshot Services), where he tries to patch together the victims of the violence, Gamini has 'chosen not to deal with the dead' and instead gives his all to try to preserve life (p. 212). His struggles and determination increasingly dominate the narrative of the later sections of the novel. However, his noble motives are questioned to a degree – in repairing the bodies of those who may go on to kill again, and refusing to dwell on the dead, he becomes 'a perfect participant in the war' (p. 224).

The ending of the novel restates each of the strategies presented for dealing with the trauma of war, though each has to some degree been modified and developed. Sarath has seemed at times sceptical of Anil's urge metonymically to prove the horrors of the war despite believing 'as an archaeologist' in the 'principle' of truth: we are told that 'he would have given his life for the truth if the truth were of any use', which initially seems a resignation to the futility of Anil's task, but eventually is revealed as a foreshadowing of the actual sacrifice he makes in helping Anil to escape the country with the evidence she has found (p. 157). Although she is absent from the final chapters of the novel, the type of knowledge gained from an impartial, external investigation into the war is by no means wholly discounted. However, the main focus of the concluding chapters is the coping mechanisms of those who stay in Sri Lanka. Gamini is confronted by the body of Sarath in his hospital's morgue and tends to his brother as if he were still alive, preserving the ethic of care he embodies in the novel, but showing also how it might extend beyond the living and administer also to the dead. In the final chapter we see the craftsman Ananda rebuilding a second head, this time that of a statue of Buddha that has been destroyed by explosives. He painstakingly restores its face but decides against hiding the seams that reveal its previous destruction. His acknowledgement of suffering yet simultaneous attempt to begin reconstruction may be the only possible way for him to avoid 'the spectres of retaliation' (p. 304). While none of these various strategies of handling atrocity – exposure, amelioration and reconstruction – is seen as sufficient for Sri Lanka, *Anil's Ghost* suggests that they all may be necessary.

SUMMARY

- The violent recent histories of many postcolonial societies during and since decolonisation may have normalised war and violence as a constant element of people's lives.
- Frantz Fanon saw anticolonial violence as necessary both to overcome colonial alienation and degradation but also to forge new national unities.
- V. S. Naipaul's bleak vision of postcolonial Africa in *A Bend in the River* suggests that the project of rejecting Western modernity inevitably turns into a cycle of destruction.
- Tahmima Anam's *A Golden Age* explores how a productive nationalist feeling, linked to familial love, can arise from an experience of civil war.
- The poems of *The Country Without a Post Office* see Agha Shahid Ali negotiating the problems of representing conflict in his beloved but distant homeland of Kashmir.
- In Giorgio Agamben's writing on the state of exception and Achille Mbembe's on necropolitics we find new formulations of the ways in which lives are appraised and controlled by sovereign powers.
- Chris Abani's 'Buffalo Women' examines how the experience of war might transform the way in which a person experiences their humanity.
- *Anil's Ghost* sees Michael Ondaatje laying out a variety of strategies for responding to martial violence and suggesting that some combination of all may be necessary.

NOTES

1. Michael Hardt and Antonio Negri, *Empire* (Cambridge, MA: Harvard University Press, 2001), pp. 210–11.
2. Tamara Sivanandan, 'Anticolonialism, National Liberation and Postcolonial Nation Formation', in Neil Lazarus (ed.), *The Cambridge Companion to Postcolonial Literary Studies* (Cambridge: Cambridge University Press, 2004), p. 42.
3. Frantz Fanon, *The Wretched of the Earth*, trans. Constance Farringdon (London: Penguin, [1961] 1990), p. 28. Further references to this edition are given in the main text.
4. Joseph Conrad, *Heart of Darkness* (London: Penguin, [1902] 2007), p. 5.
5. V. S. Naipaul, 'A New King for the Congo', *New York Review of Books*, 26 June 1975, 20.
6. Ibid., p. 9.
7. V. S. Naipaul, *A Bend in the River* (London: André Deutsch, 1979), p. 72. Further references to this edition are given in the main text.
8. Naipaul, 'A New King', p. 24.
9. Tahmima Anam, *A Golden Age* (London: John Murray, [2007] 2008), p. 47. Further references to this edition are given in the main text.
10. Tahmima Anam, 'Mango Pickles and Revolution', *Publishers Weekly*, 15 October 2007, 36.
11. Tahmima Anam, 'Bangladesh: Give Me Back My Country', *New Statesman*, 22 January 2007, 31.
12. Agha Shahid Ali, *The Country Without a Post Office: Poems* (New York: W. W. Norton, [1997] 1998), p. 34. Further references to this edition are given in the main text.
13. Agha Shahid Ali, 'Introduction', in Agha Shahid Ali (ed.), *Ravishing DisUnities: Real Ghazals in English* (Middletown, CT: Wesleyan University Press, 2000), p. 3.
14. While in Judeo-Christian texts it is Isaac who is taken by his father to be sacrificed, a strong current of thought in the Islamic tradition instead identifies his brother Ishmael as the offered victim.

15. Hannah Arendt, *The Origins of Totalitarianism* (New York: Harcourt Brace Jovanovich, 1966), p. 296.
16. Giorgio Agamben, *Homo Sacer: Sovereign Power and Bare Life*, trans. Daniel Heller-Roazen (Stanford: Stanford University Press, [1995] 1998), p. 71.
17. Ibid., p. 18.
18. Ibid., p. 146.
19. Michel Foucault, *The History of Sexuality: Volume One, An Introduction*, trans. Robert Hurley (London: Penguin, [1976] 1990), p. 137.
20. Ibid., p. 139.
21. Michel Foucault, *Society Must Be Defended: Lectures at the Collège de France*, trans. David Macey (New York: Picador, [1997] 2003), p. 255.
22. Achille Mbembe, 'Necropolitics', trans. Libby Meintjes, *Public Culture* 15(1) (2003), 40.
23. Ibid., p. 32.
24. Ibid., p. 56.
25. Ibid., p. 37.
26. Chris Abani, *Hands Washing Water* (Port Townsend, WA: Copper Canyon, 2006), p. 81. Further references to this edition are given in the main text.
27. Chris Abani, *Song for Night* (New York: Akashic, 2007).
28. Chris Abani, *Chris Abani on the Stories of Africa* (video) (2007) http://www.ted.com/talks/chris_abani_on_the_stories_of_africa.html
29. Michael Ondaatje, 'Michael Ondaatje in Conversation with Maya Jaggi', *Wasafiri* 32 (2000), 6.
30. Michael Ondaatje, *Anil's Ghost* (London: Bloomsbury, 2000), p. 156. Further references to this edition are given in the main text.
31. Michael Ondaatje, 'Pale Flags: Reflections on Writing *Anil's Ghost*', *Wasafiri* 42 (2004), 62.
32. Margaret Scanlan, '*Anil's Ghost* and Terrorism's Time', *Studies in the Novel* 36(3) (2004), 302.

CHAPTER 6

Challenging Histories

The critic Antoinette Burton reads the various attempts in *Anil's Ghost* to present alternative strategies of conceptualising events in Sri Lanka as fatally undermined by the list of studies Ondaatje cites at the end of the novel as invaluable to his research into its topic. She suggests that the empiricism of these works reveals the author's ultimate faith in a Western conception of history and 'Ondaatje's critique of History ends up being a re-inscription of western civilisation's long romance with it'. Clearly, 'History' here refers to more than just the events of the past, and the term is in addition used to indicate a particular 'analytical category'.[1] That this category may be suspect has long been an ongoing concern of postcolonial studies.

The issue of whose history can be told is not simply a question of content, but crucially one of form. Certain ways of telling historical stories necessarily favour particular kinds of narrative and an insistence that there is only one methodology for historical enquiry ensures that some histories can never be told. A notorious example of this deliberate blindness to alternative conceptions of the past can be found in the 1965 pronouncement by the influential Oxford historian Hugh Trevor-Roper that Africa has no history:

Perhaps in the future there will be some African history to teach. But at present there is none, or very little: there is only the history of Europeans in Africa. The rest is largely darkness, like the history of pre-European, pre-Columbian America. And darkness is not a subject for history.[2]

Trevor-Roper is bound to a particular notion of what counts as the source material for a historian and as such sees no way in which the practices through which non-literate societies record and transmit their past can be counted as 'history'. Only the history of Europeans in Africa can be written because it is only they who have the materials he sees as constitutive of the historian's archive.

In a provocative and influential statement, the Indian historian Dipesh Chakrabarty argued that the selectivity found in views like Trevor-Roper's was not only confined to the history of non-literate societies but that the imposition of a particular way of doing history went much further than assumptions regarding what might count as a meaningful archive. In fact, Chakrabarty argues, the concepts at the centre of the academic practice of history were inseparably tied to the world in which they were formed: '"Europe" remains the sovereign, theoretical subject of all histories, including the ones we call "Indian", "Chinese", "Kenyan", and so on.'[3] Chakrabarty's argument is based around the idea of a particular notion of historicism, the placing of events in historical time. He argues that the study of history became possible because of a guiding narrative of progress, of events leading toward a particular point in time. This model of historicism was formed in Europe and when it was extended to the rest of the world these places were seen as backwards in attaining the social and cultural features that made up the European present. An idea that the non-European world was 'not yet' at an equivalent level of development became prevalent.[4] Chakrabarty goes on to note that the demands of decolonisation, which insisted on having these things 'now', equally subscribed to the narrative of a single and homogeneous idea of progress. Against this, he suggests the need to complicate our sense of the modern world and to recognise that there may be more than one path through time. He fixes on the person of the Indian 'peasant', whom he uses to suggest 'all that is not bourgeois (in a European sense) in Indian capitalism and modernity.[5] His point is that the 'peasant' (who may not be the 'rational' subject of European history, but may instead have a worldview fundamentally determined by his relationship with the 'supernatural') is not an anachronistic anomaly in modern India but a crucial constituent of that modernity. To assume that such a figure will (or should) wither away when faced with the modern world is to reveal a failure to understand that there is more than one version of the modern world, and that the European story cannot be seen as the only one, or that to which all other societies are heading.

Chakrabarty argues that the overwhelming impulse behind the European narrative of history, that was then exported to the postcolonial world, is 'the universalisation of the nation-state as the most desirable form of political community'.[6] This reduction of history to the narrative of a nation was a key target of the set of Indian historians with which Chakrabarty was associated for much of his early career, who named themselves the Subaltern Studies group. Central among their concerns was to explore the history of the 'subaltern' peoples in Indian colonial society: those who were not part of the colonialist Raj, nor of the 'native' elite who later came to rule the postcolonial nation. For both of these latter social groups a particular notion of historical progress structured their accounts of events in the past, one that may not have been shared by the subalterns. For Ranajit Guha, another of the most important Subaltern Studies historians, the project of narrating subaltern history is not only that of refusing the ways in which a European version of modernity is read as universal, but also to recognise that the postcolonial state might also have an interest in effacing particular histories. Indeed, the task of the historian is in part to unpack the 'conflict between state and community mediated by a still far from fully formed civil society'.[7] In tracing the ways in which civil society is formed through its particular codes of social interaction and shared practice, the other histories of modernity, neither Eurocentric nor reductively nationalist, might be written.

This chapter discusses how challenging moments in history have been narrated, and the idea of history itself challenged, in works that explore the transnational spaces of the Atlantic and Indian Oceans, and others that look at the troubled history of Australia; but it begins by examining how the personal experience of history is felt within familial relationships in a pair of Indian novels. The family unit, held together not only by communal bonds, but also by a shared understanding of past events, which might often require as many things to be forgotten as remembered, can be seen as a metonym of the national community. Without needing to see the relationships between familial and national histories as allegorical, we can nonetheless find in the former useful ways of negotiating the evasions and half-truths that so often constitute the latter.

A SCAB ON THE WOUNDS OF HISTORY: ANITA DESAI, *CLEAR LIGHT OF DAY*

Writing about the difficulties inherent in contemporary attempts to come to terms with the legacy of Partition, Suvir Kaul describes the tensions between India and Pakistan as 'an impossible sibling rivalry' and notes that 'it is hard to avoid metaphors of the family when writing about the birth and contemporary existence of the two countries'.[8] Anita Desai's *Clear Light of Day* (1980) is partly an account of the drama of Partition in Delhi, but its focus is firmly on one estranged family, telling the story of the return of Tara, an ambassador's wife, to her old family home. Since their eldest brother, Raja, left to start a new family in Hyderabad, Tara's sister Bim has held charge of the decaying home and of their congeni- tally mentally disabled youngest sibling Baba. The disputes and tensions between the family, however, cannot be seen merely as a metaphorical depiction of the national situation. Rather, the sib- lings are buffeted by all sorts of histories and those internal to the family are as important as those that may structure their relation- ships from outside.

Tara feels disturbed by the way in which Bim has failed to change the decor of the house from that put in place by their parents, lamenting that 'she [had] developed no taste of her own, no likings that made her wish to sweep the old house of all its rubbish and place in it things of her own choice'.[9] Tara herself is determined to break from the past and to start life afresh. Bim's association with the old seems reinforced by her employment as a university teacher of history. We learn that her passion for history developed as a child, when she turned away from Raja's voracious reading of poetry and adventure and instead sought occupation in facts. Her brother dismissed this calling as a lack of imagination, to which Bim responded by questioning to herself 'what need of imagination when one could have knowledge instead?' (p. 121). However, this binary division, like so many others in the novel, does not ultimately seem to stand: we learn that Raja's efforts at Urdu poetry 'were really very derivative [. . .] There was no image, no metaphor, no turn of phrase that was original' and instead he just repeated what he had learned (p. 168). Equally, the history that Bim teaches to her students seems as full of romantic stories of princesses as grounded in empirical investigation (p. 18). *Clear Light of Day* refuses the separation of fact and imagination in coming to terms with history and instead reveals their inevitable and necessary intertwining. Desai has written that India has difficulty in addressing its own recent history: 'the Indian habit is to ignore what is close and gaze into the distance where nothing is visible and nothing can distract from soothing reverie'.[10] The novel seems to acknowledge this in its characters' separating themselves from their contemporary political situation. The present of the novel is the fraught situation of Indira Gandhi's Emergency (1975–7), but reference is made to this only once, when Bim presses Tara's husband Bakul to justify it (though she seems less than serious in doing so and soon lets the point drop). Bakul's stance on Indian history seems precisely to mirror the view Desai disparages. When asked by foreigners to talk of the contemporary situation in his role as ambassador, he refuses to comment and instead insists on promoting 'The Taj Mahal – the Bhagavad Gita – Indian philosophy – music – art' and arguing that 'local politics, party disputes, election malpractices, Nehru, his daughter, his grandson' are unimportant 'when compared with India, eternal India' (p. 35). This recourse to a comforting history seems not only to avoid discussing the injustices of the present, but implicitly to justify them.

At a personal level, too, the novel portrays a failure to discuss the important events of the past within the family. Bim notes at one point that time never seems to flow smoothly and instead is masked by 'momentous events' that break up an otherwise monotonous sameness, and she and Tara each seem willing to grant that particular times in their youth functioned in this all-determining way (p. 42). However, as becomes clear as the novel progresses, they each see a very different set of events as the most significant. Their mutual failure to acknowledge and understand what has shaped the world of the other is increasingly revealed as the cause of the current rift between them.

Tara's return is marked by her quest to arrive at an objective understanding of what has happened to her family, though she realises that this desire may be incapable of being fulfilled, that her childhood self was perhaps too naive to understand the nuances of what was happening around her, and that as an adult 'her vision was strewn, obscured and screened by too much of the past' (p. 148). The past is frequently masked by uncanny and ghostly presences, which can never fully be named, like the horror of the well poisoned by the carcass of a drowned cow, or the image of a figure at the periphery of one's vision that Bim finds in T. S. Eliot's modernist poem *The Waste Land* (1922) and cannot forget. This unnameable, or unconscious, spectral presence of the past perhaps cannot be articulated or exorcised but can occasionally be obscured by an explanation. Tara is haunted by a vision of her father 'killing' her mother with an injection; when she later learns that he was administering an insulin shot to treat diabetes, Tara is grateful for 'an explanation that would cover up the livid, throbbing scene in her mind as a scab covers a cut' (p. 115). The trauma is not swept away, but a means of dealing with it is perhaps offered.

Memory is revealed to be crucially unreliable in the novel. The opening paragraphs of the book see Tara nostalgically and sadly remembering the former glories of her parents' rose garden and comparing it with its present state of neglect (p. 1). However, we later revisit this memory from the perspective of the omniscient narrator and it is revealed that the roses were always unimpressive; the spectacular blooms she remembers were actually in the garden of the Hyder Alis, their sophisticated Muslim neighbours (p. 102). This moment becomes especially significant in realising what may become effaced in the work of memory. The Hyder Alis were forced to leave Delhi in the violence of Partition. They (and by extension the political tensions of 1947) become misplaced in the contemporary attempt to understand what befell the family in those years. While Tara and Bim begin to understand each other a little in the course of the novel, and Bim begins the work of understanding her 'abandonment' by Raja, the degree to which the external situation conditioned their family history is never fully accounted for. The Urdu-loving Raja, who rejected the Hindu nationalism of his college classmates, eventually fled to join the Hyder Alis in Hyderabad; Bim's determination to read this as a personal betrayal perhaps indicates a failure to address the political aspect.

Bim eventually softens in her feelings toward her siblings and decides that she needs to love them more in order to mend the 'rents and tears' between them (p. 165). In a final epiphany she recognises

> how her own house and its particular history linked and con-
> tained her as well as her whole family with all their separate
> histories and experiences – not binding them within some
> dead and airless cell but giving them the soil in which to
> send down their roots, and food to make them grow and
> spread, reach out to new experience and new lives, but always
> drawing from the same soil, the same secret darkness. (p. 182)

Bim's revelation does not go beyond the personal divisions in her family, but the novel that frames her thought does offer some suggestion that this sense of interconnectedness that provides resolution for Bim might also be extended to address the unresolved bitterness of Partition. In this way the 'scab' of explanation might start to grow over the wound of history, and healing begin.

SQUARING HISTORY'S BOOKS: ARUNDHATI ROY, *THE GOD OF SMALL THINGS*

A family haunted by the ghosts of its past is also at the heart of Arundhati Roy's *The God of Small Things* (1997), set in Kerala in the south-west of India. The series of events that culminates in the separation of the twins Estha and Rahel from each other and from their mother, Ammu, after the murder by police of Ammu's untouchable lover Velutha, also includes the death by drowning of their cousin Sophie Mol. Reflecting on these times, Rahel notes that the memory of Sophie Mol has become obscured by the years but that the fact of her absence has increasingly become palpable. It is this absence that 'ushered Rahel through childhood (from school to school) into womanhood'.[11] Like Estha, who at thirty-one years old has not spoken for years, Rahel is formed by the ghosts of the trauma that happened to her seven-year-old self. The alienation from the present that each of the twins suffers in their own way, it seems, is the necessary fate of those who cannot be reconciled with history, who are excluded from its explanatory frame.

Early in the novel the twins' uncle, Chacko, offers a vivid metaphor for history, describing it as 'an old house at night. With all the lamps lit. And ancestors whispering inside'. To understand history, he argues, they need to enter the house and listen to these voices, but they have been locked out 'and when we try to listen all we hear is a whispering' (pp. 52–3). Chacko sees this exclusion in terms of his family's Anglophilia, which has caused them to be separated from the real past of India, but it becomes clear in the novel that the commandeering of 'History' by the powerful has consistently worked to exclude the weak and vulnerable. Roy's narrator suggests that her story could be seen to have begun 'thousands of years ago' (p. 33): the multiple divisions of India, whether these take the form of ancient caste restrictions, colonial administration or neo-colonial globalised exploitation all rely on the imposition of one particular ordering logic that works to exclude alternative formulations, and to punish those who transgress these laws.

For the twins, the metaphorical History House becomes identified with the now-rotting former home of an English landlord, which is where Velutha eventually meets his violent fate. In the later timeframe of the novel we discover that it has been converted into a luxury hotel complex for foreign visitors. Here local culture is repackaged into 'toy histories': the Marxist leader E. M. S. Namboodiripad is evoked as local 'Heritage' alongside such exhibits as a 'Traditional Kerala Umbrella' and 'Traditional Bridal Dowry Box'. The ancient dances of the Keralese *kathakali* tradition are reduced from six-hour epics to 'twenty minute cameos' for the benefit of tourists with 'small attention spans' (pp. 326, 126–7). Roy has written elsewhere that 'India lives in several centuries at once' and the History House serves as a place where this is lived out: from the predatory paedophile Englishman to the blindly consuming tourists we can see the ways in which India is exploited from outside; and in the murder of Velutha for breaking caste laws we can see how this oppression is also frequently home-grown.[12] History is the place where power is felt.

The epigraph to the novel is taken from the art critic John Berger: 'Never again will a single story be told as though it's the only one.' The novel insists on the importance of small stories, and on the danger of accepting single narratives. Its structure is such that the reader is drawn along by hints and the fragments of stories: it is not until the final chapter that we can trace exactly the course of events and see how so many of the characters each contributed to the tragedy. The full story is denied to anyone within the novel and each has only a partial understanding. The gaps in what they know are filled by assumptions and lies. Roy's narrator finishes her discussion of the grief of Sophie Mol's mother, Margaret Kochamma, by noting that 'It is unreasonable to expect someone to remember what she didn't know had happened' (p. 265). No one in the novel is granted more than a partial perspective yet the tragedy seems generated by people wanting to turn these necessarily fragmented understandings into totalising explanations. The 'small things' of individual narratives are then crushed by the 'big' forces of history. Increasingly throughout the novel history itself is seen as an agent: a destructive and vengeful god that punishes those who defy socially acceptable behaviour. The murder of Velutha is described as history 'collect[ing] its dues' and 'squar[ing] its books' after it is 'caught off guard' by the desire that springs up between Ammu and Velutha (p. 176).

In making history itself culpable, *The God of Small Things* suggests that the agency of those individuals who bring about the murder is eclipsed by a power greater than themselves. The policemen who beat Velutha to death are 'only history's henchmen': 'impelled by feelings that were primal yet paradoxically wholly impersonal' (p. 308). The bleakly satiric account of how people justify brutality is most powerfully rendered in Roy's critique of the communists in Kerala, especially the local official Comrade Pillai, who is described as not planning events but 'merely slipping his hand into history's waiting glove' (p. 281). It is clear that this is an act of moral weakness and that conceding to the brutality of history is precisely what allows it to continue to oppress. Pillai and the chief policeman Inspector Thomas Mayhew are described as 'Men without curiosity. Without doubt' (p. 262). This failure of imagination, which manifests as a willingness to concede to history, is precisely what Roy is writing against. Velutha has turned to communism because of its utopian promise, the lure of a better world, but when Pillai tells him that the Party can offer no help, the Marxist dream seems empty: 'Another religion turned against itself. Another edifice constructed by the human mind, decimated by human nature' (p. 282).

However, despite the novel's pervading pessimism, there is some sense of hope remaining by its ending. Rahel and Estha incestuously make love, which may suggest some reconciliation between them, a return to the days when they were so close that they 'thought of themselves together as Me, and separately, individually, as We or Us' (p. 2). It is interesting to note that this coupling seems brought about by their shared observation of a *kathakali* performance, where the dancers erase the humiliation of their hotel shows by staging the full dances for themselves. They defy their categorisation by history, their relegation to the status of exotic heritage, and insist on their dignity. It seems that *The God of Small Things* ultimately puts its faith in such acts of persistence in defying the dominance of history. The Indian Marxist critic Aijaz Ahmad has suggested that the novel is flawed politically because it finds resolution only in sexual transgression, 'construct[ing] eroticism as that transcendence which takes individuals beyond history and society' instead of 'fac[ing] the fact that the erotic is very rarely a sufficient mode for overcoming real social oppressions; one has to make some other, more complex choices'.[13] Ahmad is no doubt correct in that the novel offers no political solutions, but perhaps too willing to accept that the sexual unions between Rahel and Estha and Ammu and Velutha are intended as resolution. Rather, they might be construed as showing both the need for such resolution in the future, and the persistence of the hope required to set such a process in motion. The final word of the novel is 'tomorrow' (p. 340): Roy is not suggesting that the problems she outlines in modern India can be fixed by an inter-caste affair, but articulating a moment where a particular demand for justice can be made upon the future, free from the binding tradition of history.

CAN THE SUBALTERN SPEAK?

The influential postcolonial theorist Gayatri Chakravorty Spivak was loosely associated with the Subaltern Studies collective of historians in the 1980s. While fascinated by their work, she was nonetheless concerned that there was a conceptual problem at the very heart of the enterprise. Her concerns centre on the notion of the subaltern, people who belong to the lowest groups in society. Spivak draws upon Ranajit Guha's own definition which identifies the subaltern as '*the demographic difference between the total Indian population and all those [. . .] described as the "elite"*'.[14] Particularly notable here is the way this definition works in terms of absence: the subaltern classes are defined precisely by what they are not. It is this sense of absence in which Spivak is most interested. Her concern is whether these figures can ever in fact be recaptured by historians in the way the Subaltern Studies group wished.

Critics of Spivak frequently misread the titular question explored in her seminal essay 'Can the Subaltern Speak?' as a refusal to grant any articulacy or agency to the dispossessed classes; however, it should not be read as an *ontological* enquiry (into how the world actually is) but rather as a *historiographical* one (into the degree to which the past can be written truly). This distinction is perhaps made most clearly in another essay written about the Subaltern Studies project where she looks to unpack some of the ways in which 'consciousness' is used as a concept in historical writing. We are familiar with the use of 'consciousness' to describe our individual sense of being alive, and associate this application of the word with such ideas as reason and agency. However, there is also a communal understanding of consciousness that we can see in the work of many historians. Here we can read the rebellious consciousness of the subaltern, for example, as revealed in the act of their rebellion. It seems reasonable to read back to the first form of (individual, interior) consciousness and thus to infer the desires of the subaltern class from their historically-recorded acts, but Spivak refuses this move and seeks to show why it is a mistake. Crucial here is the fact that the historical record is not produced by the subaltern classes themselves: 'it is only the texts of counterinsurgency or elite documentation that give us the news of the consciousness of the subaltern'. These texts are produced by the elite groups – the consciousness recorded is actually a projection of how the elite imagines the subaltern to think, a record of their fears and desires about the revolting group. The actual consciousness of the subaltern is then 'never fully recoverable' and 'effaced even as it is disclosed'.[15]

The question 'Can the Subaltern Speak?' is therefore perhaps answered in Spivak's work by her pointing out that they obviously can, but that means of transmission do not exist for us to be able to hear what they say. In effect the subaltern remains silent as their historical actions are used to support models of consciousness that were not necessarily their own but instead imposed from outside. Yet, despite this seeming pessimism about the historiographical project of the Subaltern Studies group, she does not reject the idea of searching for subaltern consciousness altogether. Rather, it should only be approached with due vigilance and a care on the part of historians to realise what they are doing in writing of the subaltern. Spivak makes a useful distinction between two senses of the word 'representation' by drawing on German, in which two different words are used. The first (*vertreten*) refers to political representation, where one individual or group aims to promote the interests of another; the second (*darstellen*) to the types of representation that take place in art.[16] Crudely, we can think of the first as 'speaking for' and the second as 'speaking of'. It is crucial for historians and activists to be aware which they are doing in trying to represent the subaltern.

Spivak ends her 'Can the Subaltern Speak?' essay with an anecdote that reveals both how hard subaltern subjects might struggle to articulate their own consciousness and also how this can still be effaced in the act of interpretation which decides how this speaking should be heard. She tells the story of Bhuvaneswari Bhaduri, a young woman who killed herself by hanging in 1926 (strictly, this middle-class woman falls outside the category of subalternity, but Spivak's example is more concerned with process than status, and how it is that any voice can be obliterated even in listening to it). Bhuvaneswari was menstruating at the time of her suicide, which Spivak sees as a deliberate refusal to have her death read within the framework of the 'sanctioned motive' for female suicide: as brought about by an illicit love affair. In fact, Bhuvaneswari had been entrusted with a political assassination she had felt unable to carry out. Her use of her body to reject the 'obvious' interpretation of her suicide seems to Spivak a significant example of how the subaltern might struggle to speak. However, Spivak goes on to describe how she went to discuss the story of Bhuvaneswari with a 'philosopher and Sanskritist' friend:

> Two responses: (a) Why, when her two sisters, Saileswari and Raseswari, led such full and wonderful lives, are you interested in the hapless Bhunvaneswari? (b) I asked her nieces. It appears that it was a case of illicit love.[17]

The first woman is uninterested in this story of tragic failure and instead wants to turn to a triumphalist narrative; her nieces explicitly reinscribe the consciousness that Bhuvaneswari had tried to refute. In this way, then, Spivak shows the difficulty, yet necessity, of trying adequately to attend to the voice of the subaltern.

MADE NOBLE IN THE FIRE: PETER CAREY, *TRUE HISTORY OF THE KELLY GANG*

The title of Peter Carey's 2000 novel *True History of the Kelly Gang* is seen by its author as signalling precisely that it is a work of fiction: Carey told an interviewer that 'anyone who says "true history" is obviously writing a novel . . . No historian would ever say that'.[18] Academic history is too careful to make such bold claims to truth or perhaps just not willing to do so in such an unsubtle manner. Yet Carey's term is precisely in keeping with the voice and beliefs of the man he ventriloquises in the novel: the bushranger Ned Kelly (1855–1880), an outlaw often seen as a folk hero in Australia. During his lifetime Kelly was deeply concerned with his popular image and determined to set the record straight if possible. This was most famously done in his Jerilderie Letter. The letter, over 7,000 words long, was a brief account of his life with particular reference to how his gang's recent killing of a posse of policemen should be seen as an act of justified self defence. During an extended bank robbery in the town of Jerilderie, Kelly had tried unsuccessfully to get the local printer to copy and distribute his letter. Following his death by hanging, however, Kelly's fame ensured that the original paper letter was preserved; and it is now kept by the National Museum of Australia.[19] The letter is an extraordinary document, written in powerful language, and it reveals Kelly's belief that if he could air his version of events then public opinion would forgive him his acts. Carey too can be seen to show a remarkable faith in the power of representation. In one sense, *True History of the Kelly Gang* is the Jerilderie Letter expanded to cover the whole of Kelly's life. By placing the events recorded in numerous histories of the gang into a prose that imitates Ned's letter in its attitudes, vocabulary and loose punctuation, Carey attempts to put Kelly right at the centre of his own history, himself dictating the terms through which he should be understood.

This act of centring Kelly's history on the man itself is matched in the novel by a desire to question how Australian history more generally should be centred, and by extension to explore to whom Australia belongs. The novel's Ned is quite sure of this, arguing that squatters (rich landlords) like R. R. McBean 'did not own that country he never could'.[20] The novel explores the popular idea that the English–descended ruling class of Australia had fewer claims on the nation than the settlers of Irish birth, usually either transported convicts or their descendents. It is frequently made clear that the Irish are a persecuted group in the Victoria colony, and to a degree they bond around their ancestry. However, although Ned as a child finds comfort in some of the old Irish legends his mother tells him, they ultimately provide insufficient succour (p. 29). Significantly, he notes that while belief in St Brigit, who could bring cows to milk, has faded amongst the transportees, they retain their belief in the spirit that foresees death, the banshee (p. 108). Only the bleak tales have travelled from Ireland and ultimately Carey's Ned sees that clinging to an Irish past is insufficient and cannot provide the ballast needed to belong fully in Australia: 'our parents would rather forget what came before so we currency [Australian-born] lads is left alone ignorant as tadpoles spawned in puddles on the moon' (p. 334). Ireland can be used as a measure for comparison in that it too suffers as a colony – as when the Australian children learn the names both of Irish traitors and those who would tell nothing to the police (p. 175) – but it remains ultimately different from the 'colony made specifically to have poor men bow down to their gaolers' (p. 181).

For Ned's mentor, Harry Power, the meaningful claim to Australia is in knowing the land, but the novel indicates that something more than that is needed (p. 343).[21] In an important scene, suggested in the novel to be one of the spurs behind the composition of the Jerilderie Letter, Ned is 'tried' by a jury of his peers as he and his co-outlaw Joe Byrne seek to defend their actions to a group of hostages in the town of Eurora. The hostages initially consider the gang cold-blooded murderers but eventually come to sympathise with them as the actions of the police are made clear. Ned argues that the turn to sympathy seen in the hostages is precisely because they are Australians and therefore knew the 'terror of the unyielding law' and have a 'historic memory of UNFAIRNESS':

> A man might be a bank clerk or an overseer he might never have been lagged for nothing but still he knew in his heart what it were to be forced to wear the white hood in prison he knew what it were to be lashed for looking a warder in the eye.[22]

The uniqueness of settler Australians is seen as consisting of the unity created through a shared experience of oppression. Ned comments at another point that 'the Queen of England should beware her prisons give a man a potent sense of justice' (p. 341). Ned's criminality can then be seen from another viewpoint as precisely a truer form of justice, in opposition to the cruel logic of the law. When he breaks into Whitty's pound to reclaim his confiscated foals he declares that 'this did not seem a crime to me not then or now' (p. 229). Ned invokes a natural law, or higher justice, that the regulations of the squatter class violate. The colonial law is usurped by a different sense of what is fair and right.

It is the fate of Australians to be 'made noble in the fire', to be turned into a new people by the oppression under which they suffer (p. 305). This is what Thomas Curnow fails to realise at the end of the book. Having betrayed Ned and saved the convoy of police who are to arrest Ned and kill his gang, Curnow '*was called a hero more than once, although less frequently and less enthusiastically than he might have reasonably expected*'. He is dismayed instead by the 'ever-growing adoration' of Ned and his gang and questions '*What is wrong with us?* [. . .] *Might not we find someone better to admire than a horse thief and a murderer?*' (p. 419). Curnow cannot see that the morality through which he judges Ned a villain is one that is inextricably tied up with a colonial order that many Australians reject. Through inverting these values Ned Kelly provides a glimpse of an alternative justice, one truer to the needs of the former transportees and their descendents.

THE SORT OF SECRETS YOU COULD USE: SALLY MORGAN, *MY PLACE*

To some degree Ned Kelly's story can be seen as 'historical' because of its public nature, its impact upon the world around him. Yet, as we have seen across the examples so far in this chapter, a frequent strategy in postcolonial novels that address the challenges of history is to reject public space (where the larger, sanctioned narratives of history hold sway) and retreat instead to the personal. The separation of non-fictional writings that deal with the past into the categories of history or autobiography is partly predicated on whether they are concerned with the public world of communal social life or the private one of the developing self within the world. However, as Bart Moore-Gilbert has noted, postcolonial life-writing has frequently demonstrated that 'subjectivity is characteristically constructed *between* individual and collective historical experience'.[23] Postcolonial autobiography, then, is frequently not a retreat from history but another way of engaging with it. Even when the topic is the formation of the individual self (the usual preoccupation of the form), autobiography may work 'to "provincialise" western paradigms of selfhood and psychic development'.[24]

Accounts of the self might in this way be as politically charged as those that deal with the social world more broadly.

Sally Morgan's *My Place* (1987) tells the story of her growing up in the 1950s and 1960s and coming to realise that she was partly of Aboriginal descent, which leads her to research some of her family's history. A bestseller in Australia, it soon became controversial. Some of the many charges laid against it are clearly articulated in Edward Hills's stinging critique that accuses the book of effacing the Aboriginal concerns it claims to promote, in favour of offering an easily consumed reconciliation of identity where Sally's non-threatening whiteness is ultimately affirmed, even as she appropriates Aboriginal experience: 'the book absolves white guilt by promoting cathartic release at the expense of collective responsibility'. He lays much of the blame for this on the author's choice of form, attacking 'the conservative, depoliticising influence of the genre' of autobiography.[25] It is interesting therefore to trace the ways in which Morgan's book disrupts its own autobiographical form and the ways in which this unsettling of conventions can be read as revealing some of her most political impulses.

The early chapters of the book can seem very clearly within the conventions of the autobiographical form: we meet the young Sally and are led through the tragic and comic adventures of her life at home and at school. The discovering of her Aboriginality is initially seen as another life event like any of these others. At first she believes her mother and grandmother who tell her she is of Indian descent, and as she later discovers the truth it is seen as a particular challenge she will have to face: her sister Jill bemoans that 'It's a terrible thing to be Aboriginal. Nobody wants to know you [. . .] You can be Indian, Dutch, Italian, anything but not Aboriginal!'[26] Graham Huggan has written that the book is about coming to terms with memories 'without being destroyed by them' and notes how the demise of Sally's alcoholic veteran father is another example of this in the book.[27] Yet it is in the difference in the formal treatment of Sally's father's death and her discovery of Aboriginality that we can begin to pinpoint how a critique like Hills's may miss its target. Bill's death has a crucial impact upon the process of Sally's self-formation, but in a way that can comfortably be accommodated within the traditional structure of autobiography: a linear narrative focused on a single individual. Living with Aboriginality, however, registers a formal impact as enormous as the one experienced personally.

After having her right to an Aboriginal scholarship challenged, Sally begins to reflect on 'What did it mean to be Aboriginal?' recognising that this may involve more than just her darker skin colour and the prejudice she faces (p. 141). Trying to answer this question involves a fundamental fracturing of Morgan's narrative, and recognition that the standard autobiography's focus on the single, unified self will be insufficient for her purposes. Soon after this point she interrupts her story with the interposition of that of her great-uncle, Arthur, told in his own words. For Hills, Morgan 'has colonised her family's stories' in drawing them into her own narrative of personal development,[28] but the book never really returns to the clear focus on Sally's life that marked the early chapters. Shortly after Arthur's tale, Sally takes her mother to the estate where the family had once lived. In this chapter, 'Return to Corunna', dozens of characters are introduced, some with the same names as each other, as the two women learn about the complicated ways in which they are tied to so many of the people there. The narrator tells us that 'our heads were spinning' (p. 221) and it is likely the reader will feel the same way: these encounters are not neatly managed in terms of their impact on Sally's development but are confusing, frantic and frequently inconclusive. At the end of the trip, Sally reflects on how she now knows 'our place' (p. 223). However, the nature of the chapter we have read could suggest to us that this might not refer to a sense of ownership of the location, nor even of her own new identity, but rather to her recognition of her implication within a network of social relationships; a sense that she can no longer be understood just as an individual but precisely only in the collective sense that Hills sees *My Place* as denying.

The later interjections of her mother's and grandmother's stories into the text can be seen as continuing this idea of a fractured (though not necessarily a discordant) self, but they also have another purpose. In each of these two mini-narratives, as well as in Arthur's, and in the continuing (though much slimmed) story of Sally herself, the idea of autobiography survives. Morgan may disrupt autobiography but she does not abandon it. This is matched by another interesting move within the text as the book Sally is writing is nearly always referred to as a history. Both Sally and her mother argue that all history is about 'the white man' and that this needs to be redressed (pp. 161–3), and at the conclusion of Arthur's narrative he asserts that 'I'm a part of history, that's how I look on it' (p. 213). His claim seems simultaneously to assert his always-existing place within the history of Australia and also that the act of writing about him has provided him with a degree of legitimation. Inscribing her family members into a textual record is one way for Morgan to insist on the need for their public acknowledgement in Australia.

Sally encourages her grandmother to tell her story by insisting to her that secrets should not be kept 'when they're the sort of secrets you could use to help your own people' (p. 319). Ultimately, the stories revealed by Arthur and Sally's mother and grandmother shed light on some of the terrible abuses suffered by Australia's indigenous peoples, and particularly on the Stolen Generation, the enormous number of mixed-race children who were taken away from their Aboriginal families to live with white people in a eugenic government experiment to try to eliminate the Aboriginal people. An official enquiry into the Stolen Generation did not begin until 1997; at the time that Morgan's book was written, the recording of individual testimony was one of the only ways to highlight and remember what had been done. *My Place* shows a recognition of the some of the problems inherent in autobiography's usual assumption of a single, unified self, but nonetheless can also be read as a strategic deployment of the form to fill the gaps left by history and to ensure that silenced stories do not remain that way.

BEYOND THE MESMERIC POWER OF TRADITION: BLACK ATLANTIC HISTORIES

A particularly influential reimagining of historical sensibilities is given in Paul Gilroy's 1993 study *The Black Atlantic*. Attempting to situate itself between and amongst focal points of black cultures in Africa, North America, the Caribbean and Britain, this book offers the Atlantic Ocean as a meaningful unit for cultural analysis,

as distinct from the more traditionally nation-based accounts provided within cultural studies. Yet his understanding of this Atlantic
space is always historical as much as geographical and can best be
understood as an attempt to theorise 'the recent history of blacks,
as people in but not necessarily of, the western world, a history
which involves processes of political organisation that are explicitly
transnational and international in nature'.[29] Gilroy's determination to think outside of the traditional explanatory boundaries of
the nation does entail attention to processes of spatial dislocation
(two of the main chapters of his book concern the influence of the
time spent in Germany and France of two great African-American
intellectuals W. E. B. Du Bois and Richard Wright, respectively),
but the most significant propositions of his work regard the way in
which he insists on understanding diaspora as not just constructed
in space, but as entailing particular relationships of 'temporality
and historicity, memory and narrativity'; diasporas, those groups
of people who experience a sense of unity and collectivity despite
dispersal across nation borders, must be understood, for Gilroy,
as evincing particular and unique experiences of history (p. 191).[30]
Much as nations can only be understood through the double-
faced address of both geography and history (see the discussion of
Homi Bhabha in Chapter 2), so too must diasporas, even as they
disturb nationalist logic, be seen as constituted around a similar
duality.

Despite the title of his book, Gilroy actually does not offer the
Atlantic Ocean itself as the best model for understanding the processes of which he writes, but rather focuses on the 'chronotope'
of the ship. Chronotopes are encapsulations of time and space
together and Gilroy's ship reminds us that movement always takes
place within both, and that black Atlantic culture has its traditions
as well as its locations. Gilroy acknowledges his debt to anthropologist James Clifford who sought to refigure his discipline through
drawing attention to the fact that all cultures are always mobile,
and that insisting instead on stasis is always a significant political act.[31] The ship is not just an empty metaphor for Gilroy but
concretely 'focus[es] attention on the middle passage [the journey
of slaves from Africa to the New World], on the various projects
for redemptive return to an African homeland, on the circulation

of ideas and activists as well as the movement of key cultural and political artefacts' (p. 4).

Gilroy's endeavours are best understood when placed against the currents in black political and social thought that he sees as not only misleading but also possibly dangerous: those which look to postulate and invigorate an essentialist, and unchanging, notion of black selfhood, usually with reference to an African past. 'The idea of tradition,' he writes, 'has a strange, mesmeric power in black political discourse' (p. 185). He traces philosophies that look to inspire pride among black people by turning to stories of ancient African civilisations, which offer plentiful resources for productively reshaping the contemporary world, and recognises that these ideas not only have genuine appeal but can also prove, at least locally or temporarily, extremely effective. However, he is overwhelmingly concerned that such celebratory ideals can only operate by acting as if the great traumatic event of Atlantic slavery never took place and that the 'mystical and ruthlessly positive notion of Africa that is indifferent to interracial variation and is frozen at the point where blacks boarded the ships' can only ever offer, at best, a partial understanding of Atlantic black cultures, and, at worst, erases all that may be most significant about them. He argues that such retreat to invariant tradition is in fact itself a reaction to the modernity that has so often worked to exclude black people.

Gilroy wishes to mobilise a different conception of tradition, one which is 'used neither to identify a lost past nor to name a culture of compensation that would restore access to it' (p. 198). Recognising that the experiences of slavery and its aftermaths are central to modern black lives, he instead wishes to trace exactly how this brutal past might have crafted the particular articulations of black culture and also offer radical symbols of hope more generally. Gilroy argues that even as the Western discourses of rationality and human progress we call the Enlightenment were being undermined by the terrible violence of slavery and colonialism, those black subjects who laboured under this tyranny nonetheless found alternative ways of figuring the Enlightenment's noble goals. He suggests that this was more than simply a 'politics of fulfilment', demanding that the colonisers enacted their own rhetoric, and was instead a 'politics of transfiguration', identifying the contradictions at the heart of the Enlightenment project and providing better ways of achieving its utopian aims, and ensuring that 'reason is thus reunited with the happiness and freedom of individuals and the reign of justice within the collectivity' (p. 39). His sentiments are undoubtedly utopian, but the point of *The Black Atlantic* is to make possible this utopianism through mobilising a specific critical mode. It is not simply to suggest that the European traditions of humanism, which managed to find space to justify the transatlantic slave economy, can easily be redeemed, as if dogged by only minor imperfections. Rather, it is to recognise that much of this philosophy was sullied by a racist terror from the outset. Gilroy counsels that attention precisely to the greatest moral failings of Enlightenment reason (and he includes not only slavery, but the Nazi Holocaust), and, crucially, to the strategies of survival developed by their victims, might best lay the way for a renewal and rehabilitation of any utopian impulse or possibility of human progress.

NOT GOING HOME: CARYL PHILLIPS, *THE ATLANTIC SOUND*

Caryl Phillips's writing, which has frequently explored the experiences of black people at various times and locations in the modern world, can seem to share several characteristics with Gilroy's notion of the black Atlantic. He has written that, when asked by his lawyer what he wished to happen to his remains after death, 'I answered without hesitation. "I wish my ashes to be scattered in the middle of the Atlantic Ocean at a point equidistant between Britain, Africa and North America."'[32] Elsewhere in his essays he has emphasised the plural nature of his 'home', locating himself variously in the Caribbean of his birth, the Britain in which he was raised, the United States in which he now lives and the Africa of his ancestry. In each location, he writes, 'I am of, and not of, this place.'[33] Phillips wants to claim each of these places as his home yet recognises strong impediments to doing so in all of them: the image of his watery grave suggests he expects this tension to continue long after his death.

His 2000 book *The Atlantic Sound* is part travelogue and part history, mapping his travels between these various places, but also stretching back in time to find other individuals who had made similar journeys, and have similarly troubled notions of home. The book begins with Phillips re-enacting an Atlantic crossing by banana boat similar to that his parents would have taken in the 1950s. On arrival in Britain he notes that 'I am happy to be home' and that 'I have travelled towards Britain with a sense of knowledge and propriety.'[34] Yet the association with Britain is always to some degree anxious, as Phillips recognises that his history, and the history of all black people in the West, always gestures elsewhere. His next journey is to Ghana and while on the aeroplane he is asked by a Ghanaian where he is from: 'the problem question for those of us who have grown up in societies which define themselves by excluding others [. . .] Does this man not understand the complexity of his question?' Phillips makes 'the familiar flustered attempt to answer *the* question' but this is 'spoiled' by the African man's reaction: 'So, my friend, you are going home to Africa.' Phillips's silent reply to this is repeated several times: '*No, I am not going home*' (p. 98). The strength of this negation is central to Phillips's relation to the strategies for belonging developed within many black communities. While Gilroy's *The Black Atlantic* is critical of many instincts toward community, it nonetheless strives to establish others; Phillips often seems far more deeply distrustful of any such urge.

The largest section of *The Atlantic Sound* involves Phillips's stay in Ghana, which mostly revolves around attendance at Panafest, a celebration of black diasporic culture that seeks to ground this diversity in an African homeland. Phillips interviews several figures involved with this version of Pan-Africanism and often finds the philosophy wanting: from the Ghanaian Dr Mohammed Ben Abdallah who emphasises the continuity of values between Africans and the black diaspora, but then suggests that Atlantic slavery holds a different meaning for 'you people' (pp. 114–18), to Kohain Halevi, an African American who has established a community in Ghana as a site for black diasporans to come and 'cleanse their spirits' (pp. 158–65), but who finds his 'Thru the Door of No Return' ceremony quickly descending into farce (pp. 173–8). In the book's final section Phillips visits another community of 'returned' African Americans, this time in the Negev desert in Israel. In this community, where polyandry is practised and families each dress in their own uniform of coloured clothing Phillips seems to detect an absurd rejection of modernity and a refusal fully to participate in the world (the fact that Israeli citizenship is withheld from these settlers helps highlight their outlandishness). They function as an epitome of what might be wrong with the philosophy of return to Africa as a process of healing for black people: 'It is futile to walk into the face of history. As futile as trying to keep the dust from one's eyes in the desert' (p. 121).

However, Phillips equally does not advocate the wholesale rejection of history, or deny that filiative bonds may exist between diverse black populations. His vignette describing the life of Philip Quaque, an African who worked as a priest in a late-eighteenth-century missionary station/slave fort, vividly indicates how a failure to see these connections seems perverse, as Philip never once in his many letters mentions the sufferings of his fellow Africans in the dungeons below him (pp. 139–44). Elsewhere on his journeys Phillips finds people who have tried more fully to incorporate both an African past and the rupture of slavery into their understanding of contemporary black lives, but still finds these formulations to some degree inadequate. In Liverpool he meets Stephen, a young black man who campaigns against the city's 'amnesia' regarding its own slave history. Exploring the city, Phillips finds evidence of this blinkered view of the past, where the only meaningful references to the slave trade are locked away in a museum. Yet Stephen ultimately seems consumed by his anger about this and despite bemoaning the segregation of Liverpool, gleefully recounts how Jewish people have been driven from the black 'ghetto' of Toxteth (p. 89).

Phillips actually seems to find the most positive negotiation of history in the process of establishing 'home' when he travels to Charleston, South Carolina, and tells the story of Judge Julius Waties Waring, even though this man so outraged his own white community by standing up against segregation that by the end of his life 'in all but name, he was now homeless' (p. 202). Decades after the judge's courageous actions, Phillips attends a Festival of

African and Caribbean Art in the centre of Charleston. Five young black women give a display of African dance but, unlike in Ghana, this cultural affirmation is not intended to exclude and Phillips notes with pleasure white people dancing to African rhythms (pp. 211–13). Phillips certainly does not suggest that this one moment provides an answer to the extremely vexed questions of belonging he stages, but the simultaneous urge to commemorate historical belonging, yet strive for contemporary conviviality, seems to chime with his own philosophy.

A TERROR OF SYMBOLS: AMITAV GHOSH, *IN AN ANTIQUE LAND*

Much like Phillips's *The Atlantic Sound*, Amitav Ghosh's *In an Antique Land* (1992) defies simple categorisation, again blending elements of historical research with travel writing. As a doctoral anthropology student, Ghosh spent time in rural Egypt and his book is partly a recounting of these years. However, it also includes much material from a later scholarly study he made in Egypt, this time acting as a historian (his research from this time was actually published in the *Subaltern Studies* journal).[35] This research relates to a twelfth-century Jewish merchant in Cairo called Abraham Ben Yiju, and more particularly to Ben Yiju's Indian slave, whom Ghosh eventually names as Bomma. The Cairo synagogue contained a storehouse known as the Geniza, where all papers that bore the name of God would be stored rather than destroyed (and given the writing conventions of the time, this would mean nearly every piece of writing). The Geniza documents therefore provide a near-unparalleled archive of the medieval Middle East. The Indian slave upon whom Ghosh fixates is mentioned in only a couple of Ben Yiju's papers, yet Ghosh finds in this presence of an Indian serving in a Jewish household in Islamic Cairo evidence of a lost cosmopolitanism that seems belied by the current divisions across this part of the world.

However, Ghosh's historical researches are continually interrupted throughout *In an Antique Land* by the account of his initial stay in Lataifa and Nashawy. The young Indian anthropologist in these Egyptian villages frequently becomes the object of study as much as an investigator. The locals are often fascinated by India, which they perceive as a place of disturbing and ungodly rituals and superstitions. The cremation of the dead and the 'failure' to circumcise young men are particular topics for concern. After one particularly gruelling interrogation by village elders from which the young Amitav runs away, his friend Nabeel asks why he lets 'this talk of cows and burning and circumcision worry you so much? These are just customs; it's natural that people should be curious.'[36] Ghosh tells his reader that he did not share with Nabeel the reasons behind 'an Indian's terror of symbols', but he does provide the reader with a personal account of some of the horrors of Partition, 'of people killed for wearing a lungi or a dhoti [. . .] of women disembowelled for wearing veils or vermilion, of men dismembered for the state of their foreskins' (p. 210). While the curiosity of the villagers may well be innocent, Ghosh sees in it an echo of a far more dangerous discourse of separation and supremacism.

The violence that may adhere to cultural divisions seems to become more pronounced the more one moves up the ladder of education and social privilege: he writes of how educated Egyptians in particular seem to see no distinction between religion and politics, but the most telling example is in the argument he falls into with the village imam. The imam, formerly an expert in traditional healing, has embraced Western medicine and resents Ghosh's inquiries into the older methods. He aggressively responds by again attacking Hindu religious practice, but the argument quickly degenerates into each party claiming that their country is superior because it has better 'guns and bombs' (p. 236). Reflecting on this afterwards, Ghosh is disgusted by how easily he too slipped into a language of violence and military might as the only way in which cultures can meaningfully be compared in the contemporary world.

National and cultural divisions become even more pronounced when Ghosh tries to visit the tomb of a Jewish saint in Egypt. At first, the officials seem happy to welcome him, but, on learning he is not an Israeli, immediately turn hostile and question what possible interest he could have in this site. He toys with telling them the story of Ben Yuji and his slave but recognises that it would mean nothing to these officials that 'the partitioning of the past' had thoroughly been achieved (p. 340). He has a similar experience in Mangalore, India where a Muslim saint's shrine has been reinvented to venerate Vishnu, the locals 'discovering a History to replace the past' (p. 273).

Ghosh finds this partitioning of history (which he links to the geographical divide in Israel/Palestine) particularly in evidence in the way in which the Islamic high culture of Cairo allowed the Geniza documents to be sold across Europe and the United States, their removal serving to justify and confirm a stereotype of the past. Against this background, then, Ghosh's act in reviving the slave Bomma from the fragments of manuscript becomes especially significant. He has written elsewhere how fundamentalists of all religions have recently turned to 'the language of academic historiography' to justify their exclusionary beliefs.[37] His extensive descriptions that use limited textual evidence to recreate the life of twelfth-century Cairo is a counter to such trends. In emphasising in such detail the fragility and partiality of his manuscript sources, he concomitantly registers their materiality; even when he admits novelistic speculations about the past, these are explicitly grounded with reference to a concrete historical source. Early in *In an Antique Land* Ghosh writes of the discovery of the slave of MS. H.6 as providing him with 'a right to be there, a sense of entitlement' (p. 19). This seems to refer most immediately to his position as an Indian in Egypt, but it also gestures more widely to his status as a believer in the possibilities of cosmopolitanism: finding this documentation of an accommodatory past allows for an alternative to a segregatory present to be imagined. Much like many of the other writers discussed in this chapter, Ghosh's turn to history is justified ultimately by how it allows him to reimagine the future.

SUMMARY

- The ways in which histories can be imagined and written may be inseparable from colonial domination, and new forms may be needed accurately to address the past.
- Anita Desai's *Clear Light of Day* shows a family coming to terms

with its personal history, but struggling to confront the inter-related national past.

- In *The God of Small Things* Arundhati Roy frequently renders history itself as an agent enforcing divisions that disempower and alienate individuals.
- Gayatri Chakravorty Spivak has questioned the possibility of ever retrieving subaltern consciousness from colonial or elite nationalist documentation.
- By occupying the voice of a famous Australian icon, Peter Carey in *True History of the Kelly Gang* is able to suggest a way of narrating history divorced from colonial values.
- Sally Morgan's *My Place* uses and simultaneously disrupts the form of autobiography to find a space for silenced cultures.
- Paul Gilroy's Black Atlantic model offers a focus on a history of suffering to transform the humanist tradition to include those previously excluded.
- Caryl Phillips's *The Atlantic Sound* explores the problems involved in diverse strategies for imagining the history of black people in the West.
- The cosmopolitan histories traced in Amitav Ghosh's *In an Antique Land* serve as a material alternative to current modes of global division.

NOTES

1. Antoinette Burton, 'Archive of Bones: *Anil's Ghost* and the Ends of History', *Journal of Commonwealth Literature* 38(1) (2003), 50–1.
2. Hugh Trevor-Roper, *The Rise of Christian Europe* (London: Thames and Hudson, 1965), p. 9.
3. Dipesh Chakrabarty, *Provincializing Europe: Postcolonial Thought and Historical Difference* (Princeton and Oxford: Princeton University Press, 2000), p. 27.
4. Ibid., p. 7.
5. Ibid., p. 11.
6. Ibid., p. 41.
7. Ranajit Guha, 'Introduction', in Ranajit Guha (ed.), *A*

Subaltern Studies Reader, 1986–1995 (Minneapolis and London: Minnesota University Press, 1997), p. xxi.

8. Suvir Kaul, 'Introduction', in Suvir Kaul (ed.), *The Partitions of Memory: the Afterlife of the Division of India* (New Delhi: Permanent Black, 2001), p. 8.

9. Anita Desai, *Clear Light of Day* (London: Vintage, [1980] 2001), p. 21. Further references to this edition are given in the main text.

10. Anita Desai, 'An Oriental Fantasy', *The Book Review* 6(1) (1981), 35–6.

11. Arundhati Roy, *The God of Small Things* (London: Flamingo, 1997), p. 16. Further references to this edition are given in the main text.

12. Arundhati Roy, *The Algebra of Infinite Justice* (London: Flamingo, 2002), p. 167.

13. Aijaz Ahmad, 'Reading Arundhati Roy Politically', *Frontline*, 8 August 1997, 105.

14. Quoted in Gayatri Chakravorty Spivak, 'Can the Subaltern Speak?', in Cary Nelson and Lawrence Grossberg (eds), *Marxism and Interpretation of Culture* (Basingstoke: Macmillan, 1988), p. 284.

15. Gayatri Chakravorty Spivak, *In Other Worlds: Essays in Cultural Politics* (London: Methuen, 1987), p. 203.

16. Spivak, 'Can the Subaltern Speak?', pp. 275–8.

17. Ibid., p. 310.

18. Quoted in Paul Eggert, 'The Bushranger's Voice: Peter Carey's *True History of the Kelly Gang* (2000) and Ned Kelly's *Jerilderie Letter* (1879)', *College Literature* 34(3) (2007), 123.

19. A scanned image of the letter, along with a digital transcription, can be viewed at http://www2.slv.vic.gov.au/collections/treasures/jerilderieletter/index.html

20. Peter Carey, *True History of the Kelly Gang* (London: Faber and Faber, [2000] 2002), p. 234. Further references to this edition are given in the main text.

21. The imaginative connection of Australian settlers to the land is discussed at length in Chapter 2 above.

22. Ibid., p. 360.

23. Bart Moore-Gilbert, *Postcolonial Life-writing: Culture, Politics, and Self-Representation* (London: Routledge, 2009), p. 82.

24. Ibid., p. xix.

25. Edward Hills, '"What Country, Friends, is This?" Sally Morgan's *My Place* Revisited', *Journal of Commonwealth Literature* 32(2) (1997), 104, 109.

26. Sally Morgan, *My Place* (South Fremantle: Fremantle Arts Centre, 1987), pp. 39, 98. Further references to this edition are given in the main text.

27. Graham Huggan, *Australian Literature: Postcolonialism, Racism, Transnationalism* (Oxford: Oxford University Press), p. 108.

28. Hills, 'What Country', p. 105.

29. Paul Gilroy, *The Black Atlantic: Modernity and Double Consciousness* (London: Verso, 1993), p. 29. Further references to this edition are given in the main text.

30. The experience of diaspora is discussed in more detail in Chapter 4 above.

31. James Clifford, 'Traveling Cultures', in Lawrence Grossberg et al. (eds), *Cultural Studies* (New York and London: Routledge, 1992), pp. 96–116.

32. Caryl Phillips, *A New World Order: Selected Essays* (London: Secker and Warburg, 2001), p. 304.

33. Ibid. pp. 1–4.

34. Caryl Phillips, *The Atlantic Sound* (London: Faber and Faber, 2000), p. 16. Further references to this edition are given in the main text.

35. Amitav Ghosh, 'The Slave of MS. H.6', in Partha Chatterjee and Gyanendre Pandey (eds), *Subaltern Studies VII: Writings on South Asian History and Society* (New Delhi: Oxford University Press, 1992).

36. Amitav Ghosh, *In an Antique Land* (London: Granta, 1992), p. 204. Further references to this edition are given in the main text.

37. Amitav Ghosh, *Incendiary Circumstances: a Chronicle of the Turmoil of our Times* (New York: Mariner, 2005), p. 124.

Conclusion

The reader of this introduction to postcolonial literature has been taken through a selection of recent literary texts produced in a range of locations that continue variously to negotiate the pressures of living with a history of colonialism and a present where the patterns of domination and subordination established during that era continue to shape lives. Through arranging this discussion into a group of themes it is hoped that readers have begun to develop a sense of some of the ways in which this greatly diverse body of writing might be usefully compared, but also noted some of the ways in which the notable differences between the texts can be detected, even when they deal with similar ideas. Of course, such general themes as coming of age and the complicated, though necessary, working through of historical inheritance manifest in very varied ways, depending upon the specificities of geographical and historical location, as well as the idiosyncrasies of each writer's, and each text's, particular purpose. Many of these themes are also not confined to postcolonial writers, but reflect aspects of life that writers across all places and times may have touched upon. Nonetheless, the thematic approach is intended to give a (necessarily selective) account of some of the key ideas we can trace in postcolonial literature, and an idea of how, despite the necessary differences, a comparative approach might allow for enhanced insight into the way individual texts operate.

Postcolonial literature has spawned an extensive body of critical

writing and in the Guide to Further Reading that follows this conclusion the reader will find details of some of the most interesting
work done in examining the literature discussed in the preceding
chapters, both in terms of general studies of the field and also
work that looks closely at particular texts. However, choosing the
themes that have structured the discussion so far has inevitably
involved the exclusion of some particularly interesting work that
has approached postcolonial writing in other ways, and found
through such engagement other perspectives which can allow for
productive readings of this literature. It is fitting then to finish
this introduction by looking at some recent critical approaches
that have been neglected in the body of the study, but which may
offer useful tools for examining postcolonial literature further,
or to challenge some of the readings offered so far. Every act of
literary criticism is necessarily partial and the present study is no
exception, but a brief account of some of the roads not taken in the
six chapters above might serve to some degree to acknowledge the
range of other equally valid ways of assessing our topic.

In a pair of recent essays published in the journal *New Literary
History*, the important postcolonial thinkers Robert Young and
Dipesh Chakrabarty reflected on some of the challenges facing
postcolonial studies in the new millennium; identifying what
distinctive social phenomena might need investigation, and the
degree to which postcolonial studies in its existing forms might
be equipped to address them. Looking briefly to these statements
offers a way into opening up the field of postcolonial literary
enquiry beyond those approaches discussed in detail above.

Young's essay picks out three particular areas that he sees as
requiring immediate attention within postcolonial studies. These
include the continuing oppression of the indigenous communities who continue to labour under the burden of settler colonialism, and the growth of transnational networks based on Islam,
topics which have been addressed in part in the discussions above.
However, his third proposed focus for future research, the vast
numbers of people currently engaged in acts of migration, frequently as refugees or because of other pressures which ensure that
their displacements cannot be seen as voluntary, is also a very relevant issue in recent postcolonial literary studies.[1] Extant models of

diaspora need to be radically revised at least to take account of how the specifics of forced migration in the twenty-first century have resulted in new forms of cultural expression that aim to capture the uniqueness of this experience. David Farrier's *Postcolonial Asylum* is an important intervention that maps how the precarious situation of refugees within privileged nations can itself be seen as a continuation of the colonial project, but, perhaps more importantly, revises the theoretical models through which we might understand the concept of hospitality and how these communities negotiate the asylum offered or denied within the spaces they find themselves.[2] The collection *Postcolonial Europe* offers a number of explorations into how the fortress mentality of many contemporary states acts to continue to exclude postcolonial subjects from participation in many of the benefits of twenty-first century life and thereby perpetuates the global division of material advantage.[3] The essays contained here are invaluable in reminding us that these new movements of people inaugurate changes across societies far more broadly than just within the communities themselves.

Chakrabarty's essay agrees with Young in noting the importance of the fact that 'the new subalterns of the global economy – refugees, asylum seekers, illegal workers – can be found all over Europe', but he considers the most important challenge of the twenty-first century to be the need to address climate change. He argues that our models of the human might need revising to account for the situation in which rational humanity may trouble itself over the damage that continues to be inflicted upon our environment, but our species existence seems tied to the perpetuation of this assault.[4] The relationship of humans to their natural environment has, however, been a concern of postcolonial literary studies for some time. The contemporary exploitation of the environment takes very different forms in diverse global locations and it is frequently within the postcolonial world that the most brutally destructive assaults on ecosystems can be found. At the same time, the ways in which postcolonial societies have related to their environments in the past, and the continually evolving ways in which they address present problems, can offer important alternatives to dominant modes of understanding the relationships between human beings and the natural world around them.

Graham Huggan and Helen Tiffin's *Postcolonial Ecocriticism* is a good introduction to several of the key issues in this growing field, while the essays in *Postcolonial Ecologies*, edited by Elizabeth DeLoughrey and George B. Handley, offer sophisticated ways into reading what the editors called 'the aesthetics of the earth'.[5] We are all shaped by the material conditions within which we experience our environment and this strand of postcolonial thought develops the idea that this might fundamentally shape the types of cultural text we produce, in terms of both content and form.

In a response to Chakrabarty's essay, Benita Parry argues that his view fails to recognise how environmental issues need to be thought together with economic questions 'as an immense bundle of human and extra-human relations and processes organized through the mode of production'.[6] The Marxist current within postcolonial studies, which insists always on recognising the centrality of material conditions of exploitation, is well represented in Parry's own work and elsewhere.[7] While the relationship between economic relations and the manifold forms of cultural expression is rarely straightforward, such Marxist-orientated discussion reminds us that the link should never be overlooked, and that, given how so much of everyday existence is determined by the production and distribution of economic capital, a close attention to the latter may be essential to understand how the former is worked through in literature.

Such attention to the global division of wealth has proved particularly important in theorisations of globalisation, which is perhaps the dominant model used to describe international relationships in the twenty-first century. The idea that certain cultural forms have spread to all corners of the world cannot be denied, but it is important also to note how local differences continue to shape the ways in which people relate to them. While globalisation has frequently been indicted as the new imperialism, and undoubtedly consists in part of new forms of economic exploitation, some critics have looked to explore the possibilities it may offer in allowing for a network of oppositional philosophies as much as reproducing a logic of uneven development – the local variations exerted upon the globally dominant forms may reveal that the logic of economic power might yet be challenged by its diffusion in cultural forms.

Suman Gupta has summarised these debates well and the superb range of extracts in Liam Connell and Nicky Marsh's reader contain both positive and negative responses to the global age, as well as positions that fall somewhere in between.[8]

One extremely influential attempt to draw together the structures of a global economy with the types of critique often found within postcolonial literary texts is Graham Huggan's *The Postcolonial Exotic*, which highlights how postcolonial literature frequently displays writers' awareness that the processes through which their texts are consumed in privileged societies might not be that different from other ways in which value is extracted from the postcolonial world. Rather than simply being complicit in this exploitation, Huggan argues, literature can simultaneously offer critique from its location within these networks of value.[9] Some of these ideas have been usefully extended by Sarah Brouillette, while a recent wealth of studies concerning the production, dissemination and consumption of postcolonial texts remind us that works of literature are not only the vehicles for ideas or aesthetic pleasures, but also commodities that have a very material existence in a globalised world.[10]

The reminder that postcolonial literary texts do not exist in a vacuum, and that literature is shaped as much by the logic of the market as by the possibilities of the imagination seems a useful note on which to end this study. Postcolonial literature frequently excites its readers through its aesthetic ambition, through the ways in which it takes the materials that allow for the construction of literary meaning and utilises them in producing artistically fresh and invigorating forms, but to read this literature only in terms of its imaginative achievements is to get only part of the story. Reading and comparing postcolonial literary works allows for an engagement with the multiple histories that make up our divided world, and an insight into how these imbalances might shape contemporary experiences in diverse global locations. The responses that writers offer to these situations will vary enormously, even if we might understand each unique condition a little better through comparing them to others. We hopefully become more sensitive to the continuing material struggles which people live through in different places by paying attention to the cultural texts they produce, but we are fortunate also to find in these works a powerful, compelling and frequently unexpected renewal of what the literary is able to achieve.

NOTES

1. Robert J. C. Young, 'Postcolonial Remains', *New Literary History* 43(1) (2012), 19–42.
2. David Farrier, *Postcolonial Asylum: Seeking Sanctuary before the Law* (Liverpool: Liverpool University Press, 2011).
3. *Postcolonial Europe*, special issue of *Moving Worlds* 11(2) (2011).
4. Dipesh Chakrabarty, 'Postcolonial Studies and the Challenge of Climate Change', *New Literary History* 43(1) (2012), 8, 9–15.
5. Graham Huggan and Helen Tiffin, *Postcolonial Ecocriticism: Literature, Animals, Environment* (Abingdon and New York: Routledge, 2010); Elizabeth DeLoughrey and George B. Handley, *Postcolonial Ecologies: Literatures of the Environment* (New York: Oxford University Press, 2011).
6. Mike Niblett, quoted in Benita Parry, 'What is Left in Postcolonial Studies?', *New Literary History* 43(2) (2012), 346–7.
7. Benita Parry, *Postcolonial Studies: a Materialist Critique* (London and New York: Routledge, 2004); Crystal Bartolovich and Neil Lazarus (eds), *Marxism, Modernity and Postcolonial Studies* (Cambridge and New York: Cambridge University Press, 2002).
8. Suman Gupta, *Globalization and Literature* (Cambridge and Malden, MA: Polity, 2009); Liam Connell and Nicky Marsh, *Literature and Globalization: a Reader* (Abingdon and New York: Routledge, 2010).
9. Graham Huggan, *The Postcolonial Exotic: Marketing the Margins* (London and New York: Routledge, 2001).
10. Sarah Brouillette, *Postcolonial Writers in the Global Literary Marketplace* (Basingstoke and New York: Palgrave Macmillan, 2007); Robert Fraser, *Book History through Postcolonial Eyes:*

Rewriting the Script (Abingdon and New York: Routledge, 2008); Gail Low, *Publishing the Postcolonial: Anglophone West African and Caribbean Writing in the UK, 1948–1968* (London and New York: Routledge, 2010); Bethan Benwell et al. (eds), *Postcolonial Audiences: Readers, Viewers and Reception* (London and New York: Routledge, 2012).

Student Resources

General

The student who wishes to study postcolonial literature can sometimes be put off by the complexity of postcolonial theorising, but even the toughest thinker can seem less daunting once one begins to tackle them. The essays of Homi Bhabha and Gayatri Chakravorty Spivak, for example (as collected in the former's *The Location of Culture* and the latter's *In Other Worlds* and *Outside in the Teaching Machine*), are certainly complex, but do reward careful and sustained attention. Very helpful introductions to the works of these writers have been written by Eleanor Byrne, David Huddart and Stephen Morton, while they are addressed together (along with Edward Said, completing the trinity that, certainly in the 1990s, were often together seen to have founded 'postcolonial studies') in Bart Moore-Gilbert's *Postcolonial Theory: Contexts, Practices, Politics*. Robert Young's ambitious *Postcolonialism: an Historical Introduction* attempts to draw together the political history of decolonisation with later theoretical critiques (although the reader who seeks detailed historical contexts in order to illuminate their studies of postcolonial writing would do well to consult the encyclopaedia-style *A Historical Companion to Postcolonial Literatures in English*, edited by Prem Poddar and David Johnson).

There are, of course, many writers who have contributed to the diverse corpus of postcolonial theory, and looking beyond the most famous of these can yield a number of different insights and make it clear that there are manifold ways of engaging with the postcolonial. There are a large number of anthologies available that collect some of the most significant statements made in advancing postcolonial studies; the best is still probably *The Post-Colonial Studies Reader*, edited by Bill Ashcroft, Gareth Griffiths and Helen Tiffin. The second edition of this book contains extracts from more than 120 critical works, covering a huge range of topics and approaches and including alongside some of the best-known work other texts that are far more difficult for most readers to access. Most of the material included in this reader is greatly abridged to allow for breadth of coverage; of the anthologies that offer longer versions of texts, the best may well be Gregory Castle's *Postcolonial Discourses*, which helpfully groups its texts by region. Of the many introductory books that offer discussions of issues within postcolonial studies, readers may find the clearest guide in John McLeod's *Beginning Postcolonialism*, though Jenni Ramone's *Postcolonial Theories* also introduces some key theoretical ideas through reference to a handful of literary texts.

There are several excellent theoretical studies that argue for the importance of paying close attention to literary detail in reading postcolonial texts: of particular note are studies by Nicholas Harrison, Ato Quayson and Neil Lazarus. Quayson is also the editor of the fullest survey of postcolonial literary history: the two-volume *Cambridge History of Postcolonial Literature*, which has thirty-six chapters exploring the writing of a great range of locations and tracing many diverse themes. Of the more concise literary guides, those by Elleke Boehmer and C. L. Innes are particularly useful. Nearly all introductions to postcolonial writing give over more space to prose fiction than to poetry, so two useful introductions that focus on the latter are Rajeev Patke's *Postcolonial Poetry in English* and Jahan Ramazani's *The Hybrid Muse*.

- Bill Ashcroft et al. (eds), *The Post-Colonial Studies Reader*, 2nd edn (London: Routledge, 2006).
- Homi K. Bhabha, *The Location of Culture* (London: Routledge, 1994).

- Elleke Boehmer, *Colonial and Postcolonial Literature: Migrant Metaphors*, 2nd edn (Oxford: Oxford University Press, 2005).
- Eleanor Byrne, *Homi K. Bhabha* (Basingstoke: Palgrave Macmillan, 2009).
- Gregory Castle (ed.), *Postcolonial Discourses: an Anthology* (Oxford: Blackwell, 2001).
- Nicholas Harrison, *Postcolonial Criticism: History, Theory and the Work of Fiction* (Cambridge: Polity Press, 2003).
- David Huddart, *Homi K. Bhabha* (London: Routledge, 2006).
- C. L. Innes, *The Cambridge Introduction to Postcolonial Literatures in English* (Cambridge: Cambridge University Press, 2007).
- Neil Lazarus, *The Postcolonial Unconscious* (Cambridge: Cambridge University Press, 2011).
- John McLeod, *Beginning Postcolonialism*, 2nd edn (Manchester: Manchester University Press, 2010).
- Bart Moore-Gilbert, *Postcolonial Theory: Contexts, Practices, Politics* (London: Verso, 1997).
- Stephen Morton, *Gayatri Chakravorty Spivak* (London: Routledge, 2003).
- Rajeev Patke, *Postcolonial Poetry in English* (Oxford: Oxford University Press, 2006).
- Prem Poddar and David Johnson (eds), *A Historical Companion to Postcolonial Literatures in English* (Edinburgh: Edinburgh University Press, 2005).
- Ato Quayson, *Calibrations: Reading for the Social* (Minneapolis: University of Minnesota Press, 2003).
- Ato Quayson (ed.), *The Cambridge History of Postcolonial Literature* (Cambridge: Cambridge University Press, 2012).
- Jahan Ramazani, *The Hybrid Muse: Postcolonial Poetry in English* (Chicago: University of Chicago Press, 2001).
- Jenni Ramone, *Postcolonial Theories* (Basingstoke: Palgrave Macmillan, 2011).
- Gayatri Chakravorty Spivak, *In Other Worlds: Essays in Cultural Politics* (London: Methuen, 1987).
- Gayatri Chakravorty Spivak, *Outside in the Teaching Machine* (New York: Routledge, 1993).
- Robert J. C. Young, *Postcolonialism: an Historical Introduction* (Oxford: Blackwell, 2001).

Chapter 1 Finding a Voice

While the seminal recent study of language in postcolonial writing is Ashcroft, Griffiths and Tiffin's *The Empire Writes Back*, Ashcroft's revision of some of their ideas in his more recent *Caliban's Voice* is also very useful. Elsewhere, Ismail S. Talib's *The Language of Postcolonial Literatures* offers a thorough discussion of the issues involved. Ngũgĩ wa Thiong'o's important attack on the use of English in *Decolonising the Mind* can usefully be read alongside Kamau Brathwaite's equally seminal text *The History of the Voice* which charts how a particular regional English find its uniqueness in breaking away from standard forms. The anthology (Ahmed [ed.]) *Rotten English* contains some excellent examples of post-colonial texts manipulating the English language as well as reflection from writers on the value of doing so.

Readers interested in studying Derek Walcott further will find a wealth of material discussing his work: an especially useful place to start is John Thieme's *Derek Walcott*, though other very good surveys of his work have been written by Paul Breslin and Paula Burnett, while Bruce King's biography is invaluable for tracing his development. Approaching Eavan Boland is made much easier by the existence of *Eavan Boland: A Sourcebook*, edited by Jody Ann Randolph, which collects many of Boland's own writings in both verse and prose, as well as interviews she has given over the years, and extracts from critical discussions of her work. Randolph also jointly edited a special issue of *Irish University Review* on Boland; her essay in this collection contains an excellent discussion of the poet's exploration of literary 'authority'. Nissim Ezekiel is pro-ductively read alongside two of his near contemporaries in Bruce King's *Three Indian Poets*, while the 'Indian English' poems in particular have been closely read by Vinoda and Shiv Kumar. The special issue of *Interventions* that marked the fiftieth anniversary of Chinua Achebe's *Things Fall Apart* is invaluable in tracing the influence of this seminal postcolonial text, while more general introductions to Achebe's work have been provided by Nahem Yousef and Jago Morrison. Morrison has also written an excellent article exploring the politics of Ken Saro-Wiwa's *Sozaboy*, as have Michael North and G. 'Ebinyo Ogbowei and Ibiere Bell-Gam.

Useful approaches to Keri Hulme's *The Bone People* that explore its linguistic strategies and its positing of biculturalism can be found in articles by Phillip Armstrong and Elvira Pulitano.

- Dohra Ahmed (ed.), *Rotten English: A Literary Anthology* (New York: W. W. Norton, 2007).
- Phillip Armstrong, 'Good-Eating: Ethics and Biculturalism in Reading *The Bone People*', *ARIEL: a Review of International English Literature* 32(2) (2001), 7–27.
- Bill Ashcroft, *Caliban's Voice: the Transformation of English in Post-colonial Literatures* (London: Routledge, 2009).
- Bill Ashcroft et al., *The Empire Writes Back*, 2nd edn (London: Routledge, 2002).
- Kamau Brathwaite, *History of the Voice: the Development of Nation Language in Anglophone Caribbean Poetry* (London: New Beacon, 1984).
- Paul Breslin, *Nobody's Nation: Reading Derek Walcott* (Chicago: Chicago University Press, 2001).
- Paula Burnett, *Derek Walcott: Politics and Poetics* (Gainesville: University Press of Florida, 2000).
- Bruce King, *Derek Walcott: a Caribbean Life* (Oxford: Oxford University Press, 2000).
- Bruce King, *Three Indian Poets: Ezekiel, Moraes, and Ramanujan*, 2nd edn (Delhi: Oxford University Press, 2005).
- Vinoda Kumar and Shiv Kumar, 'The Indianness of Ezekiel's "Indian English Poems": an Analysis', *Kunapipi* 9(1) (1987), 21–9.
- Jago Morrison, 'Imagined Biafras: Fabricating Nation in Nigerian Civil War Writing, *ARIEL: a Review of International English Literature* 36(1/2) (2005), 5–26.
- Jago Morrison, *The Fiction of Chinua Achebe* (Basingstoke: Palgrave Macmillan, 2007).
- Michael North, 'Ken Saro-Wiwa's *Sozaboy*: the Politics of "Rotten English"', *Public Culture* 13(1) (2001), 97–112.
- G. 'Ebinyo Ogbowei and Ibiere Bell-Gam, '*Sozaboy*: Language and a Disordered World', *English Studies in Africa* 38(1) (1995), 1–17.
- Elvira Pulitano, '"In Vain I Tried to Tell You": Crossreading

Strategies in Global Literature', *World Literature Written in English* 39(2) (2002–3), 52–70.

- Jody Ann Randolph, 'Private Worlds, Public Realities: Eavan Boland's Poetry 1967–1990', *Irish University Review* 23(1) (1993), 5–22.
- Jody Ann Randolph (ed.), *Eavan Boland: a Sourcebook: Poetry, Prose, Interviews, Reviews and Criticism* (Manchester: Carcanet, 2007).
- Ismail S. Talib, *The Language of Postcolonial Literatures: an Introduction* (London: Routledge, 2002).
- John Thieme, *Derek Walcott* (Manchester: Manchester University Press, 1999).
- *'Things Fall Apart* at 50', special issue of *Interventions* 11(2) (2009).
- Ngũgĩ wa Thiong'o, *Decolonising the Mind: the Politics of Language in African Literature* (London: James Currey, 1986).
- Nahem Yousef, *Chinua Achebe* (Tavistock: Northcote House, 2003).

Chapter 2   The Need to Belong

Sara Upstone's *Spatial Politics in the Postcolonial Novel* offers a very effective introduction to the question of how space has been explored in postcolonial fiction, while the issue of establishing space has also been usefully discussed in works by Paul Carter and Graham Huggan. Establishing belonging within the postcolonial city has been explored in John McLeod's *Postcolonial London* and Rashmi Varma's *The Postcolonial City and its Subjects*. The refiguring of the nation as a structure held together by imagination that was set in place by Benedict Anderson's *Imagined Communities* is expertly explored in diverse literary contexts in Homi Bhabha's influential collection *Nation and Narration*.

Readers who wish to know more about Patrick White will benefit from a recent collection of essays edited by Elizabeth McMahon and Brigitta Olubas, while William Walsh's general introduction is undoubtedly dated but still very useful. Steven Matthews's *Les Murray* is a thorough introduction to the poet, while the essays in Carmel Gaffney's collection explore a number of aspects of his writing in detail. Susheila Nasta's *Critical Perspectives on Sam Selvon* contains a strong selection of earlier critical material on the writer, while there are excellent discussions of *The Lonely Londoners* in the studies of black British literature written by James Procter and Ashley Dawson. No sustained critical readings have yet appeared of James Berry's *Windrush Songs* collection, but excellent essays on his earlier poetry by Stewart Brown and Wolfgang Binder set up interesting critical frameworks through which the later work can be interpreted. Coetzee's *Disgrace* has attracted enormous amounts of critical attention; some of the best can be found in the special issue of *Interventions* dedicated to the novel. The novel is also thoroughly explored in Hania Nashef's *The Politics of Humiliation in the Novels of J. M. Coetzee*, while Andrew Van der Vlies's short guide to the novel is excellent for filling in contextual details that the non-South African reader may not register.

- Benedict Anderson, *Imagined Communities: Reflections on the Origin and Spread of Nationalism*, revised edn (London: Verso, 2006).
- Homi K. Bhabha (ed.), *Nation and Narration* (London: Routledge, 1990).
- Wolfgang Binder, 'Learning to Live in London: James Berry', *Commonwealth Essays and Studies* 10(2) (1988), 26–33.
- Stewart Brown, 'James Berry – Celebration Songs', *Kunapipi* 20(1) (1988), 45–56.
- Paul Carter, *The Road to Botany Bay: an Essay in Spatial History* (London: Faber and Faber, 1987).
- Ashley Dawson, *Mongrel Nation: Diasporic Culture and the Making of Postcolonial Britain* (Ann Arbor: University of Michigan Press, 2007).
- Carmel Gaffney (ed.), *Counterbalancing Light: Essays on the Poetry of Les Murray* (Armidale: Kardoorair, 1997).
- Graham Huggan, *Territorial Disputes: Maps and Mapping Strategies in Contemporary Canadian and Australian Fiction* (Toronto: University of Toronto Press, 1994).
- 'J. M. Coetzee's *Disgrace*', special issue of *Interventions* 4(3) (2002).

- Steven Matthews, *Les Murray* (Manchester: Manchester University Press, 2001).
- John McLeod, *Postcolonial London: Rewriting the Metropolis* (London: Routledge, 2004).
- Elizabeth McMahon and Brigitta Olubas (eds), *Remembering Patrick White: Contemporary Critical Essays* (Amsterdam: Rodopi, 2010).
- Hania A. M. Nashef, *The Politics of Humiliation in the Novels of J. M. Coetzee* (Abingdon: Routledge, 2009).
- Susheila Nasta (ed.), *Critical Perspectives on Sam Selvon* (Washington, DC: Three Continents, 1988).
- James Procter, *Dwelling Places: Postwar Black British Writing* (Manchester: Manchester University Press, 2003).
- Sara Upstone, *Spatial Politics in the Postcolonial Novel* (Farnham, VT: Ashgate, 2009).
- Andrew Van der Vlies, *J. M. Coetzee's Disgrace* (London: Continuum).
- Rashmi Varma, *The Postcolonial City and its Subjects: London, Nairobi, Bombay* (London: Routledge, 2012).
- William Walsh, *Patrick White's Fiction* (Sydney: Allen and Unwin, 1977).

Chapter 3 Coming of Age, Coming into Difference

The significance of the child as a device through which writers might stage enquiries into postcolonial societies is usefully theorised in the introduction to Clare Barker's study of the disabled child in postcolonial fiction, and explored through a number of examples in Meenakshi Bharat's *The Ultimate Colony*; and a brief but helpful account of the postcolonial *bildungsroman* is given in Julie Mullaney's *Postcolonial Literatures in Context*. Jameson's essay on national allegory, and indeed Ahmad's critique of it, have become standard texts in postcolonial literary studies and a good account of the debate and ways out of its impasse has been provided by Brian Larkin; Imre Szeman has also provided useful tools for reinvigorating Jameson's argument, while Neelam Srivastava's *Secularism in the Postcolonial Indian Novel* contains a subtle development of the idea that makes the terms of the debate more precise.

The representation of sexualities that articulate differently from the norm in postcolonial societies has been interestingly explored in a number of works: Gayatri Gopinath and John Hawley have provided a couple of the best.

While it does not discuss *A Star Called Henry*, an excellent reading of Roddy Doyle's relation to the Irish nation can be found in Gerry Smyth's *The Novel and the Nation* and a detailed account of the novel itself in relation to debates around Irish history in Michael Pierse's *Writing Ireland's Working Class*; a thorough general account of the writer and his work has been written by Dermot McCarthy. While no monographs have been written about Shyam Selvadurai, Minoli Salgado's *Writing Sri Lanka* is very helpful in locating him in relation to his compatriots; meanwhile, Andrew Lesk and Sharanya Jayawickrama have authored very interesting articles on his *Funny Boy*. A special issue of the *Journal of West Indian Literature* has collected a number of excellent articles on Shani Mootoo, while first-class discussion of *Cereus Blooms at Night* can also be found in an article by Miriam Pirbhai and as part of Alison Donnell's *Twentieth-century Caribbean Literature*. Ann Elizabeth Willey and Jeanette Treiber's collection of essays offers a broad range of perspectives on Tsitsi Dangarembga's work; excellent discussions of *Nervous Conditions* can be found in works by Charles Sugnet and Ranka Primorac. Philip Tew has written an excellent introduction to the work of Zadie Smith, while diverse arguments about *White Teeth* can be found in discussions by Nick Bentley and Molly Thompson, as well as in Dave Gunning's *Race and Antiracism in Black British and British Asian Writing*.

- Aijaz Ahmad, *In Theory: Nations, Classes, Literature* (London: Verso, 1992), pp. 95–122.
- Clare Barker, *Postcolonial Fiction and Disability: Exceptional Children, Metaphor and Materiality* (Basingstoke: Palgrave Macmillan, 2011).
- Nick Bentley, 'Re-writing Englishness: Imagining the Nation in Julian Barnes's *England, England* and Zadie Smith's *White Teeth*', *Textual Practice* 21(3) (2007), 483–504.
- Meenakshi Bharat, *The Ultimate Colony: the Child in Postcolonial Fiction* (New Delhi: Allied, 2003).

- Alison Donnell, *Twentieth-century Caribbean Literature: Critical Moments in Anglophone Literary History* (Abingdon: Routledge, 2006).
- Gayatri Gopinath, *Impossible Desires: Queer Diaspora and South Asian Public Cultures* (Durham, NC: Duke University Press, 2005).
- Dave Gunning, *Race and Antiracism in Black British and British Asian Literature* (Liverpool: Liverpool University Press, 2010), pp. 126–36.
- John C. Hawley, *Postcolonial, Queer: Theoretical Intersections* (Albany: SUNY Press, 2001).
- Fredric Jameson, 'Third-world Literature in the Era of Multinational Capitalism', *Social Text* 15 (1986), 65–88.
- Sharanya Jayawickrama, 'At Home in the Nation? Negotiating Identity in Shyam Selvadurai's *Funny Boy*', *Journal of Commonwealth Literature* 40(2) (2005), 123–39.
- Brian Larkin, 'National Allegory', *Social Text* 27(3) (2009), 164–8.
- Andrew Lesk, 'Ambivalence at the Site of Authority: Desire and Difference in *Funny Boy*', *Canadian Literature* 190 (2006), 31–46.
- Dermot McCarthy, *Roddy Doyle: Raining on the Parade* (Dublin: Liffey, 2003).
- Julie Mullaney, *Postcolonial Literatures in Context* (London: Continuum, 2010).
- Michael Pierse, *Writing Ireland's Working Class* (Basingstoke: Palgrave Macmillan, 2010).
- Miriam Pirbhai, 'Sexuality as (Counter)Discourse and Hybridity as Healing Practice in Shani Mootoo's *Cereus Blooms at Night*', *Journal of Caribbean Literatures* 4(1) (2005), 174–84.
- Ranka Primorac, *The Place of Tears: the Novel and Politics in Modern Zimbabwe* (London: Taurus, 2006).
- Minoli Salgado, *Writing Sri Lanka: Literature, Resistance and the Politics of Place* (London: Routledge, 2009).
- 'Shani Mootoo: Writing, Difference and the Caribbean', special issue of *Journal of West Indian Literature* 19(2) (2011).
- Gerry Smyth, *The Novel and the Nation: Studies in the New Irish Fiction* (London: Pluto, 1997).

- Neelam Srivastava, 'Allegory and Realism', in *Secularism in the Postcolonial Indian Novel: National and Cosmopolitan Narratives in English* (Abingdon: Routledge, 2008), pp. 88–109.
- Charles Sugnet, '*Nervous Conditions*: Dangarembga's Feminist Reinvention of Fanon', in Obioma Nnaemeka (ed.), *The Politics of (M)Othering: Womanhood, Identity and Resistance in African Literature* (London: Routledge, 1997), pp. 33–49.
- Imre Szeman, *Zones of Instability: Literature, Postcolonialism and the Nation* (Baltimore: Johns Hopkins University Press, 2003).
- Philip Tew, *Zadie Smith* (Basingstoke: Palgrave Macmillan, 2009).
- Molly Thompson, '"Happy Multicultural Land"? The Implications of an "Excess of Belonging" in Zadie Smith's *White Teeth*', in Kadija Sesay (ed.), *Write Black, Write British: from Post Colonial to Black British Literature* (Hertford: Hansib, 2005), pp. 122–40.
- Ann Elizabeth Willey and Jeanette Treiber (eds), *Negotiating the Postcolonial: Emerging Perspectives on Tsitsi Dangarembga* (Trenton, NJ: Africa World, 2002).

Chapter 4 Communities, Values, Transgressions

Important recent discussions of community, its attractions and its dangers, are articulated from very different perspectives in recent works by Kwame Appiah, Zygmunt Bauman and Michael Hardt and Antonio Negri. An introduction to why questions of identity can seem so pressing in the contemporary era is given in Stuart Hall's excellent 'Who Needs Identity?' Questions of diaspora communities have been explored in works by Avtah Brah and Roger Bromley and more recently in a useful comparative collection edited by Michelle Keown, David Murphy and James Procter. Michael M. J. Fischer and Mehdi Abedi and Peter Mandaville have written helpfully on the contemporary character of the Muslim *umma*, while Amin Malak has provided useful tools for understanding the literary manifestations of Islamic ideas.

Dominic Head's introduction to Nadine Gordimer is very useful for understanding how *Burger's Daughter* fits into her developing political and aesthetic framework, while Judie Newman's 'casebook' on the novel draws together an excellent selection of critics to illuminate it. Arnold Davidson, Priscilla Walton and Jennifer Andrews's *Border Crossings* is a great introduction to the work of Thomas King while Robin Ridington helpfully unpacks the ways in which *Truth and Bright Water* contains its contexts. There are several introductions to the works of Salman Rushdie, though the recent ones by Stephen Morton and by Andrew Teverson are probably the best; the definitive reading of *The Satanic Verses* in terms of diaspora is probably Homi Bhabha's; and the diverse perspectives gathered in the *Public Culture* symposium dedicated to the novel are well worth reading. The Rushdie Affair is well documented in Malise Ruthven's book on the topic as well as in the collection of newspaper stories and other contemporary sources compiled by Lisa Appignanesi and Sara Maitland. Leila Aboulela's work is discussed at length in Geoffrey Nash's *The Anglo-Arab Encounter*, as well as in more recent pieces by Sadia Abbas and Lindsey Moore. Finally, while Hamid's *The Reluctant Fundamentalist* has not seen a huge amount of published critical material as yet, Peter Morey's and Anna Hartnell's articles indicate that it certainly contains the potential for such research.

- Sadia Abbas, 'Leila Aboulela, Religion, and the Challenge of the Novel', *Contemporary Literature* 52(3) (2011), 430–61.
- Kwame Anthony Appiah, *The Ethics of Identity* (Princeton: Princeton University Press, 2005).
- Lisa Appignanesi and Sara Maitland, *The Rushdie File* (London: Institute of Contemporary Arts, 1990).
- Zygmunt Bauman, *Community: Seeking Safety in an Insecure World* (Cambridge: Polity, 2001).
- Homi K. Bhabha, *The Location of Culture* (London: Routledge, 1994), pp. 166–70, 222–9
- Avtah Brah, *Cartographies of Diaspora: Contesting Identities* (London: Routledge, 1996).
- Roger Bromley, *Narratives for a New Belonging: Diasporic Cultural Fictions* (Edinburgh: Edinburgh University Press, 2000).
- Arnold E. Davidson et al., *Border Crossings: Thomas King's*

Cultural Inversions (Toronto: University of Toronto Press, 2003).

- Michael M. J. Fischer and Mehdi Abedi (eds), *Debating Muslims: Cultural Dialogues in Postmodernity and Tradition* (Madison: University of Wisconsin Press, 1990).
- Stuart Hall, 'Introduction – Who Needs Identity?', in Stuart Hall and Paul du Gay (eds), *Questions of Cultural Identity* (London: Sage, 1996), pp. 1–17.
- Michael Hardt and Antonio Negri, *Multitude: War and Democracy in the Age of Empire* (London: Penguin, 2005).
- Anna Hartnell, 'Moving through America: Race, Place and Resistance in Mohsin Hamid's *The Reluctant Fundamentalist*', *Journal of Postcolonial Writing* 46(3–4) (2010), 336–48.
- Dominic Head, *Nadine Gordimer* (Cambridge: Cambridge University Press, 1994).
- Michelle Keown et al. (eds), *Comparing Postcolonial Diasporas* (Basingstoke: Palgrave, 2009).
- Amin Malak, *Muslim Narratives and the Discourse of English* (Albany: SUNY Press, 2005).
- Peter Mandaville, *Transnational Muslim Politics: Reimagining the Umma* (London: Routledge, 2001).
- Lindsey Moore, 'Voyages In and Out: Two (British) Arab Muslim Women's Bildungsromane', in Rehana Ahmed et al. (eds), *Culture, Diaspora and Modernity in Muslim Writing* (London: Routledge, 2012), pp. 65–84.
- Peter Morey, 'The Rules of the Game Have Changed': Mohsin Hamid's *The Reluctant Fundamentalist* and Post-9/11 Fiction', *Journal of Postcolonial Writing* 47(2) (2011), 135–46.
- Stephen Morton, *Salman Rushdie: Fictions of Postcolonial Modernity* (Basingstoke: Palgrave Macmillan, 2008).
- Geoffrey Nash, *The Anglo-Arab Encounter: Fiction and Autobiography by Arab Writers in English* (Bern: Peter Lang, 2007).
- Judie Newman (ed.), *Nadine Gordimer's* Burger's Daughter*: a Casebook* (Oxford: Oxford University Press, 2003).
- Robin Ridington, 'Happy Trails to You: Contexted Discourse and Indian Removals in Thomas King's *Truth & Bright Water*', *Canadian Literature* 167 (2000), 89–107.

- 'The Rushdie Debate', *Public Culture* 2(1) (1989), 79–122.
- Malise Ruthven, *A Satanic Affair: Salman Rushdie and the Rage of Islam* (London: Chatto and Windus, 1990).
- Andrew Teverson, *Salman Rushdie* (Manchester: Manchester University Press, 2007).

Chapter 5 War Zones

John Marx has offered the beginnings of a typology of literature that address the types of conflict faced by postcolonial societies, while the special issue of *African Literature Today* on war develops a number of approaches specifically related to that continent. Stef Craps's *Postcolonial Witnessing* is an examination of how specifically postcolonial traumas are played out in cultural representations. Fanon's ideas are well laid out in Nigel Gibson's study, while the trend in postcolonial thought that develops his version of nationalism is perhaps best represented by Neil Lazarus's *Nationalism and Cultural Practice in the Postcolonial World*. Mbembe's view of postcolonial Africa as characterised by violence is detailed most fully in his *On the Postcolony*, while Stephen Morton and Stephen Bygraves's collection on biopolitics has several important writers reassessing how this model might explain contemporary social orders.

Rob Nixon's very critical overview of V. S. Naipaul is an important study, though Suman Gupta's is a little more balanced. Lynda Prescott's early article on *A Bend in the River* remains one of the best sources for understanding the structure of the novel. Little critical work has yet been done on Tahmima Anam's *A Golden Age*, excepting Louise Harrington's discussion of the novel, but readers can explore the history that inspires the novel, and in Nazneen Ahmed's work on the pre-1971 history of Bangladeshi cultural nationalism many of the concerns of the text can be traced. Agha Shahid Ali's *The Country without a Post Office* is read as part of Jahan Ramazani's *A Transnational Poetics* and Ananya Jahanara Kabir's *Territory of Desire* includes it as part of a wide-ranging enquiry into how the Kashmiri conflict has been represented. Generally, Chris Abani's novels have received far more attention than his poetry but the discussions of how his work has reformulated questions around human rights by Mitchum Huehls and Maureen Moynagh offer interesting insights into the project of 'Buffalo Women'. In contrast, Michael Ondaatje has been the subject of a wealth of criticism: articles by David Farrier, Victoria Burrows and Ashley Halpé are particularly good ways into exploring *Anil's Ghost*, while Lee Spinks's book on the author offers a good general overview of his work.

- Nazneen Ahmed, 'The Poetics of Nationalism: Cultural Resistance and Poetry in East Pakistan/Bangladesh, 1952–71', *Journal of Postcolonial Writing* (2012). DOI: 10.1080/17449855.2012.695745
- Victoria Burrows, 'The Heterotopic Spaces of Postcolonial Trauma in Michael Ondaatje's *Anil's Ghost*', *Studies in the Novel* 40 (1/2) (2008), 161–77.
- Stef Craps, *Postcolonial Witnessing: Trauma Out of Bounds* (Basingstoke: Palgrave, 2012).
- David Farrier, 'Gesturing Towards the Local: Intimate Histories in *Anil's Ghost*', *Journal of Postcolonial Writing* 41(1) (2005), 83–93.
- Nigel Gibson, *Frantz Fanon: the Postcolonial Imagination* (Cambridge: Polity, 2003).
- Suman Gupta, *V. S. Naipaul* (Tavistock: Northcote House, 1999).
- Ashley Halpé, '*Anil's Ghost* as Symphonic Poem: Viewed in the Context of Michael Ondaatje's Re-engagements with Sri Lanka', *Moving Worlds* 10(2), 92–9.
- Louise Harrington, 'An-Other Space: Diasporic Responses to Partition in Bengal', in Rita Christian and Judith Misrahi-Barak (eds), *India and the Diasporic Imagination* (Montpellier: Presses Universitaires de la Méditerranée, 2011), pp. 237–50.
- Mitchum Huehls, 'Referring to the Human in Contemporary Human Rights Literature', *Modern Fiction Studies* 58(1) (2012), 1–2.
- Ananya Jahanara Kabir, *Territory of Desire: Representing the Valley of Kashmir* (Minneapolis: University of Minnesota Press).
- Neil Lazarus, *Nationalism and Cultural Practice in the Postcolonial World* (Cambridge: Cambridge University Press, 1999).

- John Marx, 'Failed-State Fiction', *Contemporary Literature* 49(4) (2008), 597–633; 'War in African Literature', *African Literature Today* 26 (2008).
- Achille Mbembe, *On the Postcolony* (Berkeley: University of California Press, 2001).
- Stephen Morton and Stephen Bygrave (eds), *Foucault in an Age of Terror: Essays on Biopolitics and the Defence of Society* (Basingstoke: Palgrave, 2008).
- Maureen Moynagh, 'Human Rights, Child-Soldier Narratives and the Problem of Form', *Research in African Literatures* 42(4) (2011), 39–59.
- Rob Nixon, *London Calling: V. S. Naipaul, Postcolonial Mandarin* (Oxford: Oxford University Press, 1992).
- Lynda Prescott, 'Past and Present Darkness: Sources for V. S. Naipaul's *A Bend in the River*', *Modern Fiction Studies* 30 (1984), 547–59.
- Jahan Ramazani, *A Transnational Poetics* (Chicago and London: Chicago University Press, 2009).
- Richard Sisson and Leo E. Rose, *War and Secession: Pakistan, India, and the Creation of Bangladesh* (Berkeley: University of California Press, 1990).
- Lee Spinks, *Michael Ondaatje* (Manchester: Manchester University Press, 2008).

Chapter 6 Challenging Histories

Some of the most significant historical enquiries of the Subaltern Studies Collective, together with theoretical reflections on the project, are gathered in a handful of anthologies (edited by Vinayak Chaturvedi, Ranajit Guha, and Guha and Spivak), while Rochona Majumdar's *Writing Postcolonial History*, aimed at student historians, is a very clear guide to many of the important debates. Spivak's theorising of the subaltern is usefully explored in an interview with Donna Landry and Gerald MacLean, and Rosalind Morris's book offers a range of perspectives on the impact of Spivak's influential essay. The afterlife of Paul Gilroy's *The Black Atlantic* is summarised skilfully in Lucy Evans's review of responses to the study and the possibilities it opens for new frameworks of research are mapped in a collection by Bénédicte Ledent and Pilar Cuder-Domínguez.

Elaine Ho's book on Anita Desai provides a good general introduction to her work, while articles by Dieter Riemenschneider and Jasbir Jain offer useful perspectives on *Clear Light of Day*. Alex Tickell's study guide on *The God of Small Things* is comprehensive in reviewing criticism up to its date of publication; since then, particularly interesting discussions have been written by Elizabeth Outka and as part of Paul Jay's *Global Matters*. Paul Eggert's extended comparison of the *Jerilderie Letter* and Carey's *True History of the Kelly Gang* is invaluable in reading the latter. Bruce Woodcock has provided a good general account of Carey's work, while Andreas Gaile's collection of essays on Carey contains a couple of very good ones on *True History of the Kelly Gang*. Sally Morgan's *My Place* is located in a variety of critical contexts in discussions by Bain Attwood, Sarah Nuttall and Subhash Jaireth. Study of Caryl Phillips can profitably begin with Bénédicte Ledent and Daria Tunca's collection of essays on the writer, which include several discussions of *The Atlantic Sound*, while other interesting takes on the novel have been offered by Elvira Pulitano and Elena Machado Sáez. Finally, Anshuman Mondal's *Amitav Ghosh* is a fine introduction to the writer, while discussions of *In an Antique Land* by Javed Majeed, Shirley Chew and Gaurav Desai all reward attention.

- Bain Attwood, 'Portrait of an Aboriginal as an Artist: Sally Morgan and the Construction of Aboriginality', *Australian Historical Studies* 99 (1992), 302–18.
- Vinayak Chaturvedi (ed.), *Mapping Subaltern Studies and the Postcolonial* (London: Verso, 2000).
- Shirley Chew, 'Texts and Worlds in Amitav Ghosh's *In an Antique Land*', in Maureen Bell et al. (eds), *Reconstructing the Book* (Aldershot: Ashgate, 2001), pp. 197–209.
- Gaurav Desai, 'Old World Orders: Amitav Ghosh and the Writing of Nostalgia', *Representations* 85 (2004), 125–48.
- Paul Eggert, 'The Bushranger's Voice: Peter Carey's *True History of the Kelly Gang* (2000) and Ned Kelly's *Jerilderie Letter* (1879)', *College Literature* 34(3) (2007), 120–39.

- Lucy Evans, 'The Black Atlantic: Exploring Gilroy's Legacy', Atlantic Studies 6(2) (2009), 225–68.
- Andreas Gaile (ed.), Fabulating Beauty: Perspectives on the Fiction of Peter Carey (Amsterdam: Rodopi, 2005).
- Ranajit Guha (ed.), A Subaltern Studies Reader, 1986–1995 (Minneapolis: Minnesota University Press, 1997).
- Ranajit Guha and Gayatri Chakravorty Spivak (eds), Selected Subaltern Studies (Oxford: Oxford University Press, 1988).
- Elaine Yee Lin Ho, Anita Desai (Tavistock: Northcote, 2006).
- Jasbir Jain, 'Airing the Family Ghosts: Anita Desai's Clear Light of Day', World Literature Written in English 24(2) (1984), 416–22.
- Subhash Jaireth, 'The 'I' in Sally Morgan's My Place: Writing of a Monologised Self', Westerly 40(3) (1995), 69–78.
- Paul Jay, Global Matters: the Transnational Turn in Literary Studies (Ithaca, NY: Cornell University Press, 2010).
- Bénédicte Ledent and Daria Tunca (eds), Caryl Phillips: Writing in the Key of Life (Amsterdam: Rodopi, 2012).
- Bénédicte Ledent and Pilar Cuder-Domínguez (eds), New Perspectives on The Black Atlantic: Definitions, Readings, Practices, Dialogues (Bern: Peter Lang, 2012).
- Elena Machado Sáez, 'Postcoloniality, Atlantic Orders, and the Migrant Male in the Writings of Caryl Phillips', Small Axe 9(1) (2005), 17–39.
- Javed Majeed, 'Amitav Ghosh's In an Antique Land: the Ethnographer-Historian and the Limits of Irony', Journal of Commonwealth Literature 30(2) (1995), 45–55.
- Rochona Majumdar, Writing Postcolonial History (London: Bloomsbury, 2010).
- Anshuman A. Mondal, Amitav Ghosh (Manchester: Manchester University Press, 2007).
- Rosalind C. Morris (ed.), Can the Subaltern Speak? Reflections on the History of an Idea (New York: Columbia University Press, 2010).
- Sarah Nuttall, 'History and Identity in Contemporary Australian Women's Autobiography', Women's Writing 5(2) (1998), 189–99.
- Elizabeth Outka, 'Trauma and Temporal Hybridity in Arundhati

Roy's *The God of Small Things*, *Contemporary Literature* 52(1) (2011), 21–53.

- Elvira Pulitano, 'Re-mapping Caribbean Land(Sea)scapes: Aquatic Metaphors and Transatlantic Homes in Caryl Phillips's *The Atlantic Sound*', in Annalisa Oboe and Anna Scacchi, *Recharting the Black Atlantic: Modern Cultures, Local Communities, Global Connections* (New York: Routledge, 2008), pp. 301–18.
- Dieter Riemenschneider, 'History and the Individual in Anita Desai's *Clear Light of Day* and Salman Rushdie's *Midnight's Children*', *World Literature Written in English* 23(1) (1984), 53–66.
- Gayatri Chakravorty Spivak, 'Subaltern Talk: an Interview with the Editors', in Donna Landry and Gerald MacLean (eds), *The Spivak Reader* (London: Routledge, 1996), pp. 287–308.
- Alex Tickell, *Arundhati Roy's* The God of Small Things (Abingdon: Routledge, 2007).
- Bruce Woodcock, *Peter Carey*, 2nd edn (Manchester: Manchester University Press, 2003).

WRITING ABOUT POSTCOLONIAL LITERATURE

Although in some university English departments you may be able to study courses that specialise in a particular field of postcolonial literature, demarcated by region or by theme, or by some combination of the two, it is more likely that you will encounter the kinds of text explored in this guide on general survey courses of postcolonial writing, which may include texts drawn from very different times and places. The discussion here is offered largely for those students tackling a broad syllabus like this, though may also prove useful even in those cases where the corpus for study has been more strictly limited. The huge diversity of contexts and types of writing you may find on a postcolonial literature course can make it hard to postulate any meaningful unity between the works you study; indeed, it is likely that whoever designed your syllabus has deliberately sought to give a flavour of the diversity of writing that falls under this label, and thereby made it more difficult to get any clear sense of shared features that draw texts together. It is likely, also, that you will be introduced to some of the key ideas of postcolonial theory, possibly with different theories brought to bear on different texts. There are clear benefits to approaching postcolonial literature in this way, and the ability to understand theory through use of clear examples is no less valuable than achieving familiarity with a good range of postcolonial texts. However, each of these factors can lead to some potential problems for students who come to write about postcolonial literature, so it is valuable to point out some potential pitfalls, and how they can be avoided.

You may be required to write on postcolonial literature for a short coursework assignment, for a much longer piece like a dissertation or final-year project, or under the conditions of a timed exam. In all cases, though, there are common aspects to the type of writing you will do. Writing an essay can be seen foremost as the presentation of a particular argument, and all good arguments display some similar aspects: your points need to be relevant, they need to be precise and they need to be well supported by evidence. This holds for any type of essay you may be required to write, but these requirements might manifest themselves in particular ways in constructing an argument about postcolonial literature.

Relevance

The essays you write for an examination will usually be responses to particular questions asked by your tutor, but for a dissertation you would usually be expected to write your own question; coursework assignments may take either form. In all cases, though, you are required to work out your approach to the question for yourself. When the question has been set by someone else, this would usually mean paying close attention to the key words used – what possible positions or debates might be suggested by them; what assumptions are being made about the literature or how it may be read? A good answer will ensure that it works within the boundaries of these key ideas, but there will nonetheless be space for the development of a unique position – what particular interpretation of the key words do *you* want to make; how will it allow you to explore the works in which you are interested? When you are creating your own title, it is your responsibility to choose the key terms around which your essay will articulate; however, this does not mean that the requirement to ensure relevance is any less important. It is your responsibility in this case to ensure that the concepts and contexts through which you wish to locate the literary discussion are appropriate and meaningful.

In both cases, you are likely to need to read (or, in the case of exams, already to have read) widely around your topic. The conceptual terms that delimit the topic of an essay have a history, and can always be better grasped if this is known. In some cases this history might be more straightforwardly found than others: an essay on 'subalternity' would most likely have to make some reference to the ideas of Gayatri Spivak, while one on 'identity' or 'community' might be able to choose more widely from where it begins. One of the key dangers in ensuring relevance in writing about postcolonial literature, however, is to ensure that the concepts you use are relevant to the texts to which you apply them: a concept specifically developed in relation to Maori oral forms is unlikely to be applicable unproblematically in the description of oral cultures in the Caribbean. This does not mean that such a borrowing may not result in useful insights (indeed, postcolonial criticism has often achieved great things when using 'travelling' theory in this way), but it does require a sensitivity to context that allows you to map exactly what is different about the texts in order better to capture what similarities there may be. Ensuring relevance in studying postcolonial literature is often about showing due attention to context: it is important to know out of what literary or cultural traditions a text may spring, and also the particular social and political environment in which it was created. You are unlikely to have been asked merely to elucidate these conditions as your assignment, and this material may in fact only form a small part of the actual essay you finally write, but it is a crucial aspect of your research: knowing exactly from which environment a literary work arises should help avoid making untenable connections, but equally may allow for meaningful ones to become more apparent.

Precision

The criteria of precision cannot be wholly separated from those of relevance – the reader will be more clearly made aware of the relevance of your discussion if the vocabulary you use to elucidate it is fully up to the task of doing so. Again this would often require reading around a text's context, to ensure that you are alive to as much of its meaning as possible. If a novel for example explores real historical events it is important to have a clear idea what actually happened; not in order simply to present this information in your essay, but rather to appreciate better which aspect the writer has chosen to highlight, and which they may have ignored. Knowing which parts are fact, which are fiction and which might have a more ambiguous status is often invaluable to appreciating exactly how such a novel is developing its project.

However, precision is most likely to be an issue in writing about postcolonial literature when it comes to questions of theory. It was mentioned in the introduction to this guide that the Procrustean application of theory to literary texts is unlikely to lead to particularly edifying results: assuming that a particular postcolonial theory can neatly explain a literary work is likely to involve ignoring aspects of the theory, the text, or both. Rather, a strong argument is likely to be sensitive to the places where the theory and the literary work are in conflict; when different strategies and models for explaining the world are in play. One way to avoid relying on theory to explain texts, and thus to limit your discussion, is to think of the theory as a tool for guiding your exploration, rather than the end point of it. This can be tied neatly to the goal of precision. It was argued above that all concepts have their own histories: these can often be found in the realm of theoretical debates. The meanings of terms have frequently been contested and different justifications have been offered for how and when to use them. Becoming aware of these debates can in part be seen as a development of your ability to use the language of the field accurately and with confidence. The conceptual terms you use in any essay require precise definition: one of the best reasons to read theory is that it will enable you to do this more effectively. Really good definitions often acknowledge the fault lines within concepts, the places where they have been subject to debate; showing an awareness of these can allow for far more careful and useful terms through which to structure your investigation of literary texts.

Examples

In literary studies you are rarely (if ever) asked only to paraphrase a text you are studying. Rather than simply noting what happens in a work, literary study is usually concerned to think about *how* and *why* these things appear as they do, to explore the internal features of a work that help to create its meaning, or to account for the external factors that may have led a writer to proceed as they did. While you may occasionally come across characterisations of these literary approaches as diametrically opposed (divided into 'formalist' and 'historicist' camps, for example), in reality most literary critics explore these questions together, examining how particular aesthetic effects are created and simultaneously questioning why these have been deployed in this particular text. In fact, the confluence of the internal style and external conditions are often precisely what makes texts interesting to study, and your readings of postcolonial literature are likely to have such investigations at their heart. Central to this kind of enquiry is the use of examples. Concrete examples allow you to show precisely how a particular stylistic trait is deployed, or how a social question might be framed in a work of fiction. The general argument you wish to work will in large part stand or fall according to the quality of the examples you offer in support of it – they need wholly to justify the point you are making (and it is important that you take the time to explain *how* they do this) – but the examples should also always be able to redirect the argument you are making, and in doing so make it more sophisticated and better able to account for the phenomena you describe. As noted above, comparisons between texts produced in very different environments, and drawing on very different traditions, can constitute both some of the greatest pitfalls and some of the most rewarding opportunities in postcolonial literary studies. It is in close attention to the example that our justification for reading different writings alongside one another (though never suggesting their equivalence) can be found. It is hoped that this guide has provided you with precisely a sense of how examples from very different works might interrelate, and has inspired you to continue this work for yourself and to develop your own arguments about this vast and exciting literary field.

Index